MW01095092

# ISLAND IN THE SKY

*Mount Rainier, from the south part of Admiralty Inlet. By W. Alexander from a sketch taken on the spot by J. Sykes. Published in London, May 1798.*

# ISLAND IN THE SKY

## Pioneering Accounts of Mount Rainier 1833–1894

### PAUL SCHULLERY, Editor

The Mountaineers
Seattle

THE MOUNTAINEERS: Organized 1906
". . . to explore, study, and enjoy
the natural beauty of the Northwest."

© 1987 by The Mountaineers
All rights reserved

Published by The Mountaineers
306 Second Avenue West, Seattle, Washington 98119

Published simultaneously in Canada by Douglas & McIntyre
1615 Venables Street, Vancouver, British Columbia V5L 2H1

Cover photos: Background—Mount Rainier from south (Bob and Ira Spring).
Inset—Amsden, Longmire, Fuller and Smith, bound for summit, 1890 (Photo
courtesy Aubrey L. Haines).


Manufactured in the United States of America

**Library of Congress Cataloging-in-Publication Data**

Island in the sky.

   Bibliography: p.
   Includes index.
   1. Mountaineers—United States—Biography.
2. Mountaineering—Washington (State)—Rainier, Mount—
History—19th century.   3. Rainier, Mount (Wash.)—
Description and travel.   I. Schullery, Paul.
GV199.9.I83   1987       796.5'22'0922 [B]       86-23887
ISBN 0-89886-123-3 (pbk.)


0  9  8  7  6
5  4  3  2  1

To Doug Houston

# Contents

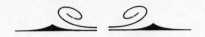

# Acknowledgments

This book grew out of a research project I conducted for the National Park Service at Mount Rainier in 1983 — a project that culminated in a report entitled *A History of Native Elk in Mount Rainier National Park*. It was while conducting a literature search of early accounts of the park for this report that I came across the material in this book. I must, therefore, thank the staff of the park, especially Superintendent William Briggle and resource management personnel Stan Schlegel, Bob Dunnagan, and Joanne Michalovic for their help with this project. Park librarian Lynn Arthur was of continual assistance in searching out obscure items.

Others who helped with material that eventually found its way into *Island in the Sky* were Aubrey Haines, whose own book *Mountain Fever* is such a superb chronicle of this period and who opened his considerable file of early accounts to me; the staffs of The Mountaineers Library, the Washington State Library in Olympia, the Pacific Northwest Collection at the University of Washington in Seattle, and the Washington State Historical Society in Tacoma; Ellen Traxel and Stephanie Toothman of the National Park Service Regional Office in Seattle; Robert Wethern of Union, Washington; and Alec Jackson of Kenmore, Washington.

The idea for the book was first suggested to me by Douglas Houston, National Park Service, Olympic National Park.

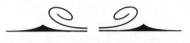

# Introduction

Mount Rainier occupies the most prominent historical position among the great peaks of the Pacific Northwest. Not only is it the greatest in elevation, it has been the most celebrated in print and certainly the most eagerly sought by pioneer climbers of the region. The mountain is of interest to many people, most of whom would never try to climb it, and quite a few who would.

The history of Mount Rainier reveals that there are almost as many ways to enjoy a mountain as there are people seeking enjoyment. Mount Rainier, with its abundant wildlife, fabulous wildflower meadows, and extraordinary scenery, provides us with recreation in the fullest sense of the word, though most of us will never try to stand on its summit. On the other hand, it is hardly likely that many visitors, even the most car-bound and comfort-addicted, will not wonder briefly about that greatest of adventures in the park, climbing the mountain itself.

There are several books that deal with Mount Rainier climbing adventures. The two best are Aubrey Haines's *Mountain Fever*, a chronicle of events and climbs that led to the establishment of the park in 1899, and Dee Molenaar's *The Challenge of Rainier*, which tells of the climbing exploration of the mountain to modern times. Both are narrative histories that recount major conquests (and failures) and put the story of the mountain into a historical context we can easily appreciate. *Island in the Sky* is not offered as competition for them. Rather, it is a companion volume, providing something their formal presentations do not: the actual firsthand accounts of the original climbers and explorers of Mount Rainier.

A good part of the enjoyment of outdoor life is found in anticipation before the event and remembrance afterward. I know a great many anglers who, when unable to fish, take solace in reading about it. Most kinds of nature appreciation have generated rich literatures that help us fill in the gaps between days afield, just as they help us better appreciate what we find when we are outdoors. Many of us are not content merely to enjoy nature; we long to share our experiences, to learn about the experiences of others, maybe even to measure ours against theirs. So it is, I think, with visiting a national park, and so it is that the

accounts reprinted in *Island in the Sky* have a great deal to offer. We have
here the thoughts and experiences—sometimes a little self-conscious,
sometimes a little varnished—of the real pioneers of Mount Rainier recreation. Their accounts are much more than recitations of climbing
milestones; like all travelers, they recorded their own impressions along
the way, impressions often very much like our own. What makes these
impressions different—and more exciting—is that these travelers were
here first.

There is no simple way to determine exactly when the "pioneer" period ended at Mount Rainier. In some ways it is still going on, as climbers search out new routes, park managers explore new perspectives on
how the park may be best appreciated, and new generations of visitors
make their first acquaintance with the mountain. True, the selection of
accounts that follows is to some extent arbitrary, based in part on my
personal conviction that something began and ended in the period they
represent. But I'm not so much interested in formal history here as in
the elemental human experience of the mountain. From these early visitors and climbers, we have inherited a lively, engaging, and telling literary legacy. It is how we relate to that legacy that most interests me,
and that makes these accounts worth reading. I wonder how different
our responses are today to these experiences, and I wonder if those dif-
ferences tell us anything about the pioneers, or about ourselves.

In the following selections we see the early days on the mountain
through many eyes. We see the lower slopes through the eyes of a busi-
nesslike botanist, William Fraser Tolmie, an employee of the Hudson's
Bay Company and in 1833 the first known white man to enter the present park area. He was collecting plants, not conquering peaks, but his
understated diary reveals a serious interest in alpine exploration. We
see the upper slopes, even the summit, through the eyes of little-known
early parties that climbed in 1852 and 1854; it is now assumed that the
Ford party did not quite reach the peak and that the "unknown climbers" did, but both attempts are remarkable for their time.

We also see the mountain through smokier eyes, those of a tale-teller.
Hamitchou's legend, which comes down to us through Theodore Winthrop, is even further removed from "real" history than the other
accounts. Not only is it legend rather than reminiscence, but it is twice-
confused by being legend transcribed by an overly imaginative and un-
scholarly white man. Winthrop's original diary of his encounter with
Hamitchou gives only a short paragraph on the legend. It concludes

with the diarist's note to himself to "work up artistically" these few lines into something grander. Hamitchou's legend, as it was published in Winthrop's book *The Canoe and the Saddle* (1862), is indeed grander, but it is an accepted part of the mountain's folklore now, and I recommend enjoying it on its own terms. It may be retread legend, but it's still quite a story.

From these earliest, often hazy accounts, we enter the bright light of more trustworthy (and historically significant) reports with the unsuccessful 1857 attempt on the mountain by August Kautz, an assault so determined and heroic that it seems almost unfair to call it a failure. It was followed by what many still regard as *the* first successful climb, that of Philemon Van Trump and Hazard Stevens in 1870. They may not actually have been first, but for subsequent climbers they were first in importance because their route became known and because Van Trump guided others to the top later.

After including every known ascent account through the Van Trump/Stevens climb, I began to pick and choose. I did not include the 1870 ascent by Samuel Emmons and A. D. Wilson, as much because the narrative is unexciting as for any historical reason. The accounts of George Bayley (1883), J. Warner Fobes (1884), and Allison Brown (1886) are included primarily because they tell their stories well, but also because they reveal something of the variety of earliest approaches to the mountain. Brown's is now seen as both the most unusual and the least certain of the three: There is no doubt the climb occurred, but there is considerable question over how high the party climbed.

I see John Muir's account (1888) as representing the beginning of yet a third period in the early climbing annals of Mount Rainier. Though even at that late date, only a handful of men had stood at the summit, several successful ascents (including repeat climbs by Van Trump) had taken some of the edge off the exploratory glamour of the achievement. The accounts by Fay Fuller (the first woman to reach the summit, though two others followed the next year) in 1890, George Dickson in 1892, Van Trump yet again in 1892, and Olin Wheeler in 1894 were chosen from almost twenty that occurred in the six years following Muir's ascent. If the climb was losing a bit of its pioneer luster (though certainly none of its physical challenge) by the time of Muir's ascent, it was well tarnished by 1894, when Wheeler was part of a climb intended mostly to promote tourism. In the following years, huge outings organized by regional mountaineering clubs took scores of people to the summit. Mount Rainier entered a new era as a climbing challenge about the same time it became a national park.

The historian in me is unable to resist offering a word of warning about these accounts. Remember that they were written in the last century; do not use them for up-to-date information about the mountain. Much has changed at Mount Rainier since these early climbers made their ascents. If you want to know more about Mount Rainier, a host of excellent publications exists to satisfy your curiosity, and I hope that *Island in the Sky* inspires you to seek them out. Don't let unfamiliar and now-discarded names, or odd spellings of familiar names, in the following accounts distract you, unless you want to look into the entertaining and often heated controversy over the mountain's "proper" name (Rainier? Tacoma? Tahoma?).

Historical changes are part of the ongoing process by which we have learned to understand the mountain and what it can mean to us. For some, that understanding will always be limited more to books and documents than to ice-climbing gear and thin air, but no matter how second-hand or vicarious our enjoyment of Mount Rainier may be, we are participants in its great pageant. Whether our views of the mountain are from a distant interstate highway or from somewhere above Camp Muir, whether we climb it ourselves or as armchair adventurers in the company of its pioneers, Mount Rainier has something for us, something durable and fulfilling.

The title of this collection is taken from a remark made by John Muir about the view from the summit, from which he said he could see the other great volcanic peaks—Adams, Hood, St. Helens—standing out above a shroud of smoke like "islands in the sky." An early geologist used a similar analogy in describing the mountain as "an arctic island in a temperate zone." Today we might further develop the analogy and call it an island of wilderness in a rapidly developing countryside, or, more philosophically, an "island of hope," as one modern writer has described all the national parks. But the accounts in this book take us from these weightier ruminations to a simpler time, a time when the mountain was still something of an island of mystery, and civilization itself was still an island in the great wilderness of the Pacific Northwest. We aren't likely to have it that way again, even if we should wish it so, but here, through these accounts, we can share a little of that era's drama and color and adventure.

# William Fraser Tolmie*
# 1833

In 1833 the Hudson's Bay Company post of Fort Nisqually, on the southeast shore of Puget Sound, was still new and unfinished; it would eventually prosper not as a fur-trading center but as an agricultural one. However, at that early date the post was hardly established, and there was relatively little to occupy the time of a young Scotsman, Dr. William Fraser Tolmie, who had arrived there that summer. Being an enthusiastic botanist, Tolmie got permission to make a brief "botanizing excursion" to Mount Rainier, which he could see in the distance. Thus, around the first of September he became the first known white man to set foot in what would become Mount Rainier National Park.

Tolmie was accompanied, as he explains in the following account, by a few Nisqually and Puyallup Indians, who went along in the hope of finding some good elk hunting. In that regard the trip was a disappointment; it was also troubled by persistent bad weather. Only after some coaxing by Tolmie were the Indians persuaded to continue with him as he followed the Mowich River into the present park and climbed what is now called Mount Pleasant, a 6,400-foot ridge northwest of Mount Rainier. From there he got his best and closest view of the mountain, to which he would never return despite many years' residence at Fort Nisqually. He seemed at least to entertain the notion of an ascent during his September 3 observation of the peak, but he could have been thinking of the likelihood that someone else would make the climb.

Tolmie's account, which is presented here from his diary deposited in the Provincial Archives in Victoria, is a kind of prelude, really, to the later and more serious attempts to climb the mountain. He was the first white man to approach it, but he was also the first to assay the possibility of doing more. That and his vivid firsthand descriptions of the trip make his account an appropriate beginning.

*Reprinted from William Fraser Tolmie, Manuscript Diary, 1833, Provincial Archives, Victoria, British Columbia.

## Tuesday August 27

Wrote Hughes today [sending] an order for £7–5/—obtained Mr.
Heron's consent to making a botanizing excursion to Mt. Rainier; for
which he has allowed 10 days—Have engaged 2 horses from a chief
living in that quarter who came here tonight & Lachalet is to be my
guide—Told the Indians I am going to Mt. Rainier to gather herbs of
which to make medicine part of which is to be sent to Britain & part
retained in case Intermittent Fever should visit us when I will prescribe
for the Indians.

## Wednesday August 28

A tremendous thunder storm occurred last night succeeded by torrents
of rain—The thunder was very loud and the lightning flashing in completely enlightened my apartment—Was cloudy thermom 62° Sunst:
P.M. Have been chatting with Mr. H. about colonizing Whidbey's island a project of which he is at present quite full—more anon. No
horses have appeared—Understand that the mountain is four days journey distant the first of which can only be performed on horseback—If
they do appear tomorrow shall start with Lachalet on foot—Began Dr.
Hookers letter—

## Thursday Augt. 29—Prairie 8 miles N. of House—sunset

Finished all the letters this forenoon—made a packet of them for Vancouver in case an opportunity occurs before my return—Mentioned to
my father that I would write a lick on my return—Busier afterward in
making arrangments for journey & while thus occupied the guide arrived with 3 horses—Started about 3 mounted on a strong iron grey
stallion—my companions disposing of themselves on the other two
horses—except one who walked—We were 6 in number—I have
engaged Lachalet for a blanket & his nephew Lashima for ammunition
to accompany me & Nuckalkut a Poyallip (whom I took for a native of
Mt. Rainier) with two horses to be guide on the mountain & after leaving the horse track & Quilniash his relative, a very active strong fellow
has volunteered to accompany us—The Indians are in great hopes of
killing Elk & Chevreuil & Lachalet has already been selling & promising the grease he is to get—It is in a great measure the expectation of
finding game that urges them to undertake the journey—Cantered

*William Fraser Tolmie, from a portrait made late in life. (Courtesy National Park Service)*

slowly along the prairie & are now at the residence of Nuckalkuts' father, under the shade of a lofty pine in a grassy amphitheatre beautifully interspersed & surrounded with oaks & through the gaps in the circle we see the broad plain extending southwards to Nusqually—in a hollow immediately behind, is a small lake whose surface is almost one sheet of water lillies about to flower—Have supped on sallal & at dusk, shall turn in—

**Friday August 30** Sandy beach of Poyallipa River

Slept ill last night & as I dozed in the mg- was aroused by a stroke across the thigh from a large decayed branch which fell from the pine overshadowing us—A drizzling rain fell during most of the night—Got up about dawn & finding thigh stiff & painful thought a stop was put to the journey, but after moving about it felt easier—Started about sunrise—I mounted on a spirited brown mare & the rest on passable animals except Nuckalkut, who bestrode a foal—made a northeasterly course thru prairie—Breakfasted at a small marsh on Bread Sallal Dried Cockles & a small piece of Chevrueil saved from the last nights repast of my companions (for I cannot call them attendants)—The point of wood now became broader & the intervening plain degenerated into prairions

—Stopped about 1 P.M. at the abode of 3 Tekatat families—who met us rank & file at the door to shake hands—Their sheds were made of bark resting upon a horizontal pole supported at each end by tripods & showed an abundance of elk's flesh, dried, within. Two kettles were filled with this & after smoking my Indians made a savage repast on the meat & bouillon Lachalet saying it was the Indian custom to eat a great deal at once & afterwards abstain for a time—he however has twice eaten since! Traded some dried meat for 4 balls & 3 rings & mounting rode off in the midst of a heavy shower—Ascended & descended at different times several steep banks & passed through dense & tangled thickets occaisionally coming on a prairion—The soil throughout was of the same nature as that of Nusqually—After descending a very steep bank, came to the Poyallip—Lashima carried the baggage across on his head—Rode [to] the opposite side through a rich alluvial plain 3 or 4 miles in length & 3/4 to 1 in breadth—it is covered with fern about 8 feet high in some parts—Passed through woods & crossed river several times—about 7 P.M. dismounted & the horses & accoutrements were left in a wood at the river's brink—Started now on foot for a house Nuckalkut knew & after traversing woods & twice crossing the torrents "on the unsteadfast footing" of a log arrived at the house which was a deserted one & encamped on the dry part of river's bed—along which our course lies tomorrow—The Poyallip flows rapidly & is about 10 or 12 yards broad—Its banks are high & covered with lofty cedars & pines—the water is of a dirty white colour, being impregnated by white clay—Lachalet has tonight been trying to dissuade me from going to the snow on the mountain—

## Saturday 31st August

Slept well & in morning, two salmon [were] caught on which are to breakfast before starting—after breakfast Quillihaish stuck the gills and sound of the fish on a spit which stood before the fire so that the next comer might know that salmon could be obtained there—Have travelled nearly the whole day through a wood of cedar & pine, surface very uneven & after ascending the bed of river a couple of miles are now encamped about 10 yards from its margin in the wood. Find myself very inferior to my companions in the power of enduring fatigue—their pace is a smart trot which soon obliges me to rest—The waters of the Poyallip are still of the same colour—Can see a short distance up two lofty hills covered with wood—Evg cloudy & rainy—Showery all day—

**Sunday Septr 1. 1833** Bank of Poyallip River

It has rained all night & is now 6 a m pouring down—Are a good deal sheltered by the trees—my companions are all snoozing—Shall presently arouse them & hold a council of war—the prospect is very discouraging—our provisions will be expended today & Lachalet said about [it] he thought the river would be too high to be fordable in either direction—Had dried meat boiled in a cedar bark kettle for breakfast—I got rigged out in green blanket without trousers in Indian style & trudged on through the woods—afterwards exchanged blanket with Lachalet for Ouvrie's Capot, which had been on almost every Indian at Nusqually—however I found it more convenient than blanket—Our course lay up the river, which we crossed frequently—the bed is clayey in most parts—Saw the Sawbill duck once or twice riding down on a log & I fired twice unsuccessfully. Have been flanked on both sides with the high pineclad hills & on some a short distance above encampment snow can be seen—It having rained almost incessantly—have encamped under a shelving bank which had been undermined by the river—immense stones only held in situ by dried roots form the roof & the floor is very rugged. Have supped on berries, which when heated with stones in kettle taste like Lozenges—Propose tomorrow to ascend one of the snowy peaks above—

**Monday Septr 2** Summit of a snowy peak immediately under Rainier

Passed a very uncomfortable night in our troglodytic mansion—Ascended the river for 3 miles to where it was shut in by amphitheatre of Mountains & could be seen bounding over a lofty precipice above—Ascended that which showed most snow—our track lay at first through a dense wood of pine but we afterwards emerged into an exuberantly verdant gully closed on each side by lofty precipices—Followed gully to near the summit & found excellent berries in abundance—It contained very few alpine plants—afterwards came to a grassy mound where the sight of several decayed trees enduced us to encamp—After tea I set out with Lachalet & Nuckalkut for the summit which was deep with snow for ¼ mile downwards— The summit terminated in abrupt precipie directed Nwards & bearing NE from Mt. [Rainier] the adjoining peak—The mists were at times very dense but a puff of SW wind occaisionally dispelled them—On the S. side of Poyallip is a range of snow dappled mountains & they as well as that on the N. side terminates in Mt. Rainier a short distance to E. Collected a vasculum of plants at the snow & having examined & packed them shall turn in. Lachalet by his own request is to be my bedfellow—Thermom: at base 54° at summit of ascent 47°—

## Tuesday Septr 3 Woody islet on Poyallip

It rained heavily during night but about dawn, the wind, shifting to N.E. dispersed the clouds & frost set in. Lay shivering all night & roused my swarthy companion twice to rekindle the fire—At sunrise, accompanied by Quilliliash, went to the summit & found the tempr of the air 33°—the snow was spangled and sparkled brightly in the bright sun shine—it was crisp and only yielded a couple of inches to the pressure of foot in walking—Mt. Rainier appeared surpassingly splendid & magnificent, it bore, from the peak on which I stood S.S.E. & was separated from it only by a narrow glen, whose sides however were formed by inaccessible precipices—Got all my bearings more correctly today the atmosphere being clear & every object distinctly perceived—The river flows at first in a northerly direction from the mountain—The snow on the summit of the mountain adjoining Rainier on western side of Poyallip is [continuous] with that of latter, & thus the S. Western aspect of Rainier seemed [the most accessible—by ascending] the first mountain through a gulley in its northern side you reach the eternal snow of Rainier & for a long distance afterwards the ascent is very gradual, but then it becomes abrupt from the sugarloaf form assumed by the Mt—Its eastern side is steep—on its northern aspect a few glaciers were seen on the conical portion, below that the mountain is composed of bare rock, apparently volcanic, which about 50 yards in breadth reaches from the snow to the valley beneath & is bounded on each side by bold bluff crags scantily covered with stunted pines—Its surface is generally smooth but here & there raised into small points or knobs or arrowed with short & narrow longitudinal lines in which snow lay—From the snow on western border the Poyallipa arose—in its course down this rocky slope was fenced in to eastward by a regular elevation of the rock in the form of a wall or dyke which (at the distance I viewed it at) seemed about 4 feet high & 400 yards in length—Two large pyramids of rock arose from the gentle acclivity at S.W. extremity of mountain & around each the drifting snow had accumulated in large quantity forming a basin apparently of great depth—Here I also perceived, peeping from their snowy covering two lines of dyke similar to that already mentioned.

# 2

# The Ford Party*
# 1852

By the early 1850s there were enough whites in the Puget Sound area to provide a lively atmosphere of boosterism for the region. Among their greatest desires was a road from Puget Sound across the Cascades to the Yakima Valley. The four members of the Ford party—Robert Bailey, Sidney Ford, John Edgar, and (with a "probably" inserted by historian Aubrey Haines) Benjamin Shaw—all would become prominent citizens of the region, and all shared an interest in seeing it promoted and opened up to development and settlement. Their trip to Mount Rainier seems to have been part of a broader interest they had in exploring the Cascades for the best route across.

They did not, according to recent historians, reach the true summit, but they probably came close, say, in the neighborhood of 14,000 feet. They traveled up the Nisqually River, demonstrating the practicality of such a route for later climbers and pioneering what was to become the most popular approach for the rest of the century. Though brief, the following account offers many of the elements that would characterize later accounts, including exclamations of wonder at the scenery, comments on the abundance of wildlife and plant life, and pronouncements that the weather could be both an exhilarating and frustrating element of the climb. We see here also an early combination of adventure writing and promotional journalism, a combination not uncommon in later accounts.

About four weeks ago, a party of young men, consisting of Messrs. R. S. Bailey, S. S. Ford, jr., and John Edgar, undertook an expedition to Mt. Ranier [sic] for the purpose of ascending that mountain as far as circumstances might warrant. Ranier, as all are aware, is situated in the main Cascade range, distant from its base to Olympia about fifty-five

*Reprinted from "Visit to Mt. Ranier," [sic] Olympia Columbian, September 18, 1852.

miles. On arriving at the foot of the mountain the party secured their
animals, and pursued their way upward by the back-bone ridge to the
main body of the mountain, and to the heighth, as near as they could
judge, of nine or ten miles.—the last half mile over snow of the depth of
fifty feet, but perfectly crusted and solid. The party were two days in
reaching their highest altitude, and they describe the mountain as extremely rugged, and difficult of ascent; on the slopes and table land
they found a luxuriant growth of grass, far exceeding in freshness and
vigor any afforded by the prairies below. On some of these table lands
they found beautiful lakes—from a half to a mile in circumference—
formed from mountain streams, and the melting of snow. The party remained at their last camp, upward, two days and nights, where they
fared sumptuously on the game afforded by the mountain, which they
found very numerous, in the shape of brown bear, mountain goat,
deer, etc., with an endless variety of the feathered genus; the side of the
mountain was literally covered with every description of berries, of
most delicious flavor.

The party had a perfect view of the Sound and surrounding country
—recognising the numerous prairies with which they were familiar, to
which were added in their observations, several stranger prairies, of
which they had no knowledge, and which, probably, have never been
explored. The evenings and mornings were extremely cold, with a
wind strong and piercing—the noon-day sun oppressively warm.

They describe their view of the surrounding country and scenery as
most enchanting, and consider themselves richly rewarded for their toil
in procuring it. This is the first party of whites, we believe, that has
ever attempted to ascend Ranier.

Not being provided with instruments for taking minute observations, and there being a constant fog and mist along the range of the
mountains, the party were unable to make any satisfactory discoveries
in relation to a practicable route across them; yet Mr. Ford informs us,
that he noticed several passes at intervals through the mountains,
which, as far as he could see, gave satisfactory evidence that a good
route could be surveyed, and a road cut through with all ease.

Who can calculate the benefit—to the Puget Sound country, had its
citizens taken sufficient interest in the project to have located a
road—Let the people on the Sound be true to their interests the coming
year, and turn their attention as early next spring as practicable, in surveying a route and establishing a road across the Cascades. . . .

# 3

# Theodore Winthrop and Hamitchou's Legend*
## 1853

Hamitchou's legend has the least to do with the history of climbing at Mount Rainier of any of the accounts here, but it is for several reasons an important part of the mountain's early lore. Theodore Winthrop, a popular young travel writer in the early 1860s (several of his books appeared after 1861, the year he died in the Civil War), traveled across the Cascades in 1853. In the following excerpt from his book *The Canoe and the Saddle* (1862), he introduces the legend by telling us he heard it at Fort Nisqually from an Indian named Hamitchou, through a translation by William Tolmie.

In the process of doing other research I have come across at least four variants of this legend, ascribing it to a Nisqually, a Puyallup, or possibly a Cowlitz or Klickitat Indian. It has been the most pervasive and enduring of Indian legends relating to the mountain and definitely one of the most uncertain in origin. Winthrop's own journals, published many years after his death, reveal that he did not take down more than the barest outline of what Tolmie was translating for him. He concluded his one paragraph of notes on what would later become a lengthy "legend" with the remark that he must "work up artistically" this material into something of greater palatability to the general reader. This is not the sort of approach that comforts anthropologists seeking accurate information on native American lore.

Nonetheless, Hamitchou's legend is of considerable interest in the pioneering history of Mount Rainier. It reveals native American interest in the highest part of the mountain. And it reveals the extent to which the mountain was even then an object of fantasy and wonder in the cultures—both native and European—that encountered it. Read it, then, as a "period piece," entertaining not only as a legendary tale but also as one culture's portrayal of another culture's perspective.

---

*Reprinted from Theodore Winthrop, The Canoe and the Saddle, New York: Ticknor and Fields, 1862, 123–176.

Up to Tacoma, or into some such solitude of nature, imaginative men must go, as Moses went up to Sinai, that the divine afflatus may stir within them. The siwashes appreciate, according to their capacity, the inspiration of lonely grandeur, and go upon the mountains, starving and alone, that they may become seers, enchanters, magicians, diviners,—what in conventional lingo is called "big medicine." For though the Indians here have not peopled these thrones of their world with the creatures of an anthropomorphic mythology, they yet deem them the abode of Tamanoüs. Tamanoüs is a vague and half-personified type of the unknown, of the mysterious forces of nature; and there is also an indefinite multitude of undefined emanations, each one a tamanoüs with a small t, which are busy and impish in complicating existence, or equally active and spritely in unravelling it. Each Indian of this region patronizes his own personal tamanoüs, as men of the more eastern tribes keep a private manitto, and as Socrates kept a daimôn. To supply this want, Tamanoüs with a big T undergoes an avatar, and incarnates himself into a salmon, a beaver, a clam, or into some inanimate object, such as a canoe, a paddle, a fir-tree, a flint, or into some elemental essence, as fire, water, sun, mist; and tamanoüs thus individualized becomes the "guide, philosopher, and friend" of every siwash, conscious that otherwise he might stray and be lost in the unknown realms of Tamanoüs.

Hamitchou, a frowzy ancient of the Squallyamish, told to Dr. Tolmie and me, at Nisqually, a legend of Tamanoüs and Tacoma, which, being interpreted, runs as follows:—

## HAMITCHOU'S LEGEND.

"Avarice, O Boston tyee," quoth Hamitchou, studying me with dusky eyes, "is a mighty passion. Now, be it known unto thee that we Indians anciently used not metals nor the money of you blanketeers. Our circulating medium was shells,—wampum you would name it. Of all wampum, the most precious is Hiaqua. Hiaqua comes from the far north. It is a small, perforated shell, not unlike a very opaque quill toothpick, tapering from the middle, and cut square at both ends. We string it in many strands, and hang it around the neck of one we love,—namely, each man his own neck. We also buy with it what our hearts desire. He who has most hiaqua is best and wisest and happiest of all the northern Haida and of all the people of Whulge. The mountain horsemen value it; and braves of the terrible Blackfeet have been known, in the good old days, to come over and offer a horse or a wife for a bunch of fifty hiaqua.

"Now, once upon a time there dwelt where this fort of Nisqually now stands a wise old man of the Squallyamish. He was a great fisher-man and a great hunter; and the wiser he grew, much the wiser he thought himself. When he had grown very wise, he used to stay apart from every other siwash. Companionable salmon-boilings round a com-mon pot had no charms for him. 'Feasting was wasteful,' he said, 'and revellers would come to want.' And when they verified his prophecy, and were full of hunger and empty of salmon, he came out of his hermitage, and had salmon to sell.

"Hiaqua was the pay he always demanded; and as he was a very wise old man, and knew all the tideways of Whulge, and all the enticing ripples and placid spots of repose in every river where fish might dash or delay, he was sure to have salmon when others wanted, and thus bagged largely of its precious equivalent, hiaqua.

"Not only a mighty fisher was the sage, but a mighty hunter, and elk, the greatest animal of the woods, was the game he loved. Well had he studied every trail where elk leave the print of their hoofs, and where, tossing their heads, they bend the tender twigs. Well had he searched through the broad forest, and found the long-haired prairies where elk feed luxuriously; and there, from behind palisade fir-trees, he had launched the fatal arrow. Sometimes, also, he lay beside a pool of sweetest water, revealed to him by gemmy reflections of sunshine gleaming through the woods, until at noon the elk came down, to find death awaiting him as he stooped and drank. Or beside the same foun-tain the old man watched at night, drowsily starting at every crackling branch, until, when the moon was high, and her illumination declared the pearly water, elk dashed forth incautious into the glade, and met their midnight destiny.

"Elk-meat, too, he sold to his tribe. This brought him pelf, but, alas for his greed, the pelf came slowly. Waters and woods were rich in game. All the Squallyamish were hunters and fishers, though none so skilled as he. They were rarely in absolute want, and, when they came to him for supplies, they were far too poor in hiaqua.

"So the old man thought deeply, and communed with his wisdom, and, while he waited for fish or beast, he took advice within himself from his demon,—he talked with Tamanoüs. And always the question was, 'How may I put hiaqua in my purse?'

"Tamanoüs never revealed to him that far to the north, beyond the waters of Whulge, are tribes with their under lip pierced with a fish-bone, among whom hiaqua is plenty as salmonberries are in the woods what time in mid-summer salmon fin it along the reaches of Whulge.

"But the more Tamanoüs did not reveal to him these mysteries of na-ture, the more he kept dreamily prying into his own mind, endeavoring to devise some scheme by which he might discover a treasure-trove of the beloved shell. His life seemed wasted in the patient, frugal indus-try, which only brought slow, meagre gains. He wanted the splendid elation of vast wealth and the excitement of sudden wealth. His own peculiar tamanoüs was the elk. Elk was also his totem, the cognizance of his freemasonry with those of his own family, and their family friends in other tribes. Elk, therefore, were every way identified with his life; and he hunted them farther and farther up through the forests on the flanks of Tacoma, hoping that some day his tamanoüs would speak in the dying groan of one of them, and gasp out the secret of the mines of hiaqua, his heart's desire.

"Tacoma was so white and glittering, that it seemed to stare at him very terribly and mockingly, and to know his shameful avarice, and how it led him to take from starving women their cherished lip and nose jewels of hiaqua, and to give them in return only tough scraps of dried elk-meat and salmon. When men are shabby, mean, and grasping, they feel reproached for their grovelling lives by the unearthliness of nature's beautiful objects, and they hate flowers, and sunsets, mountains, and the quiet stars of heaven.

"Nevertheless," continued Hamitchou, "this wise old fool of my legend went on stalking elk along the sides of Tacoma, ever dreaming of wealth. And at last, as he was hunting near the snows one day, one very clear and beautiful day of late summer, when sunlight was magi-cally disclosing far distances, and making all nature supernaturally vis-ible and proximate, Tamanoüs began to work in the soul of the miser.

" 'Are you brave,' whispered Tamanoüs in the strange, ringing, dull, silent thunder-tones of a demon voice. 'Dare you go to the caves where my treasures are hid?'

" 'I dare,' said the miser.

"He did not know that his lips had syllabled a reply. He did not even hear his own words. But all the place had become suddenly vocal with echoes. The great rock against which he leaned crashed forth, 'I dare.' Then all along through the forest, dashing from tree to tree and lost at last among the murmuring of breeze-shaken leaves, went careering his answer, taken up and repeated scornfully, 'I dare.' And after a silence, while the daring one trembled and would gladly have ventured to shout, for the companionship of his own voice, there came across from the vast snow wall of Tacoma a tone like the muffled, threatening plunge of an avalanche into a chasm, 'I dare.'

" 'You dare,' said Tamanoüs, enveloping him with a dread sense of an unseen, supernatural presence; 'you pray for wealth of hiaqua. Listen!'

"This injunction was hardly needed; the miser was listening with dull eyes kindled and starting. He was listening with every rusty hair separating from its unkempt mattedness, and outstanding upright, a caricature of an aureole.

" 'Listen,' said Tamanoüs, in the noonday hush. And then Tamanoüs vouchsafed at last the great secret of the hiaqua mines, while in terror near to death the miser heard, and every word of guidance toward the hidden treasure of the mountains seared itself into his soul ineffaceably.

"Silence came again more terrible now than the voice of Tamanoüs, —silence under the shadow of the great cliff,—silence deepening down the forest vistas,—silence filling the void up to the snows of Tacoma. All life and motion seemed paralyzed. At last Skai-ki, the Blue-Jay, the wise bird, foe to magic, sang cheerily overhead. Her song seemed to refresh again the honest laws of nature. The buzz of life stirred everywhere again, and the inspired miser rose and hastened home to prepare for his work.

"When Tamanoüs has put a great thought in a man's brain, has whispered him a great discovery within his power, or hinted at a great crime, that spiteful demon does not likewise suggest the means of accomplishment.

"The miser, therefore, must call upon his own skill to devise proper tools, and upon his own judgment to fix upon the most fitting time for carrying out his quest. Sending his squaw out to the kamas prairie, under pretence that now was the season for her to gather their winter store of that sickish-sweet esculent root, and that she might not have her squaw's curiosity aroused by seeing him at strange work, he began his preparations. He took a pair of enormous elk-horns, and fashioned from each horn a two-pronged pick or spade, by removing all the antlers except the two topmost. He packed a good supply of kippered salmon, and filled his pouch with kinni kinnick for smoking in his black stone pipe. With his bow and arrows and his two elk-horn picks wrapped in buckskin hung at his back, he started just before sunset, as if for a long hunt. His old, faithful, maltreated, blanketless, vermilion-less squaw, returning with baskets full of kamas, saw him disappearing moodily down the trail.

"All that night, all the day following, he moved on noiselessly by paths he knew. He hastened on, unnoticing outward objects, as one with a controlling purpose hastens. Elk and deer, bounding through the trees, passed him, but he tarried not. At night he camped just below the snows of Tacoma. He was weary, weary, and chill night-airs blowing down from the summit almost froze him. He dared not take his fire-sticks, and, placing one perpendicular upon a little hollow on the flat side of the other, twirl the upright stick rapidly between his palms until the charred spot kindled and lighted his 'tipsoo,' his dry, tindery wool of inner bark. A fire, gleaming high upon the mountain-side, might be a beacon to draw thither any night-wandering savage to watch in ambush, and learn the path toward the mines of hiaqua. So he drowsed chilly and fireless, awakened often by dread sounds of crashing and rumbling among the chasms of Tacoma. He desponded bitterly, almost ready to abandon his quest, almost doubting whether he had in truth received a revelation, whether his interview with Tamanoüs had not been a dream, and finally whether all the hiaqua in the world was worth this toil and anxiety. Fortunate is the sage who at such a point turns back and buys his experience without worse befalling him.

"Past midnight he suddenly was startled from his drowse, and sat bolt upright in terror. A light! Was there another searcher in the forest, and a bolder than he? That flame just glimmering over the tree-tops, was it a camp-fire of friend or foe? Had Tamanoüs been revealing to another the great secret? No, smiled the miser, his eyes fairly open, and discovering that the new light was the moon. He had been waiting for her illumination on paths heretofore untrodden by mortal. She did not show her full, round, jolly face, but turned it askance as if she hardly liked to be implicated in this night's transactions.

"However, it was light he wanted, not sympathy, and he started up at once to climb over the dim snows. The surface was packed by the night's frost, and his moccasins gave him firm hold; yet he travelled but slowly, and could not always save himself from a *glissade* backwards, and a bruise upon some projecting knob or crag. Sometimes, upright fronts of ice diverted him for long circuits, or a broken wall of cold cliff arose, which he must surmount painfully. Once or twice he stuck fast in a crevice, and hardly drew himself out by placing his bundle of picks across the crack. As he plodded and floundered thus deviously and toil-somely upward, at last the wasted moon gan pale overhead, and under foot the snow grew rosy with coming dawn. The dim world about the mountain's base displayed something of its vast detail. He could see, more positively than by moonlight, the far-reaching arteries of mist marking the organism of Whulge beneath; and what had been but a black chaos now resolved itself into the Alpine forest whence he had come.

"But he troubled himself little with staring about; up he looked, for the summit was at hand. To win that summit was wellnigh the attain-ment of his hopes, if Tamanoüs were true; and that, with the flush of morning ardor upon him, he could not doubt. There, in a spot Tama-noüs had revealed to him, was hiaqua,—hiaqua that should make him the richest and greatest of all the Squallyamish.

"The chill before sunrise was upon him as he reached the last curve of the dome. Sunrise and he struck the summit together. Together sun-rise and he looked over the glacis. They saw within a great hollow all covered with the whitest of snow, save at the centre, where a black lake lay deep in a well of purple rock.

"At the eastern end of this lake was a small, irregular plain of snow, marked by three stones like monuments. Toward these the miser sprang rapidly, with full sunshine streaming after him over the snows.

"The first monument he examined with keen looks. It was tall as a giant man, and its top was fashioned into the grotesque likeness of a salmon's head. He turned from this to inspect the second. It was of similar height, but bore at its apex an object in shape like the regular flame of a torch. As he approached, he presently discovered that this was an image of the kamas-bulb in stone. These two semblances of prime necessities of Indian life delayed him but an instant, and he hastened on to the third monument, which stood apart on a perfect level. The third stone was capped by something he almost feared to be-hold, lest it should prove other than his hopes. Every word of Tamanoüs had thus far proved veritable; but might there not be a bitter deceit at the last? The miser trembled.

"Yes, Tamanoüs was trustworthy. The third monument was as the old man anticipated. It was a stone elk's-head, such as it appears in ear-liest summer, when the antlers are sprouting lustily under their rough jacket of velvet.

"You remember, Boston tyee," continued Hamitchou, "that Elk was the old man's tamanoüs, the incarnation for him of the universal Tamanoüs. He therefore was right joyous at this good omen of protection; and his heart grew big and swollen with hope, as the black salmon-berry swells in a swamp in June. He threw down his 'ikta'; every impediment he laid down upon the snow; and, unwrapping his two picks of elk-horn, he took the stoutest, and began to dig in the frozen snow at the foot of the elk-head monument.

"No sooner had he struck the first blow than he heard behind him a sudden puff, such as a seal makes when it comes to the surface to breathe. Turning round much startled, he saw a huge otter just clambering up over the edge of the lake. The otter paused, and struck on the snow with his tail, whereupon another otter and another appeared, until, following their leader in slow and solemn file, were twelve other otters, marching toward the miser. The twelve approached, and drew up in a circle around him. Each was twice as large as any otter ever seen. Their chief was four times as large as the most gigantic otter ever seen in the regions of Whulge, and certainly was as great as a seal. When the twelve were arranged, their leader skipped to the top of the elk-head stone, and sat there between the horns. Then the whole thirteen gave a mighty puff in chorus.

*Theodore Winthrop, a chalk sketch made about the time of his western trip. (Courtesy Aubrey Haines)*

"The hunter of hiaqua was for a moment abashed at his uninvited ring of spectators. But he had seen otter before, and bagged them. These he could not waste time to shoot, even if a phalanx so numerous were not formidable. Besides, they might be tamanoüs. He took to his pick, and began digging stoutly.

"He soon made way in the snow, and came to solid rock beneath. At every thirteenth stroke of his pick, the fugleman otter tapped with his tail on the monument. Then the choir of lesser otters tapped together with theirs on the snow. This caudal action produced a dull, muffled sound, as if there were a vast hollow below.

"Digging with all his force, by and by the seeker for treasure began to tire, and laid down his elk-horn spade to wipe the sweat from his brow. Straightway the fugleman otter turned, and, swinging his tail, gave the weary man a mighty thump on the shoulder; and the whole band, imitating, turned, and, backing inward, smote him with centripetal tails, until he resumed his labors, much bruised.

"The rock lay first in plates, then in scales. These it was easy to remove. Presently, however, as the miser pried carelessly at a larger mass, he broke his elkhorn tool. Fugleman otter leaped down, and, seizing the supplemental pick between his teeth, mouthed it over to the digger. Then the amphibious monster took in the same manner the broken pick, and bore it round the circle of his suite, who inspected it gravely with puffs.

"These strange, magical proceedings disconcerted and somewhat baffled the miser; but he plucked up heart, for the prize was priceless, and worked on more cautiously with his second pick. At last its blows and the regular thumps of the otters' tails called forth a sound hollower and hollower. His circle of spectators narrowed so that he could feel their panting breath as they bent curiously over the little pit he had dug.

"The crisis was evidently at hand.

"He lifted each scale of rock more delicately. Finally he raised a scale so thin that it cracked into flakes as he turned it over. Beneath was a large square cavity.

"It was filled to the brim with hiaqua.

"He was a millionnaire.

"The otters recognized him as the favorite of Tamanoüs, and retired to a respectful distance.

"For some moments he gazed on his treasure, taking thought of his future proud grandeur among the dwellers by Whulge. He plunged his arm deep as he could go; there was still nothing but the precious shells. He smiled to himself in triumph; he had wrung the secret from Tamanoüs. Then, as he withdrew his arm, the rattle of the hiaqua recalled him to the present. He saw that noon was long past, and he must proceed to reduce his property to possession.

"The hiaqua was strung upon long, stout sinews of elk, in bunches of fifty shells on each side. Four of these he wound about his waist; three he hung across each shoulder; five he took in each hand;—twenty strings of pure white hiaqua, every shell large, smooth, unbroken, beautiful. He could carry no more; hardly even with this could he stagger along. He put down his burden for a moment, while he covered up the seemingly untouched wealth of the deposit carefully with the scale stones, and brushed snow over the whole.

"The miser never dreamed of gratitude, never thought to hang a string from the buried treasure about the salmon and kamas tamanoüs stones, and two strings around the elk's head; no, all must be his own, all he could carry now, and the rest for the future.

"He turned, and began his climb toward the crater's edge. At once the otters, with a mighty puff in concert, took up their line of procession, and, plunging into the black lake, began to beat the water with their tails.

"The miser could hear the sound of splashing water as he struggled upward through the snow, now melted and yielding. It was a long hour of harsh toil and much backsliding before he reached the rim, and turned to take one more view of this valley of good fortune.

"As he looked, a thick mist began to rise from the lake centre, where the otters were splashing. Under the mist grew a cylinder of black cloud, utterly hiding the water.

"Terrible are storms in the mountains; but in this looming mass was a terror more dread than any hurricane of ruin ever bore within its wild vortexes. Tamanoüs was in that black cylinder, and as it strode forward, chasing in the very path of the miser, he shuddered, for his wealth and his life were in danger.

"However, it might be but a common storm. Sunlight was bright as ever overhead in heaven, and all the lovely world below lay dreamily fair, in that afternoon of summer, at the feet of the rich man, who now was hastening to be its king. He stepped from the crater edge and began his descent.

"Instantly the storm overtook him. He was thrown down by its first assault, flung over a rough bank of iciness, and lay at the foot torn and bleeding, but clinging still to his precious burden. Each hand still held its five strings of hiaqua. In each hand he bore a nation's ransom. He staggered to his feet against the blast. Utter night was around him,— night as if daylight had forever perished, had never come into being from chaos. The roaring of the storm had also deafened and bewildered him with its wild uproar.

"Present in every crash and thunder of the gale was a growing under-tone, which the miser well knew to be the voice of Tamanoüs. A deadly shuddering shook him. Heretofore that potent Unseen had been his friend and guide; there had been awe, but no terror, in his words. Now the voice of Tamanoüs was inarticulate, but the miser could divine in that sound an unspeakable threat of wrath and vengeance. Floating upon this undertone were sharper tamanoüs voices, shouting and screaming always sneeringly, 'Ha ha, hiaqua!—ha, ha, ha!'

"Whenever the miser essayed to move and continue his descent, a whirlwind caught him, and with much ado tossed him hither and thither, leaving him at last flung and imprisoned in a pinching crevice, or buried to the eyes in a snow-drift, or bedded upside down on a shaggy boulder, or gnawed by lacerating lava jaws. Sharp torture the old man was encountering, but he held fast to his hiaqua.

"The blackness grew ever deeper and more crowded with perdition; the din more impish, demoniac, and devilish; the laughter more appalling; and the miser more and more exhausted with vain buffeting. He determined to propitiate exasperated Tamanoüs with a sacrifice. He threw into the black cylinder storm his left-handful, five strings of precious hiaqua."

"Somewhat long-winded is thy legend, Hamitchou, Great Medicine-Man of the Squallyamish," quoth I. "Why didn't the old fool drop his wampum,—shell out, as one might say,—and make tracks?"

"Well, well!" continued Hamitchou; "when the miser had thrown away his first handful of hiaqua, there was a momentary lull in elemen-tal war, and he heard the otters puffing around him invisible. Then the storm renewed, blacker, louder, harsher, crueller than before, and over the dread undertone of the voice of Tamanoüs, tamanoüs voices again screamed, 'Ha, ha, ha, hiaqua!' and it seemed as if tamanoüs hands, or the paws of the demon otters, clutched at the miser's right-handful and tore at his shoulder and waist belts.

"So, while darkness and tempest still buffeted the hapless old man, and thrust him away from his path, and while the roaring was wickeder than the roars of tens and tens of tens of bears when ahungered they pounce upon a plain of kamas, gradually wounded and terrified, he flung away string after string of hiaqua, gaining never any notice of such sacrifice, except an instant's lull of the cyclon and a puff from the invisible otters.

"The last string he clung to long, and before he threw it to be caught and whirled after its fellows, he tore off a single bunch of fifty shells. But upon this, too, the storm laid its clutches. In the final desperate struggle the old man was wounded so sternly that, when he had given up his last relic of the mighty treasure, when he had thrown into the formless chaos, instinct with Tamanoüs, his last propitiatory offering, he sank and became insensible.

"It seemed a long slumber to him, but at last he awoke. The jagged moon was just paling overhead, and he heard Skai-ki, the Blue-Jay, foe to magic, singing welcome to sunrise. It was the very spot whence he started at morning.

"He was hungry, and felt for his bag of kamas and pouch of smoke-leaves. There, indeed, by his side were the elk-sinew strings of the bag, and the black stone pipe-bowl,—but no bag, no kamas, no kinni-kinnik. The whole spot was thick with kamas plants, strangely out of place on the mountain-side, and overhead grew a large arbutus-tree, with glistening leaves, ripe for smoking. The old man found his hard-wood fire-sticks safe under the herbage, and soon twirled a light, and, nurturing it in dry grass, kindled a cheery fire. He plucked up kamas, set it to roast, and laid a store of the arbutus-leaves to dry on a flat stone.

"After he had made a hearty breakfast on the chestnut-like kamas-bulbs, and, smoking the thoughtful pipe, was reflecting on the events of yesterday, he became aware of an odd change in his condition. He was not bruised and wounded from head to foot, as he expected, but very stiff only, and as he stirred, his joints creaked like the creak of a lazy paddle upon the rim of a canoe. Skai-ki, the Blue-Jay, was singularly familiar with him, hopping from her perch in the ar-butus, and alighting on his head. As he put his hand to dislodge her, he touched his scratching-stick of bone, and attempted to pass it, as usual, through his hair. The hair was matted and interlaced into a network reaching fully two ells down his back. 'Tamanoüs,' thought the old man.

"Chiefly he was conscious of a mental change. He was calm and content. Hiaqua and wealth seemed to have lost their charms for him.

Tacoma, shining like gold and silver and precious stones of gayest lustre, seemed a benign comrade and friend. All the outer world was cheerful and satisfying. He thought he had never awakened to a fresher morning. He was a young man again, except for that unusual stiffness and unmelodious creaking in his joints. He felt no apprehension of any presence of a deputy tamanoüs, sent by Tamanoüs to do malignities upon him in the lonely wood. Great Nature had a kindly aspect, and made its divinity perceived only by the sweet notes of birds and the hum of forest life, and by a joy that clothed his being. And now he found in his heart a sympathy for man, and a longing to meet his old acquaintances down by the shores of Whulge.

"He rose, and started on the downward way, smiling, and sometimes laughing heartily at the strange croaking, moaning, cracking, and rasping of his joints. But soon motion set the lubricating valves at work, and the sockets grew slippery again. He marched rapidly, hastening out of loneliness into society. The world of wood, glade, and stream seemed to him strangely altered. Old colossal trees, firs behind which he had hidden when on the hunt, cedars under whose drooping shade he had lurked, were down, and lay athwart his path, transformed into immense mossy mounds, like barrows of giants, over which he must clamber warily, lest he sink and be half stifled in the dust of rotten wood. Had Tamanoüs been widely at work in that eventful night?—or had the spiritual change the old man felt affected his views of the outer world?

"Travelling downward, he advanced rapidly, and just before sunset came to the prairies where his lodge should be. Everything had seemed to him so totally altered, that he tarried a moment in the edge of the woods to take an observation before approaching his home. There was a lodge, indeed, in the old spot, but a newer and far handsomer one than he had left on the fourth evening before.

"A very decrepit old squaw, ablaze with vermilion and decked with countless strings of hiaqua and costly beads, was seated on the ground near the door, tending a kettle of salmon, whose blue and fragrant steam mingled pleasantly with the golden haze of sunset. She resembled his own squaw in countenance, as an ancient smoked salmon is like a newly-dried salmon. If she was indeed his spouse, she was many years older than when he saw her last, and much better dressed than the respectable lady had ever been during his miserly days.

"He drew near quietly. The bedizened dame was crooning a chant, very dolorous,—like this:

'My old man has gone, gone, gone,—
My old man to Tacoma has gone.
To hunt the elk, he went long ago.
When will he come down, down, down,
Down to the salmon-pot and me?'

'He has come from Tacoma down, down, down,—
Down to the salmon-pot and thee,'

shouted the reformed miser, rushing forward to supper and his faithful
wife."

"And how did Penelope explain the mystery?" I asked.

"If you mean the old lady," replied Hamitchou, "she was my grand-
mother, and I'd thank you not to call names. She told my grandfather
that he had been gone many years;—she could not tell how many, having dropped her tally-stick in the fire by accident that very day. She
also told him how, in despite of the entreaties of many a chief who
knew her economic virtues, and prayed her to become mistress of his
household, she had remained constant to the Absent, and forever kept
the hopeful salmon-pot boiling for his return. She had distracted her
mind from the bitterness of sorrow by trading in kamas and magic
herbs, and had thus acquired a genteel competence. The excellent
dame then exhibited with great complacency her gains, most of which
she had put in the portable and secure form of personal ornament, making herself a resplendent magazine of valuable frippery.

"Little cared the repentant sage for such things. But he was rejoiced
to be again at home and at peace, and near his own early gains of hiaqua
and treasure, buried in a place of security. These, however, he no
longer over-esteemed and hoarded. He imparted whatever he possessed, material treasures or stores of wisdom and experience, freely to
all the land. Every dweller by Whulge came to him for advice how to
chase the elk, how to troll or spear the salmon, and how to propitiate
Tamanoüs. He became the Great Medicine Man of the siwashes, a
benefactor to his tribe and his race.

"Within a year after he came down from his long nap on the side of
Tacoma, a child, my father, was born to him. The sage lived many
years, beloved and revered, and on his deathbed, long before the Boston tilicum or any blanketeers were seen in the regions of Whulge, he
told this history to my father, as a lesson and a warning. My father,
dying, told it to me. But I, alas! have no son; I grow old, and lest this
wisdom perish from the earth, and Tamanoüs be again obliged to inter-

pose against avarice, I tell the tale to thee, O Boston tyee. Mayest thou and thy nation not disdain this lesson of an earlier age, but profit by it and be wise."

So far Hamitchou recounted his legend without the palisades of Fort Nisqually, and motioning, in expressive pantomime, at the close, that he was dry with big talk, and would gladly wet his whistle.

# The Unknown Climbers*
## 1854

Here is one of the great mysteries of Mount Rainier: In about 1854, two white men, whose names have never been determined, recruited a young Yakima man, Sluskin (also spelled Saluskin, Sluiskin, and a variety of other ways) to lead them to Mount Rainier for a climb. The only surviving evidence of this climb was the memory of that Yakima when he was interviewed by historian Lucullus McWhorter in 1915. McWhorter's introduction sets the stage and explains the frequent confusion over this Sluskin and another—the one who guided Philemon Van Trump and Hazard Stevens in 1870.

Though there is no way to authenticate this story, the circumstances of its telling and its internal evidence have led authorities to believe that it is probably true. It is both ironic and entertaining that, if the story is true, Mount Rainier, one of the great early "trophies" of climbers in this country, should have first been ascended by men who did not even bother to take credit for their accomplishment.

McWhorter chose the spelling "Sluskin," though more recent historians have leaned toward "Saluskin." However the name be spelled, its owner is responsible for one of the most intriguing (and, ultimately, frustrating) chapters in Mount Rainier history. Approaching from the Yakima country east of the mountain, the unknown climbers established a camp near Mystic Lake on the north side of the mountain and, leaving Sluskin there, made their approach across Winthrop Glacier. Apparently they came down the same day.

In the correspondence and statements which went the rounds of some of the Coast papers during October, 1915, a great injustice was done Chief Sluskin, of the Yakimas. The interview of the chief by an over-

---

*Reprinted from Lucullus McWhorter, "Chief Sluskin's True Narrative," Washington Historical Quarterly 8(1917): 96–101.

zealous correspondent, reported that the aged Indian acted as guide for the Stevens-Van Trump expedition to the great mountain in 1870. Chinook jargon is, at best, a very unsatisfactory medium of conversation when questions of importance are at stake, and, unfortunately, the chief was credited with statements he did not make. Sluskin has never claimed to have acted as guide for the explorers of 1870. Inadvertently I was led to corroborate the published error, but when my attention was directed to it, I determined to sift the affair directly with the chief. This I did in November, 1915, in four different interviews, and with two interpreters. The narrative was given to a Tacoma paper, after which I had a fifth talk with the venerable tribesman, in which a few minor errors were corrected and some new data obtained. The result is here given in full. It is the clear, simple statement of the Sluskin of today, devoid of perversive injections. Those who are closely acquainted with Chief Sluskin believe him incapable of willful prevarication. Seemingly he had no knowledge of the 1870 expedition. To a direct query, he plainly stated that he knew nothing of this exploration of later years. That the chief did act as guide for two white men who visited the mountain just subsequent to the treaty at Walla Walla, should now be conceded. The facts are too obvious to be ignored.

Who were those mysterious strangers? While the chief may be in error a year or two, either way, it is not at all possible that the explorers were either Dr. Tolmie, who visited the mountain in 1833, or General Kautz, some twenty-four years later. The riddle is one for the student and historian to solve.

Chief Sluskin's narrative is as follows:

"I am thinking of my people—the old people who are no more—and of this country which once belonged to us. I was raised here since the sun was created, and I do not want to speak the lie. You white people, you big men, I know what you are thinking, but you ought to listen to me. You were lucky to come here, but I am sorry the way you have treated us. You now have all but a little of our land. I wanted everything straight. Governor Stevens was to settle all the troubles, and for this, he called the big Indians to Walla Walla in council. I was there as a boy to care for the horses of Chief Owhi. After the treaty Governor Stevens finished the work [arrangements] and in about four years we were to go on the reservation.

"It was, I think, one or two years after this, our people were camping above the [now] Moxee bridge [about two miles east of North Yakima]. For a long time a big topis [pine] tree stood there.[1]

*Distant view of Mount Rainier. From Olin Wheeler's* Mount Rainier: Its Ascent by a Northern Pacific Party.

"One day an old man, Ya-num-kun, came to me and said: 'Two King George men come.' I look and see them. Both were short [scarce] middle age. They came to us. One was a short man—black eyes like Indian. Fine looking man, clean face. Some old Indians said: 'He is Mexican.' His clothes looked like corduroy. He wore a hat, and had a big, banded, flint-lock pistol. It shot big bullets.

"The other man was tall, slender, not good looking, but about right. He had brown, not quite red, hair on upper lip. Had light hair and brown eyes. He looked some mixed blood with white, just little mixed. He had gray clothes and cap. Had long flint-lock gun with ilquis [wood] all along the barrel.[2] Barrel was round and shot big ball wrapped in blanket [patching]. I found the short man had strongest mind.

"They rode Indian horses, one blue [or roan]. Had two packhorses, one buckskin. No big, or American horses, here then. All cayuses. No white men here. Old man Thorp had not come.[3]

"They wanted to know a man who could go to Tahoma, the 'White Mountain.' The old people were afraid and said: 'Do not show them the trail. They want to find money [mineral]. Then the Indians asked: 'Why do you go to the White Mountain?' The men said: 'We are Governor Stevens' boys [employes]. We came up the river from Walla Walla, and are looking for reservation line made at treaty.' They had long glass to look through.

"Then the old people said: 'All right!' They told me to show the white men the trail. I am old man Sluskin now. I was young then. My father raised me here. I knew the trail. I asked my father if I must go. He said: 'Yes.' I was not afraid. It was about the middle of June, and patches of snow still in mountains.

"I started, leading the buckskin pack-horse and my extra saddle-horse. I took them to mouth of Tieton and camped. We got lots of trout—plenty of fish.

"Next day we traveled and camped in Tieton Basin. The white men catch plenty of fish again.

"Next day we went to Ai-yi [trout] and camped. [This was Fish Lake.] We camped at mouth of river at head of lake.

"We went on big ridge near head of Natches River and camped. Next morning the men looked with glass every way.

"Then we started and went to Tahoma, the big 'White Mountain.' The men look all around; south side is bad. They asked me about west side. Yes, I knew it. On sunny side [east] water comes out, called mook-mook. Dirty water from middle of mountain and ice. The tall man killed young yamis [deer] as we crossed the mook-mook. Shot it as it passed in front of us. This was all the game killed.

"We got to ridge-like place and found plenty green grass and nice lake, good sized, called Wah-tum. We camped there. The men looked everywhere with glass.

"The Sum-sum [sharp ridge] runs down from the mountain. It was covered with wou [mountain sheep].

"The men ask if I could catch sheep for them. I told them 'No! Only when they have young one.' They said, 'If you catch one we will buy it. Big one.' I never try to catch that sheep. Too wild. That night we roast yamis for supper.

"Next morning we went to a lake, not a big lake, only tenas [little] big, at foot of mountain. We got there about one hour after noon, camped and had dinner. This was north side of mountain.

"Next morning the men took glass up the mountain and looked. They asked if I could take them to top of mountain. I did not know the trail. Too many splits in ice. No! I was not afraid of bad spirits. Maybe that is all lie. We camped over night and roasted yamis. The men said, 'In morning we go somewhere.'

"Next morning I saw them put lunch in pockets and leave camp. I did not know where they go, but they start up the mountain. They put on shoes to walk on ice. No! not show-shoes, but shoes with nails in two places like this [heel and toe]. They started early at daylight and came back after dark same day. I stayed in camp all day and thought they fell in ice split and died. At night I saw smoke go up from top of mountain, and I heard it like low thunder. [Here the chief gave an imitation of the noise he heard, in a deep, gutteral throat sound, not unlike the distant rumble of thunder]. The men did not tell me if they heard this sound.

"The white men told me they went on top of mountain and looked with glass along Cascades toward Okanogan and British Columbia, Lake Chelan and everywhere. They said, 'We find lines.' They told me they set stick, or rock on top of mountain. I did not understand much Chinook, and could not tell if wood or stone. They said, 'Ice all over top, lake in center, and smoke [or steam] coming out all around like sweat-house.'

"Next day I started home and did not know where these men went. I left them there. I do not know if they got other Indians to guide. Before I left, each man gave me a double blanket and shirt. They gave me a cotton handkerchief, big and green striped. A finger ring [plain brass band] lots of pins and fish hooks. Too-nes [steel], and sow-kus [flint] to make fire, a file and [common] hatchet. They gave me a lunch of yamis. I was two days and a half getting home.

"On this trip," concluded the chief, "I tasted bread for first time. It was nice. We had no coffee, only some kind of tea made from berries I did not know."

When asked if he ever heard of any other strangers visiting the "White Mountain" in the early days, he answered:

"Soon, not many snows after, I guided these men; we heard that four white men were in the Cowlitz. All the big men [chiefs] held council and said, 'We will go see what these men want.' We started to Cowlitz about berry-time and went to Fish Lake. There came to our camp, Poniah, Kom-kane and Koo-ciash, whose hand, I forget which one, had been broken. It was crooked in the joints. We had council and these old men told us the white men had two horses and two mules.

"After council we went to see the white men. One of them was old man Longmire.[4] We asked, 'Why are you here?' They said, 'Only to see the country. We are looking for a mine found by Poniah.' Then we would not bother them, because they only came to see the mine."

To a question:

"Yes, I was there. I saw those men. Most white men coming here came to see me. I was born here, grew up here and in the Cowlitz country. I knew all the trails. I am telling the truth. I am not fooling. Longmire at that time looked to be about thirty or thirty-five years old, not very tall, but near middle size, not very heavy."

In answer to further questions, the chief replied:

"I did not think either of the men I took to Tahoma were sons of Governor Stevens. They only worked for him, his boys. Most Indians thought they were King George men. I did not know their names. They did not tell me.

"There were no white people living here when I guided to the white mountain. We saw lots of deer, lots of sheep and plenty of yeet-tah [goats].

"The name of the white mountain is Tahoma. It was called that before the white people came. It was Tahoma, standing up to the skies. We sometimes called it the White Mountain.

"We met but two persons, Indian boys, Charley Toom-kins [possibly Tompkins] was one of them. Met them this side of Tieton Basin.

"I am no relation to the Sluiskin [note difference in the name] with the crippled hand [guide to the Stevens-Van Trump expedition]. He was half-brother to my wife on the father's side. He used to live at Thoppenish [corrupted to Toppenish] about six miles below Mool-mool [Fort Simcoe]. He worked at the Agency. He went to Cowlitz and married two sisters, daughters of Poniu. He wore two sleigh-bells, suspended under each arm, and they thought him a big chief. His little finger on right hand was gone. He was drowned in the Yakima River several years ago. Never found his body. I never heard he took two men to the White Mountain. My crippled thumb [right hand] I broke in a fight with four Columbia River Indians. We were gambling. My thumb was caught in blanket.

"The Sluskin hanged at Old Town [Yakima City] for helping kill the Perkins' people, was a Columbia River Indian, and not a Yakima. I am a Yakima, and no kin to him. My father's mother was a Cowlitz woman. My mother was a Yakima named So-patkt. My father was a Yakima, named We-owkt. He was a chief.

"If you do not understand my talk—if not interpreted straight—then you will write it as a lie. It must be right. Chinook [jargon] is not good for story. I am glad to have two interpreters. You must get this story as I tell it.

"White people are always making me stand up and talk. Why is this? I do not understand what they want. They get me tangled. Then the temis [paper] tells my talk different from my words. I do not want this. It is a lie. It is same as stealing. I did not show the White Mountain to Stevens and another man. I only guided the two strange men there. I have given you my true story. It is all that I have told to anyone. I never told it but once before this. I did not know what they wanted. You are the first man to tell me about the Stevens man going to the White Mountain. But you say that he went there long time after we had all gone on the reservation. I know nothing about this. It was before we went on the reservation that I took the white men over the trail to Tahoma.

Lucullus V. McWhorter.
North Yakima, November, 1916.

NOTES
1. The Yakimas were camped on the Moxee side of the Yakima River, east of the present city of North Yakima. The large pine tree, still remembered by many of the older white settlers, was in later years cut down.

2. Chief Sluskin's statement that these men were armed with flint-locks has been cited as reflecting on the truth of his entire narrative that such weapons were at that time obsolete. I brought this fact to his notice and he vehemently insisted that he was correct. He came to my house and I showed him both a flint-lock musket and rifle. He discarded the former and taking the rifle, pointed out wherein it was like the one carried by the taller of the strangers. The only difference was in the barrels. That owned by the explorer was **round,** while the one examined is **octagon.** Taking the powder horn, the aged Indian showed in pantomime how it was loaded. After the powder was measured and poured into the muzzle, the large bullet was put in a **"blanket"** and rammed home, after which priming placed in the "pan." The older Indians generally use the term **"musket"** in describing all guns used in an early day. The ground taken by the critics is not well founded. It is an historical fact that flint-locks were in use in many isolated localities long after the introduction of the precussion cap. Captain Boggess' company of militia called out in Lewis County (now), West Virginia, at the commencement of the Civil War, were armed with flint-lock muskets. Captain McNeill's company of Confederate Spartans, when surrendered at the close of the war, were to lay down their arms above Romney, on the Wappatomaka, Virginia. Nothing but antiquated guns, including many flint-locks, were found. It is said that the men concealed their better arms and the old guns were procured for the purpose of carrying out the terms of surrender. No more than a quarter of a century ago an old hunter in West Virginia killed a bear with his ancient flint-lock.

3. F. M. Thorp was the first settler in the Yakima Valley. He came there in 1861 and his homestead was in the Moxee. He had come to Oregon in 1844.

4. Mr. David Longmire, son of "old man Longmire," tells me that this description and location of the mining party tallies with the known facts in the case.

# ～ 5 ～

# August Kautz*
# 1857

German-born August Valentine Kautz was a distinguished lifetime military man whose nearly-fifty-year career saw him rise to the rank of brigadier general. Among his many other historical associations was his participation as a member of the military board that tried President Lincoln's assassination conspirators in 1865. He was an ambitious young lieutenant when, after four years of dreaming about it, he made his attempt on Mount Rainier in 1857.

Kautz's climb was not successful in reaching the summit, and its price was high: The entire party suffered a variety of physical ills, some lingering for years, from the exhaustion and strain of the climb. Like the Ford party, they reached a point fairly near the summit, probably about 14,000 feet.

The party approached the mountain by way of the Nisqually River valley, and Kautz made his ascent by a glacier on the south slope of the mountain; the glacier was later named in his honor.

Kautz's achievement was a matter of some public controversy almost forty years later, when an engineer and climber-guide named Fred Plummer published a story stating that Kautz had reached the top. This story disturbed another claimant for that honor, Philemon Van Trump (whose successful ascent is described in Chapter 6). Kautz, in his sixties when Plummer's story was published, was recruited to the fight, and though he defended his own achievement, he acknowledged that he had reached "the divide between the middle peak and the south peak." This clarified just how far he had gotten and apparently left him room to feel confident that with a little more time he could have reached the actual summit. Disagreements of this kind often long outlast the participants in the climbs. Sometimes disputes over who first climbed a peak are carried on by fans and descendants for many years. Luckily, Kautz's position was made clear; he nearly made it, but he did not.

---

*Reprinted from August Kautz, "Ascent of Mount Rainier," Overland Monthly 14(1876): 393–403.

In the summer of 1857 I was stationed at Fort Steilacoom, Washington Territory. This post was located near the village of Steilacoom, on the waters of Puget Sound. The post and the village took their names from a little stream near by, which is the outlet of a number of small lakes and ponds emptying into the sound. Quite a family of Indians made their permanent home in the vicinity of this creek in former years, and were known as "Steilacoom Tillicum." According to the Indian pronunciation of the name it should have been spelled "Steelacoom," dwelling long on the first syllable.

I was at that time a first-lieutenant, young, and fond of visiting unexplored sections of the country, and possessed of a very prevailing passion for going to the tops of high places. My quarters fronted Mount Rainier, which is about sixty miles nearly east of Fort Steilacoom in an air line. On a clear day it does not look more than ten miles off, and looms up against the eastern sky white as the snow with which it is covered, with a perfectly pyramidal outline, except at the top, which is slightly rounded and broken. It is a grand and inspiring view, and I had expressed so often my determination to make the ascent, without doing it, that my fellow-officers finally became incredulous, and gave to all improbable and doubtful events a date of occurrence, when I should ascend Mount Rainier.

My resolution, however, took shape and form about the first of July. Nearly all the officers had been very free to volunteer to go with me as long as they felt certain I was not going; but when I was ready to go, I should have been compelled to go alone but for the doctor, who was on a visit to the post from Fort Bellingham.

I made preparations after the best authorities I could find, from reading accounts of the ascent of Mont Blanc and other snow mountains. We made for each member of the party an *alpenstock* of dry ash with an iron point. We sewed upon our shoes an extra sole, through which were first driven four-penny nails with the points broken off and the heads inside. We took with us a rope about fifty feet long, a hatchet, a thermometer, plenty of hard biscuit, and dried beef such as the Indians prepare.

Information relating to the mountain was exceedingly meagre; no white man had ever been near it, and Indians were very superstitious and afraid of it. The southern slope seemed the least abrupt, and in that direction I proposed to reach the mountain; but whether to keep the high ground, or follow some stream to its source, was a question. Leshi, the chief of the Nesquallies, was at that time in the guard-house, awaiting his execution, and as I had greatly interested myself to save him from his fate, he volunteered the information that the valley of the Nesqually River was the best approach after getting above the falls. He had some hope that I would take him as a guide; but finding that out of the question, he suggested Wah-pow-e-ty, an old Indian of the Nesqually tribe, as knowing more about the Nesqually than any other of his people.

Mount Rainier is situated on the western side of the Cascade Range, near the forty-seventh parallel. The range to which it belongs averages about 7,000 to 8,000 feet in height, and snow may be seen along its summit-level the year round, while Rainier with its immense covering of snow towers as high again above the range. In various travels and expeditions in the territory, I had viewed the snow-peaks of this range from all points of the compass, and since that time having visited the mountain regions of Europe, and most of those of North America, I assert that Washington Territory contains mountain scenery in quantity and quality sufficient to make half a dozen Switzerlands, while there is on the continent none more grand and imposing than is presented in the Cascade Range north of the Columbia River.

About noon on the 8th of July we finally started. The party consisted of four soldiers—two of them equipped to ascend the mountain, and the other two to take care of our horses when we should be compelled to leave them. We started the soldiers on the direct route, with orders to stop at Mr. Wren's, on the eastern limit of the Nesqually plains, ten or twelve miles distant, and wait for us, while the doctor and I went by the Nesqually Reservation in order to pick up old Wah-pow-e-ty, the Indian guide.

We remained all night at Wren's, and the next morning entered that immense belt of timber with which the western slope of the Cascade Range is covered throughout its entire length. I had become familiar with the Indian trail that we followed, the year previous, in our pursuit of Indians. The little patches of prairie are so rare that they constitute in that immense forest landmarks for the guidance of the traveler. Six miles from Wren's we came to Pawhtummi, a little *camas* prairie about 500 yards long, and 100 in breadth, a resort for the Indians in the proper season to gather the *camas*-root. Six miles farther we came to a similar prairie, circular in form, not more than 400 yards in diameter, called Koaptil. Another six or seven miles took us to the Tanwut, a small stream with a patch of prairie bordering it, where the trail crossed. Ten or twelve miles more brought us to the Mishawl Prairie, where we camped for the night, this being the end of the journey for our horses, and the limit of our knowledge of the country.

This prairie takes its name from the stream near by, and is situated between it and the Owhap on a high table-land or bluff, not more than one or two miles from where these enter the Nesqually. It is perhaps half a mile long, and 200 or 300 yards wide at the widest point. The grass was abundant, and it was an excellent place to leave our horses. Fifteen months before, I had visited this spot, and camped near by with a small detachment of troops, searching for Indians who had hidden away in these forests, completely demoralized and nearly starving. A family of two or three men, and quite a number of women and children, had camped in the fork of the Mishawl and Nesqually, about two miles from this prairie, and were making fishtraps to catch salmon. When we fell in with them we learned that the Washington Territory volunteers had been before us, and with their immensely superior force had killed the most of them without regard to age or sex. Our own little command in that expedition captured about thirty of these poor, half-starved, ignorant creatures, and no act of barbarity was perpetrated by us to mar the memory of that success.

We accordingly camped in the Mishawl Prairie. When I was here before it was in March, and the rainy season was still prevailing; the topographical engineer of the expedition and I slept under the same blankets on a wet drizzly night, and next morning treated each other to bitter reproaches for having each had more than his share of the covering. Now the weather was clear and beautiful, and the scene lovely in comparison. I can imagine nothing more gloomy and cheerless than a fir-forest in Washington Territory on a rainy winter day. The misty clouds hang down below the tops of the tallest trees, and although it does not rain, but drizzles, yet it is very wet and cold, and penetrates every thread of clothing to the skin. The summers of this region are in extraordinary contrast with the winters. Clear, beautiful, and dry, they begin in May and last till November; while in the winter, although in latitude 47° and 48°, it rarely freezes or snows—often, however, raining two weeks without stopping, a permeating drizzle.

On the 9th of July, 1857, the weather was beautiful; it had not rained for weeks. The Mishawl—a raging mountain torrent, when last I saw it—was now a sluggish rivulet of clear mountain-spring water. We started early on our journey, having made our preparations the evening before. We calculated to be gone about six days. Each member of the party had to carry his own provisions and bedding; everything was therefore reduced to the minimum. Each took a blanket, twenty-four crackers of hard bread, and about two pounds of dried beef. We took Dogue (a German) and Carroll (an Irishman) with us; they were both volunteers for the trip; one carried the hatchet and the other the rope. I carried a field-glass, thermometer, and a large-sized revolver. Wah-pow-e-ty carried his rifle, with which we hoped to procure some game. The soldiers carried no arms. Bell and Doneheh were left behind to take care of the horses and extra provisions, until our return.

We each had a haversack for our provisions, and a tin canteen for water. The doctor very unwisely filled his with whisky instead of water. Having sounded Wah-pow-e-ty as to the route, we learned he had once been on the upper Nesqually when a boy, with his father, and that his knowledge of the country was very limited. We ascertained, however, that we could not follow the Nesqually at first; that there was a fall in the river a short distance above the mouth of the Mishawl, and that the mountains came down so abrupt and precipitous that we could not follow the stream, and that the mountain must be crossed first and a descent made to the river above the fall.

That mountain proved a severer task than we anticipated. There was no path and no open country—only a dense forest, obstructed with undergrowth and fallen timber. The sun was very hot when it could reach us through the foliage; not a breath of air stirred, and after we crossed the Mishawl, not a drop of water was to be had until we got down to low ground again. We toiled from early morning until three o'clock in the afternoon before we reached the summit. As the doctor had taken whisky instead of water in his canteen, he found it necessary to apply to the other members of the party to quench his thirst, and our canteens were speedily empty. The doctor sought relief in whisky, but it only aggravated his thirst, and he poured out the contents of his canteen. The severe exertion required for the ascent brought on painful cramps in his legs, and at one time, about the middle of the day, I concluded that we should be obliged to leave him to find his way back to camp, while we went on without him; but he made an agreement with Wah-pow-e-ty to carry his pack for him, in addition to his own, for ten dollars, and the doctor was thus enabled to go on. Here was an illustration of the advantage of training. The doctor was large, raw-boned, and at least six feet high, looking as if he could have crushed with a single blow the insignificant old Indian, who was not much over five feet, and did not weigh more than half as much as the doctor; but, inured to this kind of toil, he carried double the load that any of the party did, while the doctor, who was habituated to a sedentary life, had all he could do, carrying no load whatsoever, to keep up with the Indian.

Early in the afternoon we reached the summit of the first ascent, where we enjoyed, in addition to a good rest, a magnificent view of the Puget Sound Valley, with Mount Olympus and the Coast Range for a background. Here on this summit, too, munching our biscuit of hard bread and our dried beef, we enjoyed a refreshing breeze as we looked down on the beautiful plains of the Nesqually, with its numerous clear and beautiful little lakes. There was nothing definite except forest—of which there was a great excess—lakes, and plains of limited area, the sound, and a great background of mountains. No habitations, farms, or villages were to be seen; not a sign of civilization or human life.

After a good rest we pushed on, taking an easterly course, and keeping, or trying to keep, on the spur of the mountain; the forest was so thick, however, that this was next to an impossibility. We were not loth to go down into ravines in the hope of finding some water, for we needed it greatly. It was a long time, and we met with many disappointments, before we could find enough to quench our thirst. Our progress was exceedingly slow on account of the undergrowth. At sundown we camped in the grand old forest, the location being chosen on account of some water in a partially dry ravine. The distance passed over from Mishawl Prairie we estimated at about ten or eleven miles. On good roads thirty miles would have wearied us much less.

We started early the next morning, and for a time tried to keep the high ground, but found it so difficult that we finally turned down to the right, and came upon the Nesqually River about the middle of the afternoon. There was no material difference in the undergrowth, but there was an advantage gained in having plenty of water to quench our thirst. We made about ten miles this day, and camped about sundown. There seemed nothing but forest before us; dark, gloomy forest, remarkable for large trees, and its terrible solitude. But few living things were to be seen. The Nesqually is a very wide muddy torrent, fordable in places where the stream is much divided by islands.

We already here began to suffer from the loss of appetite, which was to us such a difficulty throughout the entire trip. Even the four crackers and two ounces of dried beef, which was our daily limit, we found ourselves unable to master, and yet so much was necessary to keep up our strength. I have never been able to settle in my mind whether this was due to the sameness of the food or the great fatigue we underwent.

The third morning we made an early start, and followed up the stream in almost a due east direction all day until about five o'clock, when the doctor broke down, having been unable to eat anything during the day. With considerable cramming I managed to dispose of the most of my rations. We kept the north side of the river, and had no streams to cross; in fact, there did not appear to be any streams on either side putting into the river. The valley seemed several miles in width, densely timbered, and the undergrowth a complete thicket. Not more than ten miles were made by us. Just before we stopped for the night, we passed through a patch of dead timber of perhaps 100 acres, with an abundance of blackberries. Opposite our camp, on the south side of the river, there was the appearance of quite a tributary coming in from the southeast.

We did not get started until about eleven o'clock on the fourth morning. After cutting up a deer which Wah-pow-e-ty brought in early in the morning, we dried quite a quantity of it by the fire. As we anticipated, it proved of much assistance, for we already saw that six days would be a very short time in which to make the trip. By night we reached a muddy tributary coming in from the north, and evidently having its source in the melting snows of Rainier. The summit of the mountain was visible from our camp, and seemed close at hand; but night set in with promise of bad weather. The valley had become quite narrow. Our camp was at the foot of a mountain spur several thousand feet high, and the river close at hand. The gloomy forest, the wild mountain scenery, the roaring of the river, and the dark overhanging clouds, with the peculiar melancholy sighing which the wind makes through a fir forest, gave to our camp at this point an awful grandeur.

On the fifth morning the clouds were so threatening, and came down so low on the surrounding mountains, that we were at a loss what course to pursue—whether to follow up the main stream or the tributary at our camp, which evidently came from the nearest snow. We finally followed the main stream, which very soon turned in toward the mountain, the valley growing narrower, the torrent more and more rapid, and our progress slower and slower, especially when we were compelled to take to the timber. We often crossed the torrent, of which the water was intensely cold, in order to avoid the obstructions of the forest. Sometimes, however, the stream was impassable, and then we often became so entangled in the thickets as almost to despair of farther advance. Early in the evening we reached the foot of an immense glacier and camped. For several miles before camping the bed of the stream was paved with white granite bowlders, and the mountain gorge became narrower and narrower. The walls were in many places perpendicular precipices, thousands of feet high, their summits hid in the clouds. Vast piles of snow were to be seen along the stream—the remains of avalanches—for earth, trees, and rocks were intermingled with the snow.

As it was near night we camped, thinking it best to begin the ascent in the early morning; besides, the weather promised to become worse. The foliage of the pine-trees here was very dense, and on such a cloudy day it was dark as night in the forest. The limbs of the trees drooped upon the ground, a disposition evidently given to them by the snow, which must be late in disappearing in this region.

We followed thus far the main branch of the Nesqually, and here it emerged from an icy cavern at the foot of an immense glacier. The ice itself was of a dark-blue tinge. The water was white, and whenever I waded the torrent my shoes filled with gravel and sand. The wall of this immense vein of granite that was visible on both sides seemed to form a narrow throat to the great ravine, which is much wider both above and below. The water seems to derive its color from the disintegration of this granite.[1]

We made our camp under a pine of dense foliage, whose limbs at the outer end drooped near the ground. We made our cup of tea, and found the water boil at 202° Fahrenheit. Night set in with a drizzling rain, and a more solitary, gloomy picture than we presented at that camp it is impossible to conceive. Tired, hungry, dirty, clothes all in rags—the effects of our struggles with the brush—we were not the least happy; the solitude was oppressive. The entire party, except myself, dropped down and did not move unless obliged to. I went up to the foot of the glacier, and explored a little before night set in. I also tried to make a sketch of the view looking up the glacier; but I have never looked at it since without being forcibly reminded what a failure it is as a sketch.

On the morning of the sixth day we set out again up the glacier. A drizzling rain prevailed through the night, and continued this morning. We had a little trouble in getting upon the glacier, as it terminated everywhere in steep faces that were very difficult to climb. Once up, we did not meet with any obstructions or interruptions for several hours, although the slippery surface of the glacier, which formed inclined planes of about twenty degrees, made it very fatiguing with our packs. About noon the weather thickened; snow, sleet, and rain prevailed, and strong winds, blowing hither and thither, almost blinded us. The surface of the glacier, becoming steeper, began to be intersected by immense crevasses crossing our path, often compelling us to travel several hundred yards to gain a few feet. We finally resolved to find a camp. But getting off the glacier was no easy task. We found that the face of the lateral moraine was almost perpendicular, and composed of loose stones, sand, and gravel, furnishing a very uncertain foothold, besides being about fifty feet high. Wah-pow-e-ty and I finally succeeded in getting up, and with the aid of the rope we assisted our companions to do the same. When we reached the top we were a little surprised to find that we had to go down-hill again to reach the mountain side. Here a few stunted pines furnished us fuel and shelter, and we rested for the remainder of the day. I explored a little in the evening by ascending the ridge from the glacier, and discovered that it would be much the best route to pursue in ascending to the summit.

When night set in, the solitude of our camp was very oppressive. We were near the limit of perpetual snow. The water for our tea we obtained from the melting of the ice near by. The atmosphere was very different from what it was below, and singularly clear when not obstructed by fog, rain, or snow. There were no familiar objects to enable one to estimate distance. When I caught a glimpse of the top of Rainier through the clouds, I felt certain that we could reach it in three hours. The only living things to be seen were some animals, with regard to which we still labor under an error. These little creatures would make their appearance on the side of the mountain in sight of our camp, and feed upon herbage that grew on the soil where the snow left it bare. The moment anyone stirred from camp, a sound between a whistle and scream would break unexpectedly and from some unknown quarter, and immediately all the animals that were in sight would vanish in the earth. Upon visiting the spot where they disappeared, we would find a burrow which was evidently the creatures' home. Everywhere round the entrance we found great numbers of tracks, such as a lamb or kid would make. The animals that we saw were about the size of kids, and grazed and moved about so much like them, that, taken in connection with the tracks we saw, we jumped at once to the conclusion that they were mountain sheep, of which we all had heard a great deal, but none of our party had ever seen any. My report of these animals, which was published in the *Washington Republican* on our return, was severely ridiculed by some of the naturalists who were hunting for undescribed insects and animals in that country at the time. We are still at a loss to understand the habits of the creatures, and to reconcile the split hoofs which the tracks indicated with their burrow in the earth.

*A. V. Kautz, about the time of his ascent of the mountain. (Courtesy National Park Service)*

On the following morning—the seventh day from our camp on the Mishawl—the sky showed signs of clear weather, and we began the ascent of the main peak. Until about noon we were enveloped in clouds, and only occasionally did we get a glimpse of the peak. Soon after midday we reached suddenly a colder atmosphere, and found ourselves all at once above the clouds which were spread out smooth and even as a sea above which appeared the snowy peaks of St. Helens, Mount Adams, and Mount Hood, looking like pyramidal icebergs above an ocean. At first we could not see down through the clouds into the valleys. Above, the atmosphere was singularly clear, and the reflection of the sun upon the snow very powerful. The summit of Rainier seemed very close at hand.

About two o'clock in the afternoon the clouds rolled away like a scroll; in a very short time they had disappeared, and the Cascade Range lay before us in all its greatness. The view was too grand and extensive to be taken in at once, or in the short time we had to observe. The entire scene, with few exceptions, was covered with forests, with here and there barren rocky peaks that rose up out of the ridges; now and then a mountain lake, much more blue than the sky, and the Nesqually, winding like a thread of silver through the dark forests. From the foot of the glacier for several miles the bed of the river was very white, from the granite bowlders that covered the bed of the stream. The water, too, was of a decidedly chalkier color near its source.

We had no time, however, to study the beauties that lay before us. We had already discovered that there was no telling from appearances how far we had to go. The travel was very difficult; the surface of the snow was porous in some places, and at each step we sunk to our knees. Carroll and the Indian gave out early in the afternoon, and returned to camp. The doctor began to lag behind. Dogue stuck close to me. Between four and five o'clock we reached a very difficult point. It proved to be the crest of the mountain, where the comparatively smooth surface was much broken up, and inaccessible pinnacles of ice and deep crevasses interrupted our progress. It was not only difficult to go ahead, but exceedingly dangerous; a false step, or the loss of a foothold, would have been certain destruction. Dogue was evidently alarmed, for every time that I was unable to proceed, and turned back to find another passage, he would say, "*I guess, Lieutenant, we petter go pack.*"

Finally we reached what may be called the top, for although there were points higher yet, the mountain spread out comparatively flat, and it was much easier to get along. The soldier threw himself down exhausted, and said he could go no farther. The doctor was not in sight. I went on to explore by myself, but I returned in a quarter of an hour without my hat, fully satisfied that nothing more could be done. It was after six o'clock, the air was very cold, and the wind blew fiercely, so that in a second my hat which it carried away was far beyond recovery. The ice was forming in my canteen, and to stay on the mountain at such a temperature was to freeze to death, for we brought no blankets with us, and we could not delay, as it would be impossible to return along the crest of the mountain after dark. When I returned to where I had left the soldier, I found the doctor there also, and after a short consultation we decided to return.

Returning was far easier and more rapid than going. The snow was much harder and firmer, and we passed over in three hours, coming down, what required ten in going up. We were greatly fatigued by the day's toil, and the descent was not accomplished without an occasional rest of our weary limbs. In one place the snow was crusted over, and for a short distance the mountain was very steep, and required the skillful use of the stick to prevent our going much faster than we desired. The soldier lost his footing, and rolled helplessly to the foot of the declivity, thirty or forty yards distant, and his face bore the traces of the scratching for many a day after, as if he had been through a bramble-bush.

We found the Indian and Carroll in the camp. The latter had a long story to tell of his wanderings to find camp, and both stated that the fatigue was too much for them. There was no complaint on the part of any of us about the rarity of the atmosphere. The doctor attributed to this cause the fact that he could not go but a few yards at a time, near the summit, without resting; but I am inclined to think this was due to our exhaustion. My breathing did not seem to be the least affected.

We were much disappointed not to have had more time to explore the summit of the mountain. We had, however, demonstrated the feasibility of making the ascent. Had we started at dawn of the day we should have had plenty of time for the journey. From what I saw I should say the mountain top was a ridge perhaps two miles in length and nearly half a mile in width, with an angle about half-way, and depressions between the angle and each end of the ridge which give to the summit the appearance of three small peaks as seen from the east or west. When viewed from north or south, a rounded summit is all that can be seen; while viewed from positions between the cardinal points of the compass, the mountain generally has the appearance of two peaks.

The night was very cold and clear after our return. We had some idea of making another ascent; but an investigation into the state of our provisions, together with the condition of the party generally, determined us to begin our return on the morning of the eighth day. The two soldiers had eaten all their bread but one cracker each. The doctor and I had enough left, so that by a redistribution we had four crackers each, with which to return over a space that had required seven days of travel coming. We, of course, expected to be a shorter time getting back; but let it be ever so short, our prospect for something to eat was proportionately much more limited. We had more meat than bread, thanks to the deer the Indian had killed, and we depended greatly on his killing more game for us going back: but this dependence, too, was cut off; the Indian was snow-blind, and needed our help to guide him. His groans disturbed us during the night, and what was our astonishment in the morning to find his eyelids closed with inflammation, and so swollen that he looked as if he had been in a free fight and got the worst of it. He could not have told a deer from a stump the length of his little old rifle.

Our camp was about 1,000 or 1,500 feet below the last visible shrub; water boiled at 199°, and, according to an approximate scale we had with us, this indicated an elevation of 7,000 feet. We estimated the highest peak to be over 12,000 feet high. I greatly regretted not being able to get the boiling-point on the top, but it was impossible to have had a fire in such a wind as prevailed round the summit.

As we returned we had more leisure to examine and clearer weather to see the glacier than we had coming up. There was no medial moraine; but an icy ridge parallel to the lateral moraines, and about midway between them, extending as far as we ascended the glacier. The lateral moraines were not continuous, but were interrupted by the walls of the spurs where they projected into the glacier; between these points the lateral moraines existed. The glacier sloped away from the ridge to the moraines, more or less sharply, and it was no easy matter to get off the ice, owing to the steepness of the moraine. The ice melted by reflection from the face of the moraine, and formed a difficult crevasse between it and the glacier. Bowlders of every shape and size were scattered over the face of the glacier. Large ones were propped up on pinnacles of ice; these were evidently too thick for the sun to heat through. The small bowlders were sunk more or less deeply, and surrounded by water in the hot sun; but they evidently froze fast again at night.

The noise produced by the glacier was startling and strange. One might suppose the mountain was breaking loose, particularly at night. Although, so far as stillness was concerned, there was no difference between day and night, at night the noise seemed more terrible. It was a fearful crashing and grinding that was going on, where the granite was powdered that whitened the river below, and where the bowlders were polished and partially rounded.

The great stillness and solitude were also very oppressive; no familiar sounds; nothing except the whistle of the animal before mentioned and the noise of the glacier's motion was to be heard, and if these had not occurred at intervals the solitude would have been still more oppressive. We were glad to get down again to the Nesqually, where we could hear its roar and see its rushing waters. The other members of the party were so tired and worn, however, that they seemed to observe but little, and as we were now on our homeward way, their thoughts were set only on our camp on the Mishawl, with its provisions and promise of rest.

The first day we passed two of the camps we had made coming up, and reached a point where we remembered to have seen a great quantity of blackberries. It was quite dark by the time we reached the little spot of dead timber—which seems to be the favorite haunt of the creeping bramble in this country—and to gather our supper of berries we built a fire at the foot of a large dead tree. Speedily the flames were climbing to the top of the withered branches, and casting a cheerful light for a hundred yards round. But what we found very convenient for gathering berries proved to be a great annoyance when we wanted to sleep. During the night we were constantly moving our place of rest, at first on account of the falling embers, and finally for fear of the tree itself.

Blackberries are refreshing so far as the palate is concerned; but they are not very nourishing. We took our breakfast on them, and continued down the Nesqually from six in the morning until six in the evening, traveling slowly because of the difficult undergrowth and our worn-out and exhausted condition. We passed another of our camps, and finally stopped at what evidently had been an Indian camp. The cedar bark, always to be found in such places, we anticipated would make a shelter for us in case of rain, which the clouds promised us.

No rain fell, however, and we resumed our march, continuing down the river five or six miles farther than where we first struck it, to a point where the hills came close up and overhung the water. There we camped, expecting that an easy march on the morrow would enable us to reach our camp on the Mishawl. We ate our last morsel, and the next morning I was awakened by the conversation of the two soldiers. They were evidently discussing the subject of hunger, for the Irishman said: "I've often seen the squaws coming about the cook-house picking the pitaties out of the slop-barrel, an' I thought it was awful; but I giss I'd do it mesilf this mornin'."

The morning of the eleventh day we left the Nesqually to cross over to the Mishawl, and traveled on the mountain all day, until we reached the stream at night completely exhausted. We should have stopped sooner than we did, but we were almost perishing with thirst, not having had any water since we left the Nesqually in the morning. What we took along in our canteens was exhausted in the early part of the day. We were not more than two miles from the camp in the prairie, and notwithstanding that we had had nothing to eat all day, except a few berries we had picked by the way, we were so exhausted that we lay down to sleep as soon as we had quenched our thirst.

We started up-stream the next morning, thinking we had reached the Mishawl below our camp; but soon discovering our mistake, we turned down. At this point the Irishman's heart sunk within him, he was so exhausted. Thinking we were lost, he wanted to lie down in the stream and "drownd" himself. He was assured that we should soon be in camp, and we arrived there very soon after, before the men left in charge of the horses were up.

Our first thought was of something to eat. I cautioned all about eating much at first; but from subsequent results am inclined to think my advice was not heeded. I contented myself with a half cracker, a little butter, and weak coffee; and an hour after, when I began to feel the beneficial effects of what I had eaten, I took a little more substantial meal, but refrained from eating heartily.

After a short rest we caught our horses, and the doctor and I rode into Steilacoom, where we arrived after a hard ride late in the afternoon. As we approached the post, we met on the road a number of the inhabitants with whom we were well acquainted, and who did not recognize us. Nor were we surprised when we got a glimpse of our faces in a glass. Haggard and sunburnt, nearly every familiar feature had disappeared. Since the loss of my hat, my head-dress was the sleeve of a red flannel shirt, tied into a knot at the elbow, with the point at the arm-pit for a visor. Our clothes were in rags; one of the doctor's pantaloon-legs had entirely disappeared, and he had improvised a substitute out of a coffee-sack. In our generally dilapidated condition none of our acquaintances recognized us until we got to the post. We passed for Indians until we arrived there, where we were received by the officers with a shout at our ludicrous appearance. They were all sitting under the oak-trees in front of quarters, discussing what had probably become of us, and proposing means for our rescue, when we came up.

I felt the effects of the trip for many days, and did not recover my natural condition for some weeks. The doctor and I went to the village next morning, where the people were startled at our emaciated appearance. We found that the doctor had lost twenty-one pounds in weight in fourteen days, and I had lost fourteen pounds in the same time. The doctor, while we were in the village, was taken with violent pains in his stomach, and returned to his post quite sick. He did not recover his health again for three months.

*General A. V. Kautz, a*
*photograph from late in life.*
*(Courtesy Aubrey Haines)*

The two soldiers went into the hospital immediately on their return, and I learned that for the remainder of their service they were in the hospital nearly all the time. Four or five years after, Carroll applied to me for a certificate on which to file an application for a pension, stating that he had not been well since his trip to the mountain. The Indian had an attack of gastritis, and barely escaped with his life after a protracted sickness. I attribute my own escape from a lingering illness to the precautions I took in eating when satisfying the first cravings of hunger, on our return to camp.

We are not likely to have any competitors in this attempt to explore the summit of Mount Rainier. Packwood and McAllister, two citizens of Pierce County, Washington Territory, explored up the Nesqually, and crossed over to the head of the Cowlitz River, and thence by what was called Cowlitz Pass (since called Packwood Pass), to the east side of the mountains, searching for a trail to the mining regions of the upper Columbia. More recently, surveyors in the employ of the Pacific Railroad Company have been surveying through the same route for a railway passage.

When the locomotive is heard in that region some day, when American enterprise has established an ice-cream saloon at the foot of the glacier, and sherry-cobblers may be had at twenty-five cents half-way up to the top of the mountain, attempts to ascend that magnificent snow-peak will be quite frequent. But many a long year will pass away before roads are sufficiently good to induce anyone to do what we did in the summer of 1857.

NOTE

1. I have no doubt that the south branch of the Nachess, which flows to the east into the Columbia, and that the Puyallap and White rivers, which flow west into Puget Sound, have similar sources in glaciers, from the fact that in July they are all of a similar character with the Nesqually, muddy, white torrents, at a time when little rain has fallen for months.

# 6

# Hazard Stevens[*]
# 1870

This is the climb that, rightly or wrongly, has received the acclaim and honor of being first. Whether the mystery climbers of 1854 did reach the summit of Mount Rainier or not is almost irrelevant in the well-deserved fanfare that history has given Hazard Stevens and Philemon Van Trump. There was no mystery or secret about their success.

Both Stevens and Van Trump figured prominently in the history of the Northwest. Stevens was the son of Isaac Stevens, who had first come to Washington Territory in 1854 as Governor. Hazard distinguished himself as a soldier, winning the Congressional Medal of Honor as a Union officer in the Civil War and becoming, while just twenty-two, the youngest general in the entire war. He was an internal revenue collector and was studying the law at the time of his climb. Van Trump, a native of Ohio, became private secretary to the Governor of Washington in 1867, discovered almost immediately that he and Stevens shared an obsession with Mount Rainier, and spent almost three years planning a climb with him. Van Trump would go on to make several other climbs (see Chapter 13 for more of his adventures) and establish himself as a sort of grand old man of the mountain, always working to promote it. A third member of their party, Edmund Coleman, stayed behind during the ascent, and is sufficiently introduced in Stevens's following narrative.

The party came up the Nisqually valley to Bear Prairie (not far south of the present park boundary), where they set up a camp. From there Stevens and his party, which included a Yakima Indian named Sluiskin, crossed the Tatoosh Range (losing Coleman on the climb—he went back to Bear Prairie and waited for them to return). They established another camp at what is now called Sluiskin Falls, above Paradise, and from there the two white men made their ascent. They stayed one night on the summit, being the first to do so, and on the return trip Van Trump suffered a fall and injury that slowed them down on their return to the settlements. All of this appears in the following account, as does the sense of excitement and pride their accomplishment earned them.

*Reprinted from Hazard Stevens, "The Ascent of Takhoma," Atlantic Monthly 38(1876): 513–530.

When Vancouver, in 1792, penetrated the Straits of Fuca and explored the unknown waters of the Mediterranean of the Pacific, wherever he sailed, from the Gulf of Georgia to the farthest inlet of Puget Sound, he beheld the lofty, snow-clad barrier range of the Cascades stretching north and south and bounding the eastern horizon. Towering at twice the altitude of all others, at intervals of a hundred miles there loomed up above the range three majestic, snowy peaks that

> "Like giants stand
> To sentinel enchanted land."

In the matter-of-fact spirit of a British sailor of his time, he named these sublime monuments of nature in honor of three lords of the English admiralty, Hood, Rainier, and Baker. Of these Rainier is the central, situated about half-way between the Columbia River and the line of British Columbia, and is by far the loftiest and largest. Its altitude is 14,444 feet, while Hood is 11,025 feet, and Baker is 10,810 feet high. The others, too, are single cones, while Rainier, or Takhoma,[1] is an immense mountain-mass with three distinct peaks, an eastern, a northern, and a southern; the two last extending out and up from the main central dome, from the summit of which they stand over a mile distant, while they are nearly two miles apart from each other.

Takhoma overlooks Puget Sound from Olympia to Victoria, one hundred and sixty miles. Its snow-clad dome is visible from Portland on the Willamette, one hundred and twenty miles south, and from the table-land of Walla Walla, one hundred and fifty miles east. A region two hundred and fifty miles across, including nearly all of Washington Territory, part of Oregon, and part of Idaho, is commanded in one field of vision by this colossus among mountains.

Takhoma had never been ascended. It was a virgin peak. The superstitious fears and traditions of the Indians, as well as the dangers of the ascent, had prevented their attempting to reach the summit, and the failure of a gallant and energetic officer, whose courage and hardihood were abundantly shown during the rebellion, had in general estimation proved it insurmountable.

For two years I had resolved to ascend Takhoma, but both seasons the dense smoke overspreading the whole country had prevented the attempt. Mr. Philomon Beecher Van Trump, humorous, generous, whole-souled, with endurance and experience withal, for he had roughed it in the mines, and a poetic appreciation of the picturesque

*Hazard Stevens in 1863, seven years before his ascent. (Courtesy Aubrey Haines)*

and the sublime, was equally eager to scale the summit. Mr. Edward [actually, Edmund] T. Coleman, an English gentleman of Victoria, a landscape artist and an Alpine tourist, whose reputed experience in Switzerland had raised a high opinion of his ability above the snowline, completed the party.

Olympia, the capital of Washington Territory, is a beautiful, maple-embowered town of some two thousand inhabitants, situated at the southernmost extremity of Puget Sound, and west of Takhoma, distant in an air line seventy-five miles. The intervening country is covered with dense fir forests, almost impenetrable to the midday sun, and obstructed with fallen trees, upturned roots and stumps, and a perfect jungle of undergrowth, through which the most energetic traveler can accomplish but eight or nine miles a day. It was advisable to gain the nearest possible point by some trail, before plunging into the unbroken forest. The Nisqually River, which rises on the southern and western slopes of Takhoma, and empties into the sound a few miles north of Olympia, offered the most direct and natural approach. Ten years before, moreover, a few enterprising settlers had blazed out a trail across the Cascade Range, which followed the Nisqually nearly up to its source, thence deflected south to the Cowlitz River, and pursued this stream in a northeastern course to the summit of the range, thus turning the great mountain by a wide circuit. The best-informed mountain men represented the approaches on the south and southeast as by far the most favorable. The Nisqually-Cowlitz trail, then, seemed much the best, for the Nisqually, heading in the south and southwest slopes, and the Cowlitz, in the southeastern, afforded two lines of approach, by either of which the distance to the mountain, after leaving the trail, could not exceed thirty miles.

One August afternoon, Van Trump and I drove out to Yelm Prairie, thirty miles east of Olympia, and on the Nisqually River. We dashed rapidly on over a smooth, hard, level road, traversing wide reaches of prairie, passing under open groves of oaks and firs, and plunging through masses of black, dense forest in ever-changing variety. The moon had risen as we emerged upon Yelm Prairie; Takhoma, bathed in cold, white, spectral light from summit to base, appeared startlingly near and distinct. Our admiration was not so noisy as usual. Perhaps a little of dread mingled with it. In another hour we drove nearly across the plain and turned into a lane which conducted us up a beautiful rising plateau, crowned with a noble grove of oaks and overlooking the whole prairie. A comfortable, roomy house with a wide porch nestled among the trees, and its hospitable owner, Mr. James Longmire, appeared at the door and bade us enter.

The next morning we applied to Mr. Longmire for a guide, and for his advice as to our proposed trip. He was one of the few who marked out the Nisqually-Cowlitz trail years ago. He had explored the mountains about Takhoma as thoroughly, perhaps, as any other white man. One of the earliest settlers, quiet, self-reliant, sensible, and kindly, a better counselor than he could not have been found. The trail, he said, had not been traveled for four years, and was entirely illegible to eyes not well versed in woodcraft, and it would be folly for any one to attempt to follow it who was not thoroughly acquainted with the country. He could not leave his harvest, and moreover in three weeks he was to cross the mountains for a drove of cattle. His wife, too, quietly discouraged his going. She described his appearance on his return from previous mountain trips, looking as haggard and thin as though he had just risen from a sick-bed. She threw out effective little sketches of toil, discomfort, and hardship incident to mountain travel, and dwelt upon the hard fare. The bountiful country breakfast heaped before us, the rich cream, fresh butter and eggs, snowy, melting biscuits, and broiled chicken, with rich, white gravy, heightened the effect of her words.

But at length, when it appeared that no one else who knew the trail could be found, Mr. Longmire yielded to our persuasions, and consented to conduct us as far as the trail led, and to procure an Indian guide before leaving us to our own resources. As soon as we returned home we went with Mr. Coleman to his room to see a few indispensable equipments he had provided, in order that we might procure similar ones. The floor was literally covered with his traps, and he exhibited them one by one, expatiating upon their various uses. There was his ground-sheet, a large gum blanket equally serviceable to Mr. Coleman as a tent in camp and a bath-tub at the hotel. There was a strong rope to which we were all to be tied when climbing the snow-fields, so that if one fell into a chasm the others could hold him up. The "creepers" were a clumsy, heavy arrangement of iron spikes made to fasten on the foot with chains and straps, in order to prevent slipping on the ice. He had an ice-axe for cutting steps, a spirit-lamp for making tea on the mountains, green goggles for snow-blindness, deer's fat for the face, Alpine staffs, needles and thread, twine, tacks, screws, screw-driver, gimlet, file, several medical prescriptions, two boards for pressing flowers, sketching materials, and in fact every article that Mr. Coleman in his extensive reading had found used or recommended by travelers. Every one of these he regarded as indispensable. The Alpine staff was, he declared, most important of all, a great assistance in traveling through the woods as well as on the ice; and he illustrated on his hands and knees how to cross a crevasse in the ice on two staffs. This interview naturally brought to mind the characteristic incident related of Packwood, the mountain man who, as hunter and prospecter, had explored the deepest recesses of the Cascades. He had been engaged to guide a railroad surveying party across the mountains, and just as the party was about to start he approached the chief and demanded an advance to enable him to buy his outfit for the trip. "How much do you want?" asked the chief, rather anxiously, lest Packwood should overdraw his prospective wages. "Well, about two dollars and a half," was the reply; and at the camp-fire that evening, being asked if he had bought his outfit, Packwood, thrusting his hand into his pocket, drew forth and exhibited with perfect seriousness and complacency his entire outfit,—a jack-knife and a plug of tobacco.

Half a dozen carriages rattled gayly out of Olympia in the cool of the morning, filled with a laughing, singing, frolicking bevy of young ladies and gentlemen. They were the Takhoma party starting on their adventurous trip, with a chosen escort accompanying them to their first camp. They rested several hours at Longmire's during the heat of the day, and the drive was then continued seven miles farther, to the Lacamas, an irregular-shaped prairie two miles in length by half a mile in breadth. Here live two of Mr. Longmire's sons. Their farms form the last settlement, and at the gate of Mr. Elkane Longmire's house the road ends. A wooded knoll overlooking the prairie, with a spring of water at its foot, was selected as the campground. Some of the party stretched a large sail between the trees as a tent, others watered and fed the horses, and others busied themselves with the supper. Two eager sportsmen started after grouse, while their more practical companions bought half a dozen chickens, and had them soon dressed and sputtering over the fire. The shades of night were falling as the party sat down on the ground and partook of a repast fit for the Olympians, and with a relish sharpened by the long journey and a whole day's fast.

Early in the morning Mr. Longmire arrived in camp with two mules and a pack-horse, and our mountain outfit was rapidly made up into suitable bales and packed upon the horse and one of the mules, the other mule being reserved for Longmire's own riding. We assembled around the breakfast with spirits as gay and appetites as sharp as ever. Then, with many good-bys and much waving of handkerchiefs, the party broke up. Four roughly clad pedestrians moved off in single file, leading their pack animals, and looking back at every step to catch the last glimpse of the bright garments and fluttering cambrics, while the carriages drove rapidly down the road and disappeared in the dark, sullen forest.

We stepped off briskly, following a dim trail in an easterly course, and crossing the little prairie entered the timber. After winding over hilly ground for about three miles, we descended into the Nisqually bottom and forded a fine brook at the foot of the hill. For the next ten miles our route lay across the bottom, and along the bank of the river, passing around logs, following old, dry beds of the river and its lateral sloughs, ankle-deep in loose sand, and forcing our way through dense jungles of vine-maple. The trail was scarcely visible, and much obstructed by fallen trees and underbrush, and its difficulties were aggravated by the bewildering tracks of Indians who had lately wandered about the bottom in search of berries or rushes. We repeatedly missed the trail, and lost hours in retracing our steps and searching for the right course. The weather was hot and sultry, and rendered more oppressive by the dense foliage; myriads of gnats and mosquitoes tormented us and drove our poor animals almost frantic; and our thirst, aggravated by the severe and unaccustomed toil, seemed quenchless. At length we reached the ford of the Nisqually. Directly opposite, a perpendicular bluff of sand and gravel in alternate strata rose to the height of two hundred and fifty feet, its base washed by the river and its top crowned with firs. The stream was a hundred yards wide, waist-deep, and very rapid. Its waters were icy cold, and of a milk-white hue. This color is the characteristic of glacial rivers. The impalpable powder of thousands of tons of solid rocks, ground up beneath the vast weight and resistless though imperceptible flow of huge glaciers, remains in solution in these streams, and colors them milk-white to the sea. Leading the animals down the bank and over a wide, dry bar of cobble-stones, we stood at the brink of the swift, turbulent river, and prepared to essay its passage. Coleman mounted behind Van Trump on the little saddle-mule, his long legs dangling nearly to the ground, one hand grasping his Alpine staff, the other the neck-rope of the pack-mule, which Longmire bestrode. Longmire led in turn the pack-horse, behind whose bulky load was perched the other member of the party. The cavalcade, linked together in this order, had but just entered the stream when Coleman dropped the neck-rope he was holding. The mule, bewildered by the rush and roar of the waters, turned directly downstream, and in another instant our two pack-animals, with their riders, would have been swept away in the furious rapids, had not Longmire with great presence of mind turned their erratic course in the right direction and safely brought them to the opposite shore. Following the bottom along the river for some distance, we climbed up the end of the bluff already mentioned, by a steep zigzag trail, and skirted along its brink for a mile. Far below us on the right rushed the Nisqually. On the left the bluff fell off in a steep hill-side thickly clothed with woods and underbrush, and at its foot plowed the Owhap, a large stream emptying into the Nisqually just below our ford. Another mile through the woods brought us out upon the Mishell Prairie, a beautiful, oval meadow of a hundred acres, embowered in the tall, dense fir forest, with a grove of lofty, branching oaks at its farther extremity, and coered with green grass and bright flowers. It takes its name from the Mishell River, which empties into the Nisqually a mile above the prairie.

We had marched sixteen miles. The packs were gladly thrown off beneath a lofty fir; the animals were staked out to graze. A spring in the

edge of the woods afforded water, and while Mr. Coleman busied himself with his pipe, his flask, his note-book, his sketch-book, and his
pouch of multifarious odds and ends, the other members of the party
performed the duties incident to camp-life: made the fire, brought
water, spread the blankets, and prepared supper. The flags attached to
our Alpine staffs waved gayly overhead, and the sight of their bright
folds fluttering in the breeze deepened the fixed resolve to plant them
on Takhoma's hoary head, and made failure seem impossible. Mr.
Coleman announced the altitude of Mishell Prairie as eight hundred
feet by the barometer. By an unlucky fall the thermometer was broken.

The march was resumed early next morning. As we passed the lofty
oaks at the end of the little prairie, "On that tree," said Longmire,
pointing out one of the noblest, "Maxon's company hanged two Indians
in the war of '56. Ski-hi and his band, after many depredations upon
the settlements, were encamped on the Mishell, a mile distant, in
fancied security, when Maxon and his men surprised them and cut off
every soul except the two prisoners whom they hanged here."

For eight miles the trail led through thick woods, and then, after
crossing a wide "burn," past a number of deserted Indian wigwams,
where another trail from the Nisqually plains joined ours, it descended
a gradual slope, traversed a swampy thicket and another mile of heavy
timber, and debouched on the Mishell River. This is a fine, rapid,
sparkling stream, knee-deep and forty feet wide, rippling and dashing
over a gravelly bed with clear, cold, transparent water. The purity of
the clear water, so unlike the yeasty Nisqually, proves that the Mishell
is no glacial river. Rising in an outlying range to the northwest of Takhoma, it flows in a southwest course to its confluence with the Nisqually near our previous night's camp. We unsaddled for the noon-rest.
Van Trump went up the stream, fishing; Longmire crossed to look out
the trail ahead, and Coleman made tea *solitaire*.

An hour passed, and Longmire returned. "The trail is blind," said
he, "and we have no time to lose." Just then Van Trump returned; and
the little train was soon in readiness to resume the tramp. Longmire
rode his mule across the stream, telling us to drive the pack-animals after him and follow by a convenient log near by. As the mule attempted
to climb a low place in the opposite bank, which offered an apparently
easy exit from the river, his hind legs sank in a quicksand, he sat down
quickly, if not gracefully, and, not fancying that posture, threw himself
clear under water. His dripping rider rose to his feet, flung the bridle-
rein over his arm, and, springing up the bank at a more practicable

point, strode along the trail with as little delay and as perfect unconcern as though an involuntary ducking was of no more moment than climbing over a log.

The trail *was* blind. Longmire scented it through thickets of salal, fern, and underbrush, stumbling over roots, vines, and hollows hidden in the rank vegetation, now climbing huge trunks that the animals could barely scramble over, and now laboriously working his way around some fallen giant and traveling two hundred yards in order to gain a dozen yards on the course. The packs, continually jammed against trees and shaken loose by this rough traveling, required frequent repacking—no small task. At the very top of a high, steep hill, up which we had laboriously zigzagged shortly after crossing the Mishell, the little pack-horse, unable to sustain the weight of the pack, which had shifted all to one side, fell and rolled over and over to the bottom. Bringing up the goods and chattels one by one on our own shoulders to the top of the hill, we replaced the load and started again. The course was in a southerly direction, over high rolling ground of good clay soil, heavily timbered, with marshy swales at intervals, to the Nisqually River again, a distance of twelve miles. We encamped on a narrow flat between the high hill just descended and the wide and noisy river, near an old ruined log-hut, the former residence of a once famed Indian medicine man, who, after the laudable custom of his race, had expiated with his life his failure to cure a patient.

Early next morning we continued our laborious march along the right bank of the Nisqually. Towards noon we left the river, and after thridding in an easterly course a perfect labyrinth of fallen timber for six miles, and forcing our way with much difficulty through the tangled jungle of an extensive vine-maple swamp, at length crossed Silver Creek and gladly threw off the packs for an hour's rest.

A short distance after crossing Silver Creek the trail emerged upon more open ground, and for the first time the Nisqually Valley lay spread out in view before us. On the left stretched a wall of steep, rocky mountains, standing parallel to the course of the river and extending far eastward, growing higher and steeper and more rugged as it receded from view. At the very extremity of this range Takhoma loomed aloft, its dome high above all others and its flanks extending far down into the valley, and all covered, dome and flanks, with snow of dazzling white, in striking contrast with the black basaltic mountains about it. Startlingly near it looked to our eyes, accustomed to the restricted views and gloom of the forest.

After our noon rest we continued our journey up the valley, twisting in and out among the numerous trunks of trees that encumbered the ground, and after several hours of tedious trudging struck our third camp on Copper Creek, the twin brother to Silver Creek, just at dusk. We were thoroughly tired, having made twenty miles in thirteen hours of hard traveling.

Starting at daylight next morning, we walked two miles over rough ground much broken by ravines, and then descended into the bed of the Nisqually at the mouth of Goat Creek, another fine stream which empties here. We continued our course along the river bed, stumbling over rocky bars and forcing our way through dense thickets of willow, for some distance, then ascended the steep bank, went around a high hill over four miles of execrable trail, and descended to the river again, only two miles above Goat Creek. At this point the Takhoma branch or North Fork joins the Nisqually. This stream rises on the west side of Takhoma, is nearly as large as the main river, and like it shows its glacial origin by its milk-white water and by its icy cold, terribly swift and furious torrent. Crossing the Takhoma branch, here thirty yards wide, we kept up the main river, crossing and recrossing the stream frequently, and toiling over rocky bars for four miles, a distance which consumed five hours, owing to the difficulties of the way. We then left the Nisqually, turning to the right and traveling in a southerly course, and followed up the bed of a swampy creek for half a mile, then crossed a level tract much obstructed with fallen timber, then ascended a burnt ridge, and followed it for two miles to a small, marshy prairie in a wide canyon or defile closed in by rugged mountains on either side, and camped beside a little rivulet on the east side of the prairie. This was Bear Prairie, the altitude of which by the barometer was 2630 feet. The canyon formed a low pass between the Nisqually and Cowlitz rivers, and the little rivulet near which we camped flowed into the latter stream. The whole region had been swept by fire: thousands of giant trunks stood blackened and lifeless, the picture of desolation.

As we were reclining on the ground around the camp-fire, enjoying the calm and beatific repose which comes to the toil-worn mountaineer after his hearty supper, one of these huge trunks, after several warning creaks, came toppling and falling directly over our camp. All rushed to one side or another to avoid the impending crash. As one member of the party, hastily catching up in one hand a frying-pan laden with tin plates and cups, and in the other the camp kettle half full of boiling water, was scrambling away, his foot tripped in a blackberry vine and he fell outstretched at full length, the much-prized utensils scattering far and wide, while the falling tree came thundering down in the rear, doing no other damage, however, than burying a pair of blankets.

The following day Longmire and the writer went down the canyon to its junction with the Cowlitz River, in search of a band of Indians who usually made their head-quarters at this point, and among whom Longmire hoped to find some hunter familiar with the mountains who might guide us to the base of Takhoma. The tiny rivulet as we descended soon swelled to a large and furious torrent, and its bed filled nearly the whole bottom of the gorge. The mountains rose on both sides precipitously, and the traces of land-slides which had gouged vast furrows down their sides were frequent. With extreme toil and difficulty we made our way, continually wading the torrent, clambering over broken masses of rock which filled its bed, or clinging to the steep hill-sides, and reached the Cowlitz at length after twelve miles of this fatiguing work, but only to find the Indian camp deserted. Further search, however, was rewarded by the discovery of a rude shelter formed of a few skins thrown over a frame-work of poles, beneath which sat a squaw at work upon a half-dressed deer-skin. An infant and a naked child of perhaps four years lay on the ground near the fire in front. Beside the lodge and quietly watching our approach, of which he alone seemed aware, stood a tall, slender Indian clad in buckskin shirt and leggings, with a striped woolen breech-clout, and a singular head garniture which gave him a fierce and martial appearance. This consisted of an old military cap, the visor thickly studded with brass-headed nails, while a large circular brass article, which might have been the top of an oil-lamp, was fastened upon the crown. Several eagle feathers stuck in the crown and strips of fur sewed upon the sides completed the edifice, which, notwithstanding its components, appeared imposing rather than ridiculous. A long Hudson Bay gun, the stock also ornamented with brass-headed tacks, lay in the hollow of the Indian's shoulder.

He received us with great friendliness, yet not without dignity, shaking hands and motioning us to a seat beneath the rude shelter, while his squaw hastened to place before us suspicious-looking cakes of dried berries, apparently their only food. After a moderate indulgence in this delicacy, Longmire made known our wants. The Indian spoke fluently the Chinook jargon, that high-bred lingo invented by the old fur-traders. He called himself "Sluiskin" and readily agreed to guide us to Rainier, known to him only as Takhoma, and promised to report at

Bear Prairie the next day. It was after seven in the evening when we reached camp thoroughly fagged.

Punctual to promise, Sluiskin rode up at noon mounted upon a stunted Indian pony, while his squaw and pappooses followed upon another even more puny and forlorn. After devouring an enormous dinner, evidently compensating for the rigors of a long fast, in reply to our inquiries he described the route he proposed to take to Takhoma. Pointing to the almost perpendicular height immediately back or east of our camp, towering three thousand feet or more overhead, the loftiest mountain in sight, "We go to the top of that mountain to-day," said he, "and to-morrow we follow along the high, backbone ridge of the mountains, now up, now down, first on one side and then on the other, a long day's journey, and at last, descending far down from the mountains into a deep valley, reach the base of Takhoma." Sluiskin illustrated his Chinook with speaking signs and pantomime. He had frequently hunted the mountain sheep upon the snow-fields of Takhoma, but had never ascended to the summit. It was impossible to do so, and he put aside as idle talk our expressed intention of making the ascent.

We had already selected the indispensable articles for a week's tramp, a blanket apiece, the smallest coffee-pot and frying-pan, a scanty supply of bacon, flour, coffee, etc., and had made them up into suitable packs of forty pounds each, provided with slings like a knapsack, and had piled together under the lee of a huge fallen trunk our remaining goods. Longmire, who although impatient to return home, where his presence was urgently needed, had watched and directed our preparations during the forenoon with kindly solicitude, now bade us good-by: mounted on one mule and leading the other, he soon disappeared down the trail on his lonely, homeward way. He left us the little pack-horse, thinking it would be quite capable of carrying our diminished outfit after our return from Takhoma.

Sluiskin led the way. The load upon his shoulders was sustained by a broad band passing over his head, upon which his heavy, brass-studded rifle, clasped in both hands, was poised and balanced. Leaving behind the last vestige of trail, we toiled in single file slowly and laboriously up the mountain all the afternoon. The steepness of the ascent in many places required the use of both hand and foot in climbing, and the exercise of great caution to keep the heavy packs from dragging us over backwards. Coleman lagged behind from the start, and at intervals his voice could be heard hallooing and calling upon us to wait. Towards

*Philemon Van Trump as he
appeared when he made the first
ascent. (Courtesy Aubrey Haines)*

sunset we reached a level terrace, or bench, near the summit, gladly threw off our packs, and waited for Coleman, who, we supposed, could not be far below. He not appearing, we hallooed again and again. No answer! We then sent Sluiskin down the mountain to his aid. After an hour's absence the Indian returned. He had descended, he said, a long distance, and at last caught sight of Coleman. He was near the foot of the mountain, had thrown away his pack, blankets and all, and was evidently returning to camp. And Sluiskin finished his account with expressions of contempt for the "cultus King George man." What was to be done? Coleman carried in his pack all our bacon, our only supply of meat, except a few pounds of dried beef. He also had the barometer, the only instrument that had survived the jolts and tumbles of our rough trip. But, on the other hand, he had been a clog upon our march from the outset. He was evidently too infirm to endure the toil before us, and would not only be unable to reach, still less to ascend Takhoma, but might even impede and frustrate our own efforts. Knowing that he would be safe in camp until our return, we hastily concluded to proceed without him, trusting to our rifles for a supply of meat.

Sluiskin led us along the side of the ridge in a southerly direction for two miles farther, to a well-sheltered, grassy hollow in the mountain-top, where he had often previously encamped. It was after dark when we reached this place. The usual spring had gone dry, and, parched with thirst, we searched the gulches of the mountain-side for water an hour, but without success. At length the writer, recalling a scanty rill which trickled across their path a mile back, taking the coffee-pot and large canteen, retraced his steps, succeeded in filling these utensils after much fumbling in the dark and consequent delay, and returned to camp. He found Van Trump and the Indian, anxious at the long delay, mounted on the crest of the ridge some two hundred yards from camp, waving torches and shouting lustily to direct his steps. The mosquitoes and flies came in clouds, and were terribly annoying. After supper of coffee and bread, we drank up the water, rolled ourselves in our blankets, and lay down under a tree with our flags floating from the boughs overhead. Hot as had been the day, the night was cold and frosty, owing, doubtless, to the altitude of our camp.

At the earliest dawn next morning we were moving on without breakfast, and parched with thirst. Sluiskin led us in a general course about north-northeast, but twisting to nearly every point of the compass, and climbing up and down thousands of feet from mountain to mountain, yet keeping on the highest backbone between the headwaters of the Nisqually and Cowlitz rivers. After several hours of this work we came to a well-sheltered hollow, one side filled with a broad bed of snow, at the foot of which nestled a tiny, tranquil lakelet, and gladly threw off our heavy packs, assuaged our thirst, and took breakfast,—bread and coffee again. Early as it was, the chill of the frosty night still in the air, the mosquitoes renewed their attacks, and proved as innumerable and vexatious as ever.

Continuing our march, we crossed many beds of snow, and drank again and again from the icy rills which flowed out of them. The mountains were covered with stunted mountain-ash and low, stubby firs with short, bushy branches, and occasionally a few pines. Many slopes were destitute of trees, but covered with luxuriant grass and the greatest profusion of beautiful flowers of vivid hues. This was especially the case with the southern slopes, while the northern sides of the mountains were generally wooded. We repeatedly ate berries, and an hour afterwards ascended to where berries of the same kind were found scarcely yet formed. The country was much obscured with smoke from heavy fires which had been raging on the Cowlitz the last two days. But when at length, after climbing for hours an almost perpendicular peak, —creeping on hands and knees over loose rocks, and clinging to scanty tufts of grass where a single slip would have sent us rolling a thousand feet down to destruction,—we reached the highest crest and looked over, we exclaimed that we were already well repaid for all our toil. Nothing can convey an idea of the grandeur and ruggedness of the mountains. Directly in front, and apparently not over two miles distant, although really twenty, old Takhoma loomed up more gigantic than ever. We were far above the level of the lower snow-line on Takhoma. The high peak upon which we clung seemed the central core or focus of all the mountains around, and on every side we looked down vertically thousands of feet, deep down into vast, terrible defiles, black and fir-clothed, which stretched away until lost in the distance and smoke. Between them, separating one from another, the mountain-walls rose precipitously and terminated in bare, columnar peaks of black basaltic or volcanic rock, as sharp as needles. It seemed incredible that any human foot could have followed out the course we came, as we looked back upon it.

After a few hours more of this climbing, we stood upon the summit of the last mountain-ridge that separated us from Takhoma. We were in a saddle of the ridge; a lofty peak rose on either side. Below us extended a long, steep hollow or gulch filled with snow, the farther extremity of which seemed to drop off perpendicularly into a deep valley or basin. Across this valley, directly in front, filling up the whole horizon and view with an indescribable aspect of magnitude and grandeur, stood the old leviathan of mountains. The broad, snowy dome rose far among and above the clouds. The sides fell off in vertical steeps and fearful black walls of rock for a third of its altitude; lower down, vast, broad, gently sloping snow-fields surrounded the mountain, and were broken here and there by ledges or masses of the dark basaltic rock protruding above them. Long, green ridges projected from this snow-belt at intervals, radiating from the mountain and extending many miles until lost in the distant forests. Deep valleys lay between these ridges. Each at its upper end formed the bed of a glacier, which closed and filled it up with solid ice. Below the snow-line bright green grass with countless flowers, whose vivid scarlet, blue, and purple formed bodies of color in the distance, clothed the whole region of ridges and valleys, for a breadth of five miles. The beautiful balsam firs, about thirty feet in height, and of a purple, dark-green color, stood scattered over the landscape, now singly, now in groves, and now in long lines, as though planted in some well-kept park. Farther down an unbroken fir forest surrounded the mountain and clad the lower portions of the ridges and valleys. In every sheltered depression or hollow lay beds of snow with tiny brooks and rivulets flowing from them. The glaciers terminated not gradually, but abruptly, with a wall of ice from one to five hundred feet high, from beneath which yeasty torrents burst forth and rushed roaring and tumbling down the valleys. The principal of these, far away on our left front, could be seen plunging over two considerable falls, half hidden in the forest, while the roar of waters was distinctly audible.

At length we cautiously descended the snow-bed, and, climbing at least fifteen hundred feet down a steep but ancient land-slide by means of the bushes growing among the loose rocks, reached the valley, and encountered a beautiful, peaceful, limpid creek. Van Trump could not resist the temptation of unpacking his bundle, selecting one of his carefully preserved flies, and trying the stream for trout, but without a single rise. After an hour's rest and a hearty repast we resumed our packs, despite Sluiskin's protests, who seemed tired out with his arduous day's toil and pleaded hard against traveling farther. Crossing the stream, we walked through several grassy glades, or meadows, alternating with open woods. We soon came to the foot of one of the long ridges already described, and ascending it followed it for several miles through open woods, until we emerged upon the enchanting emerald and flowery meads which clothe these upper regions. Halting upon a rising eminence in our course, and looking back, we beheld the ridge of mountains we had just descended stretching from east to west in a steep, rocky wall; a little to the left, a beautiful lake, evidently the source of the stream just crossed, which we called Clear Creek, and glimpses of which could be seen among the trees as it flowed away to the right, down a rapidly descending valley along the foot of the lofty mountain-wall. Beyond the lake again, still farther to the left, the land also subsided quickly. It was at once evident that the lake was upon a summit, or divide, between the waters of the Nisqually and Cowlitz rivers. The ridge which we were ascending lay north and south, and led directly up to the mountain.

We camped, as the twilight fell upon us, in an aromatic grove of balsam firs. A grouse, the fruit of Sluiskin's rifle, broiled before the fire and impartially divided, gave a relish to the dry bread and coffee. After supper we reclined upon our blankets in front of the bright, blazing fire, well satisfied. The Indian, when starting from Bear Prairie, had evidently deemed our intention of ascending Takhoma too absurd to deserve notice. The turning back of Mr. Coleman only deepened his contempt for our prowess. But his views had undergone a change with the day's march. The affair began to look serious to him, and now in Chinook, interspersed with a few words of broken English and many signs and gesticulations, he began a solemn exhortation and warning against our rash project.

Takhoma, he said, was an enchanted mountain, inhabited by an evil spirit, who dwelt in a fiery lake on its summit. No human being could ascend it or even attempt its ascent, and survive. At first, indeed, the way was easy. The broad snow-fields, over which he had so often hunted the mountain goat, interposed no obstacle, but above them the rash adventurer would be compelled to climb up steeps of loose, rolling rocks, which would turn beneath his feet and cast him headlong into the deep abyss below. The upper snow-slopes, too, were so steep that not even a goat, far less a man, could get over them. And he would have to pass below lofty walls and precipices whence avalanches of snow and vast masses of rock were continually falling; and these would inevitably bury the intruder beneath their ruins. Moreover, a furious tempest continually swept the crown of the mountain, and the luckless adventurer, even if he wonderfully escaped the perils below, would be torn from the mountain and whirled through the air by this fearful blast. And the awful being upon the summit, who would surely punish the sacrilegious attempt to invade his sanctuary,—who could hope to escape his vengeance? Many years ago, he continued, his grandfather, a great chief and warrior, and a mighty hunter, had ascended part way up the mountain, and had encountered some of these dangers, but he fortunately turned back in time to escape destruction; and no other Indian had ever gone so far.

Finding that his words did not produce the desired effect, he assured us that, if we persisted in attempting the ascent, he would wait three days for our return, and would then proceed to Olympia and inform our friends of our death; and he begged us to give him a paper (a written note) to take to them, so that they might believe his story. Sluiskin's manner during this harangue was earnest in the extreme, and he was undoubtedly sincere in his forebodings. After we had retired to rest, he kept up a most dismal chant, or dirge, until late in the night. The dim, white, spectral mass towering so near, the roar of the torrents below us, and the occasional thunder of avalanches, several of which fell during the night, added to the weird effect of Sluiskin's song.

The next morning we moved two miles farther up the ridge and made camp in the last clump of trees, quite within the limit of perpetual snow. Thence, with snow-spikes upon our feet and Alpine staff in hand, we went up the snow-fields to reconnoitre the best line of ascent.

We spent four hours, walking fast, in reaching the foot of the steep, abrupt part of the mountain. After carefully scanning the southern approaches, we decided to ascend on the morrow by a steep, rocky ridge that seemed to lead up to the snowy crown.

Our camp was pitched on a high knoll crowned by a grove of balsam firs, near a turbulent glacial torrent. About nine o'clock, after we had lain down for the night, the firs round our camp took fire and suddenly burst out in a vivid conflagration. The night was dark and windy, and the scene—the vast, dim outlines of Takhoma, the white snow-fields, the roaring torrent, the crackling blaze of the burning trees—was strikingly wild and picturesque.

In honor of our guide we named the cascade at our feet Sluiskin's Falls; the stream we named Glacier Creek, and the mass of ice whence it derives its source we styled the Little Nisqually Glacier.

Before daylight the next morning, Wednesday, August 17, 1870, we were up and had breakfasted, and at six o'clock we started to ascend Takhoma. Besides our Alpine staffs and creepers, we carried a long rope, an ice-axe, a brass plate inscribed with our names, our flags, a large canteen, and some luncheon. We were also provided with gloves, and green goggles for snow-blindness, but found no occasion to use the latter. Having suffered much from the heat of the sun since leaving Bear Prairie, and being satisfied from our late reconnoissance that we could reach the summit and return on the same day, we left behind our coats and blankets. In three hours of fast walking we reached the highest point of the preceding day's trip, and commenced the ascent by the steep, rocky ridge already described as reaching up to the snowy dome. We found it to be a very narrow, steep, irregular backbone, composed of a crumbling basaltic conglomerate, the top only, or backbone, being solid rock, while the sides were composed of loose broken rocks and *debris*. Up this ridge, keeping upon the spine when possible, and sometimes forced to pick our way over the loose and broken rocks at the sides, around columnar masses which we could not directly climb over, we toiled for five hundred yards, ascending at an angle of nearly forty-five degrees. Here the ridge connected, by a narrow neck or saddle, with a vast square rock, whose huge and distinct outline can be clearly perceived from a distance of twenty-five miles. This, like the ridge, is a conglomerate of basalt and trap, in well-defined strata, and is rapidly disintegrating and continually falling in showers and even masses of rocks and rubbish, under the action of frost by night and melting snow by day. It lies imbedded in the side of the mountain, with one side and end projected and overhanging deep, terrible gorges, and it is at the corner or junction of these two faces that the ridge joined it at a point about a thousand feet below its top. On the southern face the strata were inclined at an angle of thirty degrees. Crossing by the saddle from the ridge, despite a strong wind which swept across it, we gained a narrow ledge formed by a stratum more solid than its fellows, and creeping along it, hugging close to the main rock on our right, laboriously and cautiously continued the ascent. The wind was blowing violently. We were now crawling along the face of the precipice almost in mid-air. On the right the rock towered far above us perpendicularly. On the left it fell sheer off, two thousand feet, into a vast abyss. A great glacier filled its bed and stretched away for several miles, all seamed or wrinkled across with countless crevasses. We crept up and along a ledge, not of solid, sure rock, but one obstructed with the loose stones and débris which were continually falling from above, and we trod on the upper edge of a steep slope of this rubbish, sending the stones at every step rolling and bounding into the depth below. Several times during our progress showers of rocks fell from the precipice above across our path, and rolled into the abyss, but fortunately none struck us.

Four hundred yards of this progress brought us to where the rock joined the overhanging edge of the vast *névé* or snow-field that descended from the dome of the mountain and was from time to time, as pressed forward and downward, breaking off in immense masses, which fell with a noise as of thunder into the great canyon on our left. The junction of rock and ice afforded our only line of ascent. It was an almost perpendicular gutter, but here our ice-axe came into play, and by cutting steps in the ice and availing ourselves of every crevice or projecting point of the rock, we slowly worked our way up two hundred yards higher. Falling stones were continually coming down, both from the rock on our right and from the ice in front, as it melted and relaxed its hold upon them. Mr. Van Trump was hit by a small one, and another struck his staff from his hands. Abandoning the rock, then, at the earliest practicable point, we ascended directly up the ice, cutting steps for a short distance, until we reached ice so corrugated, or drawn up in sharp pinnacles, as to afford a foothold. These folds or pinnacles were about two or three feet high, and half as thick, and stood close together. It was like a very violent chop sea, only the waves were sharper. Up this safe footing we climbed rapidly, the side of the mountain becoming less and less steep, and the ice waves smaller and more regular, and, after ascending about three hundred yards, stood fairly upon the broad dome of mighty Takhoma. It rose before us like a broad, gently swelling headland of dazzling white, topped with black, where the rocky summit projected above the névé. Ascending diagonally towards the left, we continued our course. The snow was hard and firm under foot, crisp and light for an inch or two, but solidified into ice a foot or less beneath the surface. The whole field was covered with the ice-waves already described, and intersected by a number of crevasses which we crossed at narrow places without difficulty. About half-way up the slope, we encountered one from eight to twenty feet wide and of profound depth. The most beautiful vivid emerald-green color seemed to fill the abyss, the reflection of the bright sunlight from side to side of its pure ice walls. The upper side or wall of the crevasses was some twelve feet above the lower, and in places overhung it, as though the snow-field on the lower side had bodily settled down a dozen feet. Throwing a bight of the rope around a projecting pinnacle on the upper side, we climbed up, hand over hand, and thus effected a crossing. We were now obliged to travel slowly, with frequent rests. In that rare atmosphere, after taking seventy or eighty steps, our breath would be gone, our muscles grew tired and strained, and we experienced all the sensations of extreme fatigue. An instant's pause, however, was sufficient to recover strength and breath, and we would start again. The wind, which we had not felt while climbing the steepest part of the mountain, now again blew furiously, and we began to suffer from the cold. Our course,—directed still diagonally towards the left, thus shunning the severe exertion of climbing straight up the dome, although at an ordinary altitude the slope would be deemed easy,—brought us first to the southwest peak. This is a long, exceedingly sharp, narrow ridge, springing out from the main dome for a mile into mid-air. The ridge affords not over ten or twelve feet of foothold on top, and the sides descend almost vertically. On the right side the snow lay firm and smooth for a few feet on top, and then descended in a steep, unbroken sheet, like an immense, flowing curtain, into the tremendous basin which lies on the west side of the mountain between the southern and northern peaks, and which is inclosed by them as by two mighty arms. The snow on the top and left crest of the ridge was broken into high, sharp pinnacles, with cracks and fissures extending to the rocks a few feet below. The left side, too steep for the snow to lie on, was vertical, bare rock. The wind blew so violently that we were obliged to brace ourselves with our Alpine staffs and use great caution to guard against being swept off the ridge. We threw ourselves behind the pinnacles or into the cracks every seventy steps, for rest and shelter against the bitter, piercing wind. Hastening forward in this way along the dizzy, narrow, and precarious ridge, we reached at length the highest point. Sheltered behind a pinnacle of ice we rested a moment, took out our flags and fastened them upon the Alpine staffs, and then, standing erect in the furious blast, waved them in triumph with three cheers. We stood a moment upon that narrow summit, bracing ourselves against the tempest to view the prospect. The whole country was shrouded in a dense sea of smoke, above which the mountain towered two thousand feet in the clear, cloudless ether. A solitary peak far to the southeast, doubtless Mount Adams, and one or two others in the extreme northern horizon, alone protruded above the pall. On every side of the mountain were deep gorges falling off precipitously thousands of feet, and from these the thunderous sound of avalanches would rise occasionally. Far below were the wide-extended glaciers already described. The wind was now a perfect tempest, and bitterly cold; smoke and mist were flying about the base of the mountain, half hiding, half revealing its gigantic outlines; and the whole scene was sublimely awful.

It was now five P.M. We had spent eleven hours of unremitted toil in making the ascent, and, thoroughly fatigued, and chilled by the cold, bitter gale, we saw ourselves obliged to pass the night on the summit without shelter or food, except our meagre lunch. It would have been impossible to descend the mountain before nightfall, and sure destruction to attempt it in darkness. We concluded to return to a mass of rocks not far below, and there pass the night as best we could, burrowing in the loose débris.

The middle peak of the mountain, however, was evidently the highest, and we determined to first visit it. Retracing our steps along the narrow crest of Peak Success, as we named the scene of our triumph, we crossed an intervening depression in the dome, and ascended the middle peak, about a mile distant and two hundred feet higher than Peak Success. Climbing over a rocky ridge which crowns the summit, we found ourselves within a circular crater two hundred yards in diameter, filled with a solid bed of snow, and inclosed with a rim of rocks projecting above the snow all around. As we were crossing the crater on the snow, Van Trump detected the odor of sulphur, and the next instant numerous jets of steam and smoke were observed issuing from the crevices of the rocks which formed the rim on the northern side. Never was a discovery more welcome! Hastening forward, we both exclaimed as we warmed our chilled and benumbed extremities over one of Pluto's fires, that here we would pass the night, secure against freezing to death, at least. These jets were from the size of that of a large steam-pipe to a faint, scarcely perceptible emission, and issued all along the rim among the loose rocks on the northern side for more than half the circumference of the crater. At intervals they would puff up more strongly, and the smoke would collect in a cloud until blown aside and scattered by the wind, and then their force would abate for a time.

A deep cavern, extending into and under the ice, and formed by the action of heat, was found. Its roof was a dome of brilliant green ice with long icicles pendent from it, while its floor, composed of the rocks and débris which formed the side of the crater, descended at an angle of thirty degrees. Forty feet within its mouth we built a wall of stones, inclosing a space five by six feet around a strong jet of steam and heat. Unlike the angular, broken rocks met with elsewhere, within the crater we found well-rounded bowlders and stones of all sizes worn as smooth by the trituration of the crater as by the action of water. Nowhere, however, did we observe any new lava or other evidences of recent volcanic action excepting these issues of steam and smoke. Inclosed within the rude shelter thus hastily constructed, we discussed our future prospects while we ate our lunch and warmed ourselves at our natural register. The heat at the orifice was too great to bear for more than an instant, but the steam wet us, the smell of sulphur was nauseating, and the cold was so severe that our clothes, saturated with the steam, froze stiff when turned away from the heated jet. The wind outside roared and whistled, but it did not much affect us, secure within our cavern, except when an occasional gust came down perpendicularly. However, we passed a most miserable night, freezing on one side, and in a hot steam-sulphur-bath on the other.

The dawn at last slowly broke, cold and gray. The tempest howled still wilder. As it grew light, dense masses of driven mist went sweeping by overhead and completely hid the sun, and enveloped the mountain so as to conceal objects scarce a hundred feet distant. We watched and waited with great anxiety, fearing a storm which might detain us there for days without food or shelter, or, worse yet, snow, which would render the descent more perilous, or most likely impossible. And when, at nine A.M., an occasional rift in the driving mist gave a glimpse of blue sky, we made haste to descend. First, however, I deposited the brass plate inscribed with our names in a cleft in a large bowlder on the highest summit,—a huge mound of rocks on the east side of our crater of refuge, which we named Crater Peak,—placed the canteen alongside, and covered it with a large stone. I was then literally freezing in the cold, piercing blast, and was glad to hurry back to the crater, breathless and benumbed.

We left our den of refuge at length, after exercising violently to start the blood through our limbs, and, in attempting to pass around the rocky summit, discovered a second crater, larger than the first, perhaps three hundred yards in diameter. It is circular, filled with a bed of snow, with a rocky rim all around and numerous jets of steam issuing from the rocks on the northern side. Both craters are inclined—the first to the west, and the latter to the east with a much steeper inclination, about thirty degrees. The rim of the second crater is higher, or the snow-field inside lower, than that of the first, and upon the east side rises in a rocky wall thirty feet above the snow within. From the summit we obtained a view of the northern peak, still partially enveloped in the driving mist. It appeared aboout a mile distant, several hundred feet lower than the centre peak, and separated from it by a deeper, more abrupt depression or gap than that separating Crater and Success peaks. Like the latter, too, it is a sharp, narrow ridge springing out from the main mountain, and swept bare of snow on its summit by the wind. The weather was still too threatening, the glimpses of the sun and sky through the thick, flying scud, were too few and fugitive, to warrant us in visiting this peak, which we named Peak Takhoma, to perpetuate the Indian name of the mountain.

Our route back was the same as on the ascent. At the steepest and most perilous point in descending the steep gutter where we had been forced to cut steps in the ice, we fastened one end of the rope as securely as possible to a projecting rock, and lowered ourselves down by it as far as it reached, thereby passing the place with comparative safety. We were forced to abandon the rope here, having no means of unfastening it from the rock above. We reached the foot of the rocky ledge or ridge, where the real difficulties and dangers of the ascent commenced, at 1.30 P.M., four and a half hours after leaving the crater. We had been seven and a half hours in ascending from this point to the summit of Peak Success, and in both cases we toiled hard and lost no time.

We now struck out rapidly and joyfully for camp. When nearly there Van Trump, in attempting to descend a snowbank without his creepers, which he had taken off for greater ease in walking, fell, shot like lightning forty feet down the steep incline, and struck among some loose rocks at its foot with such force as to rebound several feet into the air; his face and hands were badly skinned, and he received some severe bruises and a deep, wide gash upon his thigh. Fortunately the camp was not far distant, and thither with great pain and very slowly he managed to hobble. Once there I soon started a blazing fire, made coffee, and roasted choice morsels of a marmot, Sluiskin having killed and dressed four of these animals during our absence. Their flesh, like the badger's, is extremely muscular and tough, and has a strong, disagreeable, doggy odor.

Towards the close of our repast, we observed the Indian approaching with his head down, and walking slowly and wearily as though tired by a long tramp. He raised his head as he came nearer, and, seeing us for the first time, stopped short, gazed long and fixedly, and then slowly drew near, eying us closely the while, as if to see whether we were real flesh and blood or disembodied ghosts fresh from the evil demon of Takhoma. He seemed both astonished and delighted to find us safe back, and kept repeating that we were strong men and had brave hearts: "Skookum tilicum, skookum tumtum." He expected never to see us again, he said, and had resolved to start the next morning for Olympia to report our destruction.

The weather was still raw and cold. A dense cloud overhung and shrouded the triple crown of Takhoma and made us rejoice at our timely descent. The scanty shelter afforded by the few balsam firs about our camp had been destroyed by the fire, and the situation was terribly exposed to the chilly and piercing wind that blew from the great ice-fields. Van Trump, however, was too badly hurt to think of moving that night. Heating some large stones we placed them at our feet, and closely wrapped in our blankets slept soundly upon the open ground, although we awoke in the morning benumbed and chilled.

We found many fresh tracks and signs of the mountain-sheep upon the snow-fields, and hair and wool rubbed off upon rocks, and places where they had lain at night. The mountain-sheep of Takhoma is much larger than the common goat, and is found only upon the loftiest and most secluded peaks of the Cascade Range. Even Sluiskin, a skillful hunter and accustomed to the pursuit of this animal for years, failed to kill one, notwithstanding he hunted assiduously during our entire stay upon the mountain, three days. Sluiskin was greatly chagrined at his failure, and promised to bring each of us a sheep-skin the following summer, a promise which he faithfully fulfilled.

The glacial system of Takhoma is stupendous. The mountain is really the grand focal centre and summit of a region larger than Massachusetts, and the five large rivers which water this region all find their sources in its vast glaciers. They are the Cowlitz, which empties into the Columbia; the White, Puyallup, and Nisqually rivers, which empty into Puget Sound sixty, forty, and twelve miles respectively north of Olympia; and the Wenass, which flows eastward through the range and empties into the Yakima, which joins the Columbia four hundred miles above its mouth. These are all large streams from seventy to a hundred miles in length. The White, Puyallup, and Cowlitz rivers are each navigable for steamboats for some thirty miles, and like the Nisqually show their glacial origin by their white and turgid water, which indeed gives the former its name.

The southwestern sides of the mountain furnish the glaciers which form the sources of the Nisqually, and one of these, at Sluiskin's Falls, has been already described. The main Nisqually glacier issues from the deep abyss overhung by the vast rock along the face of which our route of ascent lay, and extends in a narrow and somewhat crooked canyon for two miles. The ice at its extremity rises in an abrupt wall five hundred feet high, and a noisy torrent pours out with great force from beneath. This feature is characteristic of every glacier. The main Cowlitz glacier issues from the southeast side, just to the right of our ridge of ascent. Its head fills a deep gorge at the foot of the eastern front or face of the great mass of rock just referred to, and the southern face of which overhangs the main Nisqually glacier. Thus the heads of these glaciers are separated only by this great rock, and are probably not more than half a mile apart, while their mouths are three miles apart. Several smaller glaciers serve to swell the waters of the Cowlitz. In like manner the glaciers from the western side form the Puyallup, and those from the northern and northwestern sides the White River. The principal White River glacier is nearly ten miles long, and its width is from two to four miles. Its depth, or the thickness of its ice, must be thousands of feet. Streams and rivulets under the heat of the sun flow down its surface until swallowed by the crevasses, and a lakelet of deep blue water an eighth of a mile in diameter has been observed upon the solid ice. Pouring down from the mountain, the ice by its immense weight and force has gouged out a mass upon the northeastern side a mile in thickness. The geological formation of Takhoma poorly resists the eroding power of these mighty glaciers, for it seems to be composed not of solid rock, but of a basaltic conglomerate in strata, as though the volcanic force had burst through and rent in pieces some earlier basaltic

outflow, and had heaped up this vast pile from the fragments in successive strata. On every side the mountain is slowly disintegrating.

What other peak can offer to scientific examination or to the admiration of tourists fourteen living glaciers of such magnitude, issuing from
every side, or such grandeur, beauty, and variety of scenery?

At daylight we broke up our camp at Sluiskin's Falls, and moved
slowly, on account of Van Trump's hurt, down the ridge about five
miles to Clear Creek, where we again regaled ourselves upon a hearty
repast of marmots, or "raw dog," as Van Trump styled them in deri-
sion both of the viand and of the cookery. I was convinced from the lay
of the country that Clear Creek flowed into the Nisqually, or was, perhaps, the main stream itself, and that the most direct and feasible route
back to Bear Prairie would be found by following down the valley of
these streams to the trail leading from the Nisqually to Bear Prairie. Besides, it was evidently impossible for Van Trump, in his bruised and
injured state, to retrace our rough route over the mountains. Leaving
him as comfortable as possible, with all our scanty stock of flour and
marmots, sufficient to last him nearly a week in case of need, I started
immediately after dinner, with Sluiskin leading the way, to explore this
new route. The Indian had opposed the attempt strenuously, insisting
with much urgency that the stream flowed through canyons impossible
for us to traverse. He now gradually veered away from the course of the
stream, until erelong he was leading directly up the steep mountain
range upon our former route, when I called him back peremptorily,
and kept him in the rear for a little distance. Traveling through open
timber, over ground rapidly descending, we came at the end of two
miles to where the stream is hemmed in between one of the long ridges
or spurs from Takhoma and the high mountain-chain on the south. The
stream, receiving many affluents on both sides, its clear waters soon
discolored by the yeasty glacial torrents, here loses its peaceful flow,
and for upwards of three miles rushes furiously down a narrow,
broken, and rocky bed in a succession of falls and cascades of great picturesque beauty. With much toil and difficulty we picked our way over
a wide "talus" of huge, broken granite blocks and bowlders, along the
foot of a vast mountain of solid granite on the south side of the river,
until near the end of the defile, then crossed the stream, and soon after
encountered a still larger branch coming from the north, direct from
Takhoma, the product, doubtless, of the glaciers on the southern and
southwestern sides. Fording this branch just above its confluence with
the other, we followed the general course of the river, now unmistak-

ably the Nisqually, for about four miles; then, leaving it, we struck off nearly south through the forest for three miles, and emerged upon the Bear Prairie. The distance was about thirteen miles from where we left Van Trump, and we were only some six hours in traveling it, while it took seventeen hours of terribly severe work to make the mountain-route under Sluiskin's guidance.

Without his help on the shorter route, too, it would have taken me more than twice the time it did. For the manner in which, after entering the defile of the Nisqually, Sluiskin again took the lead and proceeded in a direct and unhesitating course, securing every advantage of the ground, availing himself of the wide, rocky bars along the river, crossing and recrossing the milky flood which rushed along with terrific swiftness and fury, and occasionally forcing his way through the thick timber and underbrush in order to cut off wide bends of the river, and at length leaving it and striking boldly through the forest to Bear Prairie, proved him familiar with every foot of the country. His objections to the route evidently arose from the jealousy so common with his people of further exploration of the country by the whites. As long as they keep within the limits already known and explored, they are faithful and indefatigable guides, but they invariably interpose every obstacle their ingenuity can suggest to deter the adventurous mountaineer from exposing the few last hidden recesses that remain unexplored.

Mr. Coleman was found safe in camp, and seemed too glad to see us to think of reproaching us for our summary abandonment. He said that in attempting to follow us he climbed up so precipitous a place that, encumbered with his heavy pack, he could neither advance nor recede. He was compelled, therefore, to throw off the pack, which rolled to the very bottom of the mountain, and being thus delivered of his necessary outfit, he was forced to return to camp. He had been unable to find his pack, but having come across some cricketer's spikes among his remaining effects, he was resolved to continue his trip to, and make the ascent of Rainier by himself; he had just completed his preparations, and especially had deposited on top of the lofty mountain which overlooked the prairie two caches, or stores, of provisions.

At daylight next morning, Sluiskin, with his little boy riding one of his own ponies, himself riding our little calico-colored pack-horse, now well rested and saucy, started back for Van Trump, with directions to meet us at the trail on the Nisqually. A heavy, drizzling rain set in soon afterwards. Mr. Coleman, who had gone early to bring in the contents of his mountain-top caches, returned about noon with a very small bundle, and, packing our traps upon Sluiskin's other pony, we moved over to the rendezvous, pitched Coleman's large gumsheet as a partial shelter, made a rousing fire, and tried to be comfortable. Late in the afternoon the pony set up a violent neighing, and in a few minutes Van Trump, and Sluiskin with his little boy behind him, rode up, drenched to the skin. By following the bed of the river, frequently crossing and recrossing, the Indian had managed to ride to the very foot of the Nisqually defile, when, leaving the horses in his boy's care, he hastened to Van Trump and carefully led and assisted him down. Despite the pain of his severe hurts, the latter was much amused at Sluiskin's account of our trip, and of finding Mr. Coleman safe in camp making tea, and for long after would repeat as an excellent joke Skuiskin's remark on passing the point where he had attempted to mislead me, "Skookum tenas man hiyu goddam."

We sent the horses back by the Indian to Bear Prairie for grass, there being no indications of the rain ceasing. The storm indeed lasted three days, during which we remained sheltered beneath the gum-sheet as far as possible, and endeavored to counteract the rain by heaping up our fire in front. About eight o'clock on the second morning, Sluiskin reported himself with our horse, which he returned, he said, because he was about to return to his lodge on the Cowlitz, being destitute of shelter and food for his family on Bear Prairie. He vigorously replenished the fire, declined breakfast, jeered Coleman for turning back, although probably the latter did not comprehend his broken lingo, and departed.

Sluiskin was an original and striking character. Leading a solitary life of hardships amidst these wilds, yet of unusual native intelligence, he had contrived, during rare visits to the settlements, to acquire the Chinook jargon, besides a considerable stock of English words, while his fund of general information was really wonderful. He was possessed of a shrewd, sarcastic wit, and, making no pretense to the traditional gravity of his race, did not scruple to use it freely. Yet beneath this he cherished a high sense of pride and personal independence. Although of the blood of the numerous and powerful Yakimas, who occupied the country just east of the Cascades, he disdained to render allegiance to them, or any tribe, and undoubtedly regarded the superintendent of Indian affairs, or even the great father at Washington himself, with equally contemptuous indifference.

As the last rays of the sun, one warm, drowsy summer afternoon, were falling aslant the shady streets of Olympia, Mr. Longmire's well-

STATE HISTORICAL BUILDING. FREE TO THE PUBLIC OPEN FROM 9 to 5, Sundays 2 to 6

*Stevens (left) and Van Trump, many years later, at the State Historical Society in Tacoma with the flag they carried to the summit in 1870. (Courtesy National Park Service)*

worn family carry-all, drawn by two fat, grass-fed horses, came rattling down the main street at a most unusual pace for them; two bright flags attached to Alpine staffs, one projecting from each door, fluttered gayly overhead, while the occupants of the carriage looked eagerly forth to catch the first glimpse of welcoming friends. We returned after our tramp of two hundred and forty miles with visages tanned and sun-scorched, and with forms as lean and gaunt as greyhounds, and were received and lionized to the full, like veterans returning from an arduous and glorious campaign. For days afterward, in walking along the smooth and level pavements, we felt a strong impulse to step high, as though still striding over the innumerable fallen logs and boughs of the forest, and for weeks our appetites were a source of astonishment to our friends and somewhat mortifying to ourselves. More than two months had elapsed before Mr. Van Trump fully recovered from his hurts. We published at the time short newspaper accounts of the ascent, and, although an occasional old Puget Sounder will still growl, "They say they went on top of Mount Rainier, but I'd like to see them prove it," we were justly regarded as the first, and as I believe the only ones up to the present time, who have ever achieved the summit of Takhoma.

Hazard Stevens.

NOTE

1. Tak-ho′ma or Ta-ho′ma among the Yakimas, Klickitats, Puyallups, Nisquallys, and allied tribes of Indians, is the generic term for mountain, used precisely as we use the word "mount," as Takhoma Wynatchie, or Mount Wynatchie. But they all designate Rainier simply as Takhoma, or The Mountain, just as the mountain men used to call it the "Old He."

# 7

# George Bayley*
# 1883

The October following the Hazard Stevens-Philemon Van Trump ascent in 1870, another party reached the summit, but no more successful climbs were made until 1883 when Van Trump returned with James Longmire and George Bayley. Longmire had guided the 1870 ascent by Samuel Emmons and A. D. Wilson, though he had not gone to the summit with them. Bayley was an exceptional mountaineer, occasionally a companion of John Muir's on various climbs in California. Bayley was a California businessman with a keen interest in wild country adventure, and in the summer of 1883, after one false start on his own, he persuaded Van Trump to join him in an attempt on Mount Rainier. They then talked Longmire into guiding them and at the last minute were joined by W. C. Ewing, whose presence on the expedition is not clearly explained (though it may have been related to the fact that he was from Van Trump's home town in Ohio). Bayley's following account of the climb also introduces another enduring name associated with Mount Rainier—the Klickitat settler named Indian Henry, who traveled part of the way with the group and for whom Indian Henry's Hunting Ground, a lovely parklike area near Squaw Lake, would be named.

Like both of the 1870 parties, this group approached the summit via the Gibraltar route. It was, as Bayley vividly describes, a perilous and arduous trip, but the three returned with a sense of triumph hardly less satisfying than if they had made the first ascent. Historian Aubrey Haines has aptly summed up the feelings of the group in his book *Mountain Fever:*

> Van Trump felt it vindicated him in the eyes of some neighbors who did not believe he reached the top in 1870; Bayley felt he had at last climbed a mountain worthy of the effort; and Longmire found he was still a good man despite his sixty-three years of hardships.

*Reprinted from George Bayley, "Ascent of Mount Tacoma," Overland Monthly 8(1886): 266–278.

It was Longmire's only climb, but Van Trump and Bayley both would be back; Chapter 13 describes their 1892 attempt to reach the North Peak, a goal that eluded them in this climb.

This account also covers one of the most hotly contested issues surrounding the mountain in those days: its name. Debates over the relative appropriateness of "Mount Rainier" and "Tahoma" continued on and off for many years.

The Cascade range of mountains in Washington Territory is, without doubt, the wildest and most inaccessible region within the boundaries of the United States. Clothed with forests, whose fallen tree trunks lock together to form a continuous stockade, almost impenetrable to man or beast, furrowed by deep cañons and roaring torrents, it rises peak on peak from the valleys of the Columbia and Puget Sound to the line of perpetual snow, above which tower the culminating points of Mount Saint Helens, Mount Adams, Mount Rainier and Mount Baker. Highest, grandest, and most inaccessible of all these is Mount Rainier, or Tacoma, the home of the only living glaciers of which the American citizen can boast, if there be left out of account a few insignificant ice fields on one of the peaks of the Sierra Nevada of California, scarcely worthy the name of glacier, when compared with the majestic ice rivers of Tacoma.

As a mountain climber of some experience, I had long felt the ambition to try the difficulties of Tacoma. The spice of danger is very pungent for the moment, but it leaves a delicious after-taste; and having achieved the summits of a number of western peaks, among them Mounts Whitney, Shasta, Lyell, Dana, Hood, Pike's Peak, Lassen's Butte, and, last though not least, a mountain in the Sierra Nevada named by John Muir and myself the "California Matterhorn," I had experienced in none of them except the latter such a real sample of looking destruction in the face as the Swiss climbers seem to number among their everyday experiences. If all accounts were true, Mount Tacoma could afford the only parallel on this continent to Mount Blanc, the Jungfrau, or the Matterhorn; and to it I turned with that eagerness which can best be appreciated by those who have been infected with the same sort of ambition.

As an additional incentive, there seemed really no well authenticated records of more than one ascent having ever been made—that of General Hazzard [*sic*] Stevens, in 1870. Previous to that ascent, Gen. A. V. Kautz, then a subaltern officer in the army, made the attempt, and doubtless reached a point near the summit; but as he himself modestly says, he reached only "what may be called the top," though "there were points higher yet." This was in 1857. A most interesting and quaintly humorous account of his attempt was recently given in lecture form by the gallant general, who, as a lieutenant, braved the yellowjacket wasps and mosquitoes in the then unexplored approaches to the mountain, and frightened his Indian guide by defying the Great Spirit, Ta-ho-ma, by an invasion of his stormy home.

Following the ascent of Stevens and his brave companion, P. B. Van Trump, an essay was made by Mr. Emmons, of Clarence King's geological survey; but his description of Crater Peak is dismissed as being inadequate, he having discovered but one crater where there are two, and it is therefore surmised that he may have stopped short of the topmost peak. At all events, whether General Kautz or Mr. Emmons succeeded in reaching the top or not, it is quite certain that Mount Tacoma is not within the beaten route of tourist travel; for with the three exceptions mentioned no other white men, so far as known, had ever made the attempt to ascend it, until the writer and his staunch comrades planted their flag upon its icy crest, August 17, 1884. [Apparently Bayley was confused about the date of his climb at the time he wrote this article because his companion, Van Trump, wrote about the same climb for an Olympia newspaper in 1883 and a marker the party left on the summit recorded that the climb took place on August 16, 1883.]

Arriving at Portland, Oregon, in July, I learned by accident, and quite to my surprise, that a trail had been opened from Wilkeson station to the glaciers at the base of the mountain on the north side, and that the ascent to the summit could be made in one day. Wilkeson is the terminus of a narrow gauge railroad from Puget Sound to some coal mines, and thither I repaired without delay. I found that an excellent road had been opened through the forest some fifteen miles, ending abruptly at the foot of the grand glacier, miles in width, that pours down the northern face of the mountain. A glance was sufficient to demonstrate the impossibility of ascending the mountain on the northern and western sides, and that my information had been incorrect. I felt well repaid for the trip, however, as it brought me face to face with the most stupendous field of ice that my imagination could have conceived, and spread out before my eyes the whole mountain from base to summit.

*James Longmire, pioneer guide and hotel keeper of Mount Rainier. (Courtesy Aubrey Haines)*

Retracing my route by rail to Yelm Prairie, I resumed a search begun a year or two before to find Mr. Van Trump, who had accompanied General Stevens, in his memorable ascent fourteen years ago. My efforts were rewarded with success, and together we persuaded James Longmire, the hardy pioneer who had piloted the former party through the woods to the base of the mountain, to accompany us on another ascent. He agreed to do so if we could wait a fortnight, until he could gather his harvest—a condition which was gladly accepted.

I spent the interval very pleasantly at the Canadian metropolis of Victoria, albeit with some impatience, and gladly welcomed the letter that announced that the harvesting was over, and all was ready for the ascent.

Returning at once to Yelm Prairie, we soon completed our arrangements. Our party was increased by the addition of a fourth member—Mr. W. C. Ewing, of Ohio—and on the 10th of August we saddled our horses, packed blankets, provisions, and cooking utensils on the back of a faithful beast, and plunged into the forest.

The trip was regarded by all the neighborhood as foolhardy, if not absolutely impossible. We were told that there was no vestige of a trail,

and it was generally predicted that we should be obliged to return before reaching the foot of the mountain. Mrs. Longmire was quite pa-
thetic in her appeals to her husband to abandon the trip, and clung to
him, saying, "Jim, you jest shaan't go." But Jim's mind was made up to
go, and with true Western determination he could be deterred by nothing after the resolve was once formed. Just before starting, we were told
that a party of old woodsmen, among them Mr. Packwood, who located the old Cowlitz trail, which we proposed to try to follow, had returned a few days before, after one day's attempt to penetrate the
forest, and had reported it impassable. With these numerous dis-
couragements, we were quite prepared for the five days of toil and
struggle that followed before reaching the mountain's base.

Crossing the Nisqually within an hour after leaving Yelm Prairie, we
took advantage of a fair wagon road for twenty-five miles, gradually ascending to an altitude of eighteen hundred feet, and terminating
abruptly at Mishawl Prairie, where we passed the night, the welcome
guests of Henry, a Klickitat Indian, who had renounced allegiance to
his tribe, adopted the dress and manners of living of the whites, married three buxom squaws, and settled down as a prosperous farmer. He
had preempted a quarter section of land, fenced it, erected several good
log buildings, and planted his land to wheat and vegetables, which appeared as thrifty and prosperous as any of the farms of the white
settlers we had seen. Henry was skilled in woodcraft, and we needed
his services to guide us to the mountain. For the moderate consideration of two dollars a day, he agreed to take us by the most direct route
to the highest point that could be reached by horses, there to remain in
charge of the animals while we went forward on foot. The negotiation
was carried on in Chinook by Longmire, whose long residence among
the Indians had given him great fluency in the strange jargon, and the
eloquent gestures and contortions so essential to its interpretation.
Henry knew of the circuitous route which General Stevens had followed, and was confident he could take us by a way thirty miles
shorter. Of this Longmire expressed doubts, but all agreed to follow
our guide until we were convinced that he was in error.

On the following morning, the 11th, we were early in the saddle, and
trouble began almost immediately. The woods were on fire around us,
and we occasionally found ourselves hemmed in by flame and blinding
smoke; smouldering trunks lay across the trail and half-burned stumps
left treacherous pitfalls in our way.

Nests of yellowjackets were met with every few hundred yards, their revengeful inmates swarming out upon us with relentless fury. The horses were stung to frenzy, and snorted, kicked, and finally stampeded in reckless madness, until brought to a standstill by a barrier of logs, where they crowded together, trembling with terror. Nor was this a temporary experience, but was repeated at intervals of ten minutes throughout the day. We were thus in constant danger of having our brains dashed out against the trees by the maddened beasts. The pack animals seemed to suffer most, and kicked off their packs with charming regularity about every hour.

By dint of a vigorous use of the axe in clearing the trail, we reached the Mishawl River, a distance of five miles, in four hours. The Mishawl is a clear, sparkling stream, rising in a range of mountains to the northwest of Mount Tacoma, and betraying by its purity that its birthplace was in crystal springs uncontaminated by glaciers. Four hours more of vigorous work took us six miles further, to a small brook running into the Nisqually, and by nightfall we had traversed seventeen miles from Mishawl Prairie, and gladly pitched our camp on a grassy bar of the main Nisqually.

We all needed rest and refreshing sleep, but were denied either, for no sooner had we unpacked our animals than we were assailed by myriads of small black gnats and ravenous mosquitoes. The gnats were simply irresistible; one could not breathe without inhaling them; they buried themselves in one's flesh, burning like so many coals of fire; they got into every article of food, without however, improving its flavor; they swam in the tea in such quantities that it became a nauseating *puree* of gnat, and in fact made life quite unendurable; while the mosquitoes stung and poisoned every exposed portion of our bodies. We anointed ourselves with mud, buried our heads in our blankets, and tried to snatch a little sleep, but all to no purpose. The gnats crawled down our backs, filled our hair and ears, eyes and noses; and, in short, made us so utterly wretched that not one of us closed our eyes in slumber the whole night through. This was a poor preparation for the fatigues and hardships of the following day, but we were destined to suffer the same sleepless torture for some succeeding nights before escaping to the upper region of frost and snow.

As we proceeded on our third day's journey, the forest seemed to grow denser and more entangled with fallen tree trunks, as though arranged to form a fortified stockade.

The ax was our only weapon to enable us to penetrate the barriers. Every few minutes the Indian pony in the lead would stir up a nest of yellowjackets, and away he would dash, Henry crying out at the top of his voice, "Soldiers! Hyack claterwar!" a warning to us to look out for the yellowjackets. Pushing ahead without stopping to rest, by 3 p.m. we reached Silver Creek, or Sakatash Creek, (Chinook for wild raspberry), some fifteen miles from our last camp, and shortly after 6 p.m. made camp for the night at Copper Creek, five miles further.

What with the painful stings of the wasps, and the burning attentions of the gnats, added to the ordinary fatigues of the day, our exhaustion was complete, and we craved for sleep with an intense longing. But the gnats were, if possible, more numerous than on the previous night, and we were again disappointed.

On the morning of the fourth day, Ewing's horse having become completely exhausted, we were obliged to turn it loose, and cache the saddle and bridle till our return. Our route still followed the foaming Nisqually, which we crossed and recrossed at frequent intervals throughout the day. At times we were forced by some impassable cliff or narrow gorge to leave the river, when we would cut our way through the forest around the obstruction, and return to the river channel, as affording fewer obstacles than the wooded mountain slopes, and greater freedom from the yellowjackets; albeit the crossings of the swift torrent were full of danger, on account of the moving mass of bowlders carried along by the stream. Between 7 a.m. and 6 p.m. we succeeded in getting fifteen miles further on our way, and made our camp for the night near an extensive series of soda and iron springs of great variety, and most agreeable to the taste. Our barometer showed an altitude of 4750 feet, although we were scarcely conscious of having reached so great an elevation, as there was but little change in the character of the vegetation, or the temperature.

The black gnats never left us through the day, and were on hand in increasing numbers to partake of our supper, and cause us another miserable, sleepless night. On the morning of the fifth day, a more haggard, gaunt, blear eyed company never sat down to a breakfast of bacon and beans. In feeling and appearance we were wretchedness personified.

Just as we were about mounting for the day's journey, the pall of dense smoke that had overhung the whole country for two months lifted for a few moments, as if to revive our dejected spirits, giving us our first inspiring view of Mount Tacoma, standing out before us in clear outline, every detail distinctly marked, and bearing almost exactly northeast by compass from our position.

Our course now lay almost wholly in the rocky bed of the Nisqually River, crossing the stream with even greater frequency than the day before. Some four miles above the Soda Springs, Longmire pointed out a blaze on one of the trees, as the point where General Stevens and Van Trump had left the Nisqually for Bear Prairie in 1870. Bear Prairie lay a long distance to the south—twenty miles at least—and was only to be reached by crossing several high mountain ranges. To be sure, it gave easy access to the longest of the ridges, leading directly up to the summit of the mountain; but the way offered fresh obstacles—precipitous wooded mountains, without a trail and without water, except at long, parching intervals. As the mountain lay to the northeast, we were naturally averse to turning in the opposite direction, and were all the more ready to believe our redskin's assurance that we could continue directly up the Nisqually. To his guidance we therefore entrusted ourselves confidently, and at 11 a.m. had the satisfaction of arriving at the foot of the great Nisqually glacier, an abrupt wall of ice five hundred feet high, filling the whole valley from side to side. Here the river, born to maturity, springs like the Rhone from a dark blue cave in the ice. Our barometers marked altitude at this point of 5850 feet.

The last few miles of the ascent were exceedingly difficult and dangerous. The river bed was inclined at an angle of about twenty degrees, and the ice-cold water reached to the bellies of the horses. Several times our pack animals were in imminent danger of losing their footing, and rolling over and over. The narrow gorge echoed with the roaring, rushing sound of the waters, and the clicking of the bowlders bumping against each other as they rolled down the stream. The water, soon as it left the glacier, was white with sand, ground up from the granite by the resistless forces constantly at work under the ice river—a characteristic of all streams of glacial origin.

Crossing the stream to the south side for the last time, we unluckily pitched our luncheon bivouac over a nest of hornets—and not until the ponies had kicked themselves free of packs and other incumbrances, could we manage to secure them, and check an incipient stampede. The horses were by no means the only sufferers from this last vicious attack, as we were all badly stung, and carried the pain in swollen faces for the rest of the day.

On either side of the river, the sides of the ancient glacial moraines were precipitous for more than one thousand feet in height: the glacier in front of us was a wall; and it seemed at first sight that we had got into a box, from which the only way out was by the route we had come.

Van Trump thought we should have gone by the old route by Bear Prairie; Longmire was dubious of the outcome; but Henry was perfectly serene, and shouldering the ax, proposed cutting a zigzag trail up the mountain, as he assured us most earnestly that he could take the horses to the top of the moraine.

While the remainder of the party were engineering the trail, I started a fire, and got the dinner under way, and then eagerly ran down to examine the glacier. Its face was not so abrupt a wall as it had appeared, and I found I could climb to the top of it without difficulty. Its width was about two hundred feet, and its height over four hundred feet, confined within polished walls of grayish white granite. The river welled up from the dark blue cave at its foot, milky white, and heavily charged with fine sand. At frequent intervals quantities of large bowlders were hurled out, and went rolling down the steep cañon with a deafening noise like the roar of artillery. It was a most fascinating scene, and I left it with reluctance to return to my neglected culinary operations. The party had finished a trail in my absence, returned to camp, and finished the preparation of lunch.

Resaddling our animals, we succeeded in driving them up the trail with the greatest difficulty, and reached the top of the moraine after an hour and a half of toil and struggle. Continuing to ascend, we changed our course to due east, and in an hour emerged upon a beautiful plateau of gently rolling ground, where there was unfolded to our delighted eyes a superb panoramic view of Tacoma and all its southern and eastern approaches. The cañon of the Cowlitz, with its great glacier, lay to our right; the Nisqually glacier with its many tributaries to our left, and before us the long, sinuous, ragged ridge by which we knew lay our only hope of ascent. We were really only at the foot of the mountain, and thanks to Henry's sagacity had reached exactly the proper point, by the most direct and easiest possible route. Van Trump recognized his position and the route of approach which he and Stevens had followed from Bear Prairie, and realized the great distance that we had saved. Our way now led us through rich grassy meadows, with snowbanks jutting into them like headlands in an emerald ocean; delicate, fragrant flowers, of loveliest hue, were growing right up to the edges of the snow, and the whole scene was one of enchantment.

Across this meadow we rode for four miles, now floundering in snow, and at the next step rioting in a wilderness of flowers, coming finally to a steep, icy acclivity; ascending which, we came upon the last vestige of timber, a few stunted, gnarled, and storm-beaten balsam firs.

A few steps away lay a little gem of a meadow, some fifty feet in diameter, almost surrounded by snow, with a pretty little rivulet of ice cold water trickling through it. The meadow was thickly strewn with large blue gentians, red castilleia, yellow polygonum, white crigeron daisy, white alpine phlox, yellow and white fritillaria, yellow arinea, and a large, blue, composite flower, all of the most brilliant coloring imaginable. Here we made our final camp with our horses, and turned them loose to graze—although it seemed almost a sacrilege to see them trample and eat the dainty, gorgeously colored flowers. Our altitude here was 8200 feet, but none of us yet experienced any discomfort from the rarity of the air, or the chilliness of the atmosphere. The night was a grand one, compensating us for all the discomforts we had suffered in the lower regions. The moon shone full and clear, revealing all the landscape above and below us with startling distinctness. The long ridges of the mountains, running away to the east and south, with their barren, blackened crests cropping out above the snow; the Cowlitz winding away to the south like a silver thread in its narrow gorge, until lost in the heavy bank of smoke that had settled down some thousands of feet below us; while overtopping and overshadowing all rose the vast bulk of Mount Tacoma, glittering coldly in the moonlight.

No insects here disturbed our rest, and for the first time in several nights we slept soundly, not leaving our blankets until eight o'clock next morning, when we prepared for climbing in earnest. The saddle animals were turned loose, and the pack horses were lightly loaded with a pair of blankets for each man, provisions for two days, and a small bundle of firewood. We started at nine o'clock, bidding adieu to the last vestige of vegetation, and after ascending over four miles of snow, at times with great difficulty, at last came to a point the steepness of which forbade further progress with horses. We then unpacked them, and gave them into charge of the Indian, whom we instructed to kill some of the mountain sheep that we had seen before leaving camp.

Henry, who had not spoken a word the entire day, and had looked as blue as possible, here made a last persuasive appeal to Longmire not to persist in his foolish attempt to scale the mountain. For the rest of us he did not seem to care, but on Longmire, as an old friend and neighbor, he wasted quite an amount of Chinook eloquence, to save him from what he considered certain death. He said we should never get back alive, if we succeeded in reaching the top; while if we were permitted to go part way by the spirit who dwelt at the summit, we should return maimed for life. He doubtless felt as he spoke, and parted from us in a most dejected frame of mind, as he turned to go back with the horses.

Shouldering our packs, which were apportioned to give about twenty-five pounds to each, we traveled in an easterly direction, over the snow for about three miles, when we came to a narrow ridge of burnt and blackened rock, running north and south. All about us, to the right and to the left, were vast and terrible defiles, and before us, connected with the rock on which we stood by a steep and narrow neck, lay the last thin backbone of columnar basalt, leading directly to the summit dome of the leviathan of mountains. Beyond this point it was impossible to find a spot sufficiently level to lie down and pass the night, and as it was late in the afternoon we prepared to camp.

We lighted a fire with the few sticks of wood we brought, and prepared a place to sleep by throwing out the rocks, and making holes large enough for each to lie in. Our altitude here was about 11,300 feet; the wind was blowing strongly from the north west; and the thermometer at sundown marked 34°. We felt this sudden change of temperature keenly, on account of the wind, and gladly wrapped ourselves in our blankets.

The brilliant moonlight and the singularly clear atmosphere rendered all surrounding objects as distinct as in daylight. The sea of smoke and vapor lay six thousand feet beneath us, and as we gazed out upon its white, level expanse, so calm and limitless, it required no effort of the imagination to fancy we were on an island in mid-ocean. Mounts Saint Helena [Helens], Adams, and Hood appeared like conical islands of crystal, serene and solitary, rising from the sea far to the south of us. At times, a puff of wind would set the vapor in motion, tearing it in tatters, and rolling it up like a scroll, unveiling for a few moments the great valleys, and the vast expanse of forests, far below; and then the fog would roll back again, filling up the gaps evenly, as before.

Lying due west of us, some three miles away in an air line, was the largest glacier any of us had seen, with a length which we estimated at five miles, and a perpendicular depth of probably fifteen hundred feet. It was torn and rent with enormous fissures, the blue color of which we could clearly distinguish in the moonlight, even at so great a distance. The surface of the glacier was strewn with detached blocks or masses of ice, that appeared to have been upheaved and thrown out by some mighty power struggling underneath to escape. Some of these cubical blocks must have measured hundreds of feet in every dimension, and could be distinguished twenty miles away.

The noise all night from the grinding of the glaciers was terrific. Avalanches of snow and ice from the sides of the gorges fell with a sullen crash, and every puff of wind brought showers of stones from the tops of the crumbling cliffs to the glacier; while above all other sounds could be heard the deep boom of the bowlders rushing along the rock-bound channel underneath the glacier. The mountain seemed to be creaking and groaning, and one could almost fancy that at times it gave a mighty shudder, as if to free itself from its icy shackles.

No pen can picture the fascination of these weird sights and sounds. It was only after many hours that tired nature asserted herself, and closed the senses in sleep. We awoke next morning, the seventh day out, August 16, at four o'clock, pretty well rested, although we had suffered somewhat from the cold. As we opened our eyes, the prospect was forbidding. It was snowing and hailing briskly, and the mountain-top was hidden in fog. The wind had changed to the southwest, and all indications pointed to an imminent storm. Before we had time, however, to regret our ill fortune, the wind shifted to the north-west, and in fifteen minutes the clouds were dissipated, and we were treated to a clear, beautiful sunrise, and an unobstructed view of the mountain to its summit. Springing from our blankets, we soon had a fire started, breakfast prepared, and by five o'clock we were ready for the final ascent.

We hoped to be able to reach the summit and return to our lofty camp by nightfall; but still we feared the worst, and made what little preparation we could toward passing the night on the summit. It was out of the question to think of burdening ourselves with blankets, as they too much impeded our climbing, but we took a little food with us. Unfortunately, a bottle of alcohol, with which we expected to be able to make hot tea or soup on the summit, though carried by Van Trump with the greatest care, was broken at our last horse camp; and when that accident occurred, I threw aside as useless the spirit lamp, a tin cup, and a jar of Liebig's meat extract—not thinking of the possibility of our finding a natural steam-heating apparatus, and only having in view the necessity of lightening our load. Besides, we were certain that with so early a start from so high an altitude, we should be able to return to camp again that night. I carried one hundred feet of new manila rope; Van Trump, a hatchet and a six foot flag-staff, hewn from a dead fir; Longmire, the whisky flask; and Mr. Ewing brought up the rear with the barometer.

Starting off briskly across some three hundred yards of hard snow, we were soon climbing a black ridge of loose rock, standing at an angle of forty degrees, and requiring most dextrous and active use of hands and feet. Two hundred feet of this sort of climbing inspired Mr. Ewing with the discovery that he preferred to return to camp and watch our attempt, so the barometer was transferred to Van Trump, and we left him behind. Ascending a few hundred feet further over the crumbling rocks, which were loosened by every step, we found ourselves forced by the increasing steepness of the ridge and the volleys of stones at short range, to the edge of the glacier. This was no better. The ice lay at a frightful angle—a single misstep would have hurled us thousands of feet. We were three hours cutting some two hundred steps in the ice, a task of which we relieved each other at frequent intervals. At the end of that time we were again able to take to the rocky ridge, and held to it for over an hour, when we were forced to resume our ice chopping at the edge of the glacier, and for some time we alternated between ice steps and steep and dangerous scrambling over the loosened rocks on the side of the adjacent ridge.

Ten o'clock brought us to the top of the highest ridge, and to a view of the point of its junction with the vast *mer de glâce* that swept downward in an unbroken sheet from the summit of the mountain. Looking downward from here, the great Nisqually glacier appeared to be flowing directly below us, in a due southeast direction. The debris from the ridge on which we stood went down to meet it at an angle of nearly sixty degrees, occasionally breaking off in a sheer precipice, as the walls were exposed. The view in every direction was one of solitary grandeur.

A halt was here called, and a consultation took place as to the route by which we should proceed. Van Trump could scarcely recognize his surroundings on account of the great changes that had taken place in the face of the landscape since his first ascent, but was under the impression that we must descend, and get upon the edge of the glacier upon its western side. I was not in favor of this, feeling confident it was practicable for us to follow the ridge, and from its terminus reach the head of the glacier. We determined to proceed as we were going. Climbing over alternate ice and rocks, we finally came to a point where the ridge diminishes to a thin, crumbling knife edge, running squarely

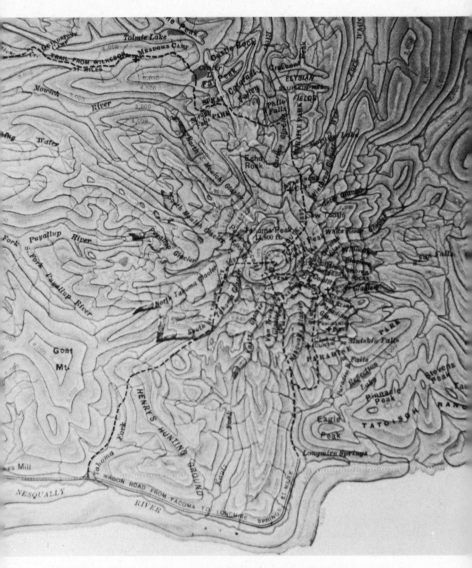

*Early map of Mount Rainier. From Olin Wheeler's* Mount Rainier: Its Ascent by a
Northern Pacific Party.

against a huge, perpendicular precipice of rock, rising grandly one thousand feet above our heads, and standing sharply out from the main bulk of the mountain, a mighty landmark, distinguishable for many miles in every direction.

Unless we could succeed in crawling around the face of this precipice, all further progress was at an end, as there were nothing but yawning chasms below us on either side of the knife ridge, reaching down hundreds of feet to glaciers in both sides; and to have scaled the face of the wall in front of us would have been as useless as it was impossible, for we should have been on an isolated rock, from which we should have had to descend again to proceed on our way. To add to our discomfiture, while we were deliberating, an avalanche of stones and dirt came over the cliff from its top, covering the head of the glacier, and loosening from the foot of the cliff tons of debris, which went booming down the ice slopes with a sound like the roar of thunder.

Feeling responsible for having brought the party into the perilous situation against Van Trump's inclination, I ran ahead as fast as I could, crawling on all fours over the dizzy knife edge, till I came squarely up against the cliff, where, to my great joy, I found a narrow ledge some four feet wide, on the face of the cliff, apparently leading around to the head of the Nisqually glacier. I shouted for my companions to follow, as the way was clear, and without waiting for them, crept on along the ledge some two hundred feet, where I found progress barred by an immense icicle, which had formed from dripping water from the top of the cliff. When the others came up with the hatchet, we soon cut a hole through the icicle, and in ten minutes more of sharp work, clinging in mid air to the side of the cliff with fingers and toes, and painfully crawling past critical points of danger, we were at the head of the glacier, which here became a steep gutter of green ice.

We had barely congratulated ourselves upon having safely run the gauntlet, when another furious shower of stones came over the cliff, falling but a few feet behind us, while a few came directly down the ice gutter, warning us that the sooner we were out of that locality, the better would be our chances for preserving whole limbs. There was no way for it but to follow up the gutter of ice; and for three quarters of an hour we experienced the severest and most perilous work of the ascent. Let the reader imagine the shady side of the steepest gothic roof he has ever seen, covered with hard, slippery ice, unsoftened by the sun, and prolonged for hundreds of feet above, and thousands of feet below, and he will have a fair idea of the situation. Every step had to be carefully selected and well chopped out of the ice. The consequences of a slip here may be readily imagined; it meant a swift slide of a thousand feet or more into the yawning jaws of a beautiful green and blue crevasse, which we had admired from the knife-edge ridge.

Laboriously and slowly carving our way up the gutter, at twelve o'clock we reached the broad stretch of billowy snow that swept unbroken to the summit, apparently within easy reach. For hours we had been looking forward to this snow-field, with pleasant anticipation of rest and relief from hard climbing. We expected to make rapid headway, and reckoned on skipping along to the summit in a few moments; but, on the contrary, we found it about the most fatiguing part of the day's work. The snow was frozen into ice-waves, running across the face of the mountain, and resembled a heavy chop sea, solidified and set up at a considerable angle—the hollows being three feet deep, hard and slippery, and the crests so softened by the sun as to make sure footing impossible. Every few moments we would fall down into the hollows, thoroughly spent and exhausted, or by a mis-step would find ourselves forcibly seated astride the ridges. After a time, we tried a new method. The man in the lead would leap upon the crest of the snow ridge, and pack the snow with his feet before the others followed, and in this way we made better progress. Every few minutes the rear man would take his turn in the lead, and by a short period of extra exertion prepared the little platforms on the snow crests to give sure footing for the others to follow. Taking frequent pauses for rest, we finally surmounted this wearisome portion of our journey, and at three o'clock p.m. we stood upon the bare rim of the eastern crater of the middle summit, with the upper edge of the crater only a few hundred yards away, and about one hundred feet higher.

Thus far on our ascent, the mountain had sheltered us from a furious gale of wind blowing from the north, which here assailed us with such force that with the greatest difficulty we accomplished the remainder of the distance, and at 3:30 p.m. planted our flag on the topmost crest, in the face of the bitterly cold blast.

The view was inexpressibly grand and comprehensive, although the whole landscape, below an altitude of five thousand feet, was swallowed up in a sea of vapor, leaving the higher mountains standing out like islands, as we had seen them the night before. An occasional gust of wind would tear open the veil for a few moments, exposing to momentary view the precipitous cañons and crags for thousands of feet down the mountain's sides. We seemed to be floating in a dark blue ocean, having no connection with the earth below, and the mountain appeared to rest gently upon its encompassing clouds.

The narrow ridge upon which we stood was the dividing line between two craters, nearly circular, opening out to the east and to the west, their rims inclining from each other at an angle of about fifteen degrees. The western crater, the larger of the two, was some four hundred yards in diameter, and filled with snow up to within sixty feet of its rocky edges. Occasional small jets of steam, issuing from the base of its ragged walls, gave evidence of former volcanic activity. We could look down into the other and slightly smaller crater, also, whose rocky walls, like those of its neighbor, stood out bare and distinct above the snow throughout their entire periphery. Jets of steam were rising from this one also at various places.

By the time we had explored both craters, another hour had passed, and all thought of descending the mountain that night had to be abandoned. Indeed, had we turned back the moment we reached the top, it would have been impossible, before the darkness overtook us, to pass under the perilous cliff, where even now we could see showers of stones flying down to the glacier below: and the attempt must have proven fatal. The only thing that could be done was to seek some sheltered nook, and pass the night as best we could.

To pass the time till dark, a suggestion was made to scale the north peak of the mountain, about a mile away; but the steadily increasing wind admonished us that we had better not run the risk of being blown over the narrow ridge by which lay our only path to the peak.

After a long search, Van Trump finally found the ice cave where General Stevens and himself had found shelter for the night in 1870; but alas! the roof had melted away, leaving only a circular well in the ice some six or eight feet in depth, and about eighteen feet in diameter. From a small and irregular hole in the center issued a scalding jet of steam about the size of one's little finger, around which still remained the loose rocks piled up by the last tenants of this rude hostelry.

Rebuilding the low wall to enclose a space large enough for their bodies to lie in, Longmire and Van Trump stowed themselves away inside the wall and on either side of the steam jet; while with hatchet and alpenstock I leveled off the stones for a short path, some seven feet long, inside the cave, and prepared to pass the night pacing to and fro to keep from freezing, preferring this weary exercise to scalding myself with the steam, which had already saturated the clothing of my companions. It was a dreary outlook for the night, as the thermometer soon fell to twenty degrees Fahrenheit, and the wind howled, and roared, and poured down into our ice-walled cave, upon our unprotected heads, with a fury that made us long for the warm blankets we left in camp. I succeeded in keeping tolerably comfortable till midnight on my feet; but finally, overcome by drowsiness, and after repeated falls and bruises on the sharp rocks, was obliged to join my comrades around the "register."

Notwithstanding the discomfort and misery of our situation, one could not but take note of the weird beauty of the night, and the brilliant prismatic effects of the full moon, directly over our heads, shining from a cloudless sky upon the blue ice-walls of our cavern. Not even the ice-palace of Montreal, illuminated with myriads of electric lights, could rival in beauty the wonderful colors displayed in our fairy grotto by moonlight.

The long night at last wore away, and by morning we were fairly cooked by the steam. We could face it but a few moments at a time, and when we turned around, our clothing was instantly frozen to sheets of ice. The monotony and discomfort of this procedure may be imagined without further elaboration.

At six the next morning, August 17th, we shivered about the steam jet, and discussed plans for the descent. The thermometer indicated sixteen degrees, and the wind was blowing at the rate of one hundred miles an hour, and shifting to the southwest, with strong indications of snow. I make this statement of the velocity of the wind with some degree of positiveness, as I once walked up Mount Washington in the face of a gale that was registered at one hundred and five miles per hour when I reached the signal station at the summit, and I could therefore judge of the effects of such a gale.

Dreading a storm, we decided not to wait for the wind to subside, and at 7 a.m. left our friendly steam jet and started on the descent. Scarcely were we outside the cavern before our clothing was frozen solid, and we were hurled with great violence upon our faces. Staggering and crawling along upon our hands and feet, we managed to reach the western rim of the large crater, where we found a partial shelter from the force of the gale behind some large rocks, which allowed us to take our breath—but so benumbed with cold as to be scarcely able to grasp our alpenstocks. We discussed the route by which we should return to the east slope of the mountain. One favored crossing the large crater and scaling its opposite wall, but the terrible wind raked it fore and aft, and we must have perished in the attempt. While the others hesitated, I set the example, and, gathering all my strength, started at my best speed along the rim of the crater.

I had not gone one hundred feet before I fell among the rocks, completely exhausted and benumbed. The others followed. Longmire also fell heavily, receiving severe cuts and bruises before reaching me. We continued crawling along slowly and painfully, a few feet at a time, all the while clinging to the rocks for dear life, to prevent being blown away by the gale, until at 9 a.m. we got around sufficiently under the lee of the mountain to be out of the wind, and reached the billowy snow field that had so wearied and vexed us on the ascent.

Following our trail of the day before, we sprang from crest to crest with accelerating pace, momentarily cheered by the fast increasing warmth of the sun. Ten o'clock brought us to the ice gutter at the head of the glacier, where we used the rope to good advantage. Two of us

*Longmire with one of his children. The pony is the one that wandered off and was found at the springs that became part of the Longmire resort. (Courtesy Aubrey Haines)*

were lowered the rope's length at a time, while the last man lowered himself by doubling the rope over projecting knobs of ice, and so getting down half the rope's length at a time. The high cliff was passed safely, although volleys of rocks fell on our path immediately after we had gone by.

Twelve o'clock found us half way down the burnt ridge, and within half an hour of camp, when we missed the trail, and wandered over a labyrinth of crumbling rocks for two hours, before we reached our bivouac, where we found Ewing, who was becoming very uneasy at our protracted absence. His little fire of two sticks served to give us a cup of hot tea, which, together with bread and butter, we devoured with the appetites of famished wolves, as we had eaten nothing in the two days of our absence. Food seemed so distasteful on the mountaintop, doubtless owing to our exhausted condition, that, though abundantly provided, we were unable to masticate it. Nature deals harshly in every way with those who have the hardihood to investigate her secrets, not alone in throwing obstacles in the way, but in the preparation of all the conditions of swift and easy destruction.

At three p.m. we resumed the downward march, and almost instantly were enveloped in a dense fog, which seemed to come from nowhere, but to form about us out of a clear sky. Luckily, the sun had not quite obliterated our tracks in the snow, and by the closest attention we groped our way down the mountain. Otherwise, we might have wandered all night, or taken a plunge to the Nisqually or the Cowlitz glaciers, by a slight deviation to the right or to the left. When we came upon the horse tracks, we had a plainer trail, and by five p.m. reached our camp at the snow line.

An unbroken stillness and solitude reigned in camp. Neither Henry nor the horse [sic] could be seen or heard. The tent was found more carefully stretched than when the party left it, a trench had been dug about it, the provisions and camp equipage had been piled and covered in the center of the tent, and at either end a scarecrow, or rather scarewolf, had been improvised—the large, fresh tracks of a wolf had been noticed on the snow not far from camp. All these preparations indicated that the Indian had made a movement not on the programme of the white man. Later in the evening, after much whooping and several revolver shots by one of the party, who had gone some distance down the slope, Henry made his appearance, and proceeded to explain—with a preliminary ejaculation of his relief from a grave responsibility. He had concluded that the party had been lost on the mountain, and he had put their house (tent) in order, removed the horses to good pasturage below, had moved his "ictas" (personal effects) to that point, provided himself with a few days' rations, and on the morrow had intended to start for home, to relate to their friends the supposed tragic fate of the mountaineers. It had been sad and mournful business for him, but his joy at our return was as genuine as his surprise, and we doubted if he really believed that we had reached the top at all.

The next morning, August 18th, there came a flurry of snow that inclined us to lie abed, and it was not till nine o'clock that we were once more underway, in full force, with blankets and all our effects packed on our horses. We adhered to the route by which we had come, and during the four succeeding days of travel encountered but a repetition of the experiences already described; a renewal of the plague of gnats and mosquitoes by night, with a running accompaniment of yellow-jackets by day. When the nests of these warm-footed little insects are stationed at intervals of one hundred yards on the trail, travel becomes lively and spirited; and when trod upon, they become an incentive to "cayuse" locomotion superior to whip or spur.

The expedition was eminently successful in all that its projectors had planned, with one exception—the southern peak was not climbed, owing to lack of time the first day, and the furious gale blowing on the second, which prevented an attempt, had we been so disposed. That peak, I believe, is still virgin soil, and may tempt the ambition of some future climber. When one has once reached the middle peak, it is only a matter of two or three hours to ascend it, provided the wind is not blowing a hurricane, as we found it. It is undoubtedly inaccessible, except by way of the middle peak.

There are indications of abundant mountain sheep on Mount Tacoma. The party obtained a view of a flock of twenty-five or thirty of them on the ascent, a long way to their right, passing from the snow to a ridge of rock, from the high comb of which they paused to view the intruding climbers. The writer has often seen them on Mount Whitney and other Californian peaks, always at high altitudes, and of the same appearance as those of Tacoma, with large curved horns and shaggy coats, very shy and most difficult to approach. Their feeding grounds are below the snow line, and they only seek the higher snowfields and precipitous rocks to escape their natural enemies. No signs of them were seen on Tacoma higher than eleven thousand feet. Our uppermost camp on the mountain was about eleven thousand feet above sea level, and was found to be the extreme limit of organic life. Among the rocks there was a little moss, a few blades of mountain grass, and a species of saxifrage; beyond this point not a vestige of animal or vegetable life, nor a fossil of either—nothing but igneous rocks, snow, and profound solitude. Since the time, ages gone by, that nature upheaved the mountain from the primal waters, the only living things the wastes of snow and rock there have known, are doubtless the few human beings who have planted weary feet upon its summit.

The achievement was a great satisfaction to all of us—to Van Trump, because it vindicated his former claims to the distinction, upon which doubts had been cast in the neighborhood; to Longmire, because it gave him renewed pride in his manly vigor which sixty winters of hardship had in no wise undermined; and to the writer, because he realized that all other mountain climbing in which he had indulged was as boys' play compared to the ascent of this—the king of all the mountains of the United States.

The name of Rainier is being gradually supplanted by the Indian appellation of Tacoma (pronounced Tachoma, with the German guttural sound to the *ach*), a name not only more appropriate on account of its antiquity, but to be preferred on account of its euphony.

# 8

# J. Warner Fobes*
# 1884

The ascent of the Fobes party is a whimsical and surprising episode in the mountain's saga. Three young men, all apparently from Snohomish, Washington (where J. Warner Fobes served as pastor of the Union Presbyterian Church), set out with no solid plans and no real climbing experience; but with their boyish zeal, they reached the summit. They approached it from what was considered the "wrong" direction, and they found a route where the veteran mountaineer George Bayley had been turned back. They ignorantly, and joyously, made several near-fatal mistakes and behaved with reckless enthusiasm where they should have trod most lightly. So uninformed were they about the mountain and the challenges of serious climbing that they did not even know it had been climbed before; they just set out to do it, and it wasn't until they were on top, celebrating their success, that they noticed evidence of earlier climbs. Would that all such casual wilderness adventures result in such a good time!

Fobes and his companions, George James and Richard Wells, pioneered a new route, this one on the north side of the mountain. At first they tried an approach up Ptarmigan Ridge; that failed, so without hesitation they shifted around to the northeast and reached the summit from the divide between Winthrop and Emmons glaciers. The ease of their success, despite their carelessness, must have been some cause for chagrin among survivors of earlier parties, but for us the result is one of the happiest, most innocent of Mount Rainier's early adventures.

Theodore Winthrop's stories have not exaggerated the beauty and charms of Puget Sound. As you look out from either Seattle or Tacoma, Nature herself gives you a thrill and inspiration of soul, such as genius on canvas or page cannot arouse. A little bay stretches out be-

*Reprinted from J. Warner Fobes, "To the Summit of Tacoma," West Shore 11(1885): 265–269.

fore you, light and pale green by the shore, but shading off toward the broad Sound to deepest amethyst; smooth as the mill pond ice, except where the leaping salmon break the surface of some bay with a hundred little fountains, or an Indian family in their black, red-edged canoe, more graceful than a gondola, glide along the shore. Above the restful waters rise up high bluffs two or three hundred feet, all forest covered, the great firs showing their giant sizes where they have fallen along the beach, outreaching the ocean steamers as they pass, three hundred feet in length. And still beyond to the westward, over the high wooded shores, rise the Olympic Mountains, their rounded summits dark green under their load of spruce and hemlock; and still above stand out against the western sky the higher peaks of Constance and Olympus, their dark rocks making a jagged outline, tinged with a ridge of white. To the east the Cascade Range raises its higher wall six to eight thousand feet, with great craggy peaks wild and rough, single precipices thousands of feet in sheer descent, black rock ribs and white lines of snow-filled ravines leading up to their snow-capped tops. Yet far up above these, so that their loftiest summits seem but pigmy foothills, towers Mount Rainier, an ideal mountain. Its broad, firm base, itself above the snow line, is planted on the wide mountain range, its steep sides rising up with their eternal snows to regions where the high clouds play; and over all, in the pure ether, bright in the sunlight, looking down from undisturbed quiet on the world, is the summit—not a thin spire, but broad and rounded, fit to be the pillar of the heavens.

Last summer, about the first of August, three of us determined to attempt to gain the summit of this Cascade monarch. As we pursued the route which will doubtless be the one used by climbers in the future, our experience may be of some value. The party consisted of a lawyer, a surveyor and myself, the latter two of us well accustomed to the woods, and all young and hardy. Although we had a far easier task than those who may have attempted the ascent years ago, yet it was fully as exciting to us because we labored under the delusion, common to most Puget Sounders, that the mountain never had really been ascended. We knew nothing of the trails or about the locality; and we went in a very plebeian manner, without guides or packers, and carrying our tent, blankets, food, etc., for ourselves.

We started from Tacoma in the morning on the Cascade Branch of the Northern Pacific. We were whirled across the Puyallup Valley, through little prairies covered with smooth oat fields and vine-covered hop yards; through the black stumps of half-made clearings; through tangled woods where maple and alder show themselves as much as hemlock or fir, and the golden rod and purple astors brighten up the open spaces. After a forty-mile journey we reached Wilkeson, a little coal mining town of about one hundred people. There the one little store furnished us the necessary supplies of flour and bacon, and the good Irish woman who kept the little miners' boarding house spread us our last dinner in civilization. Though it was rather humble fare of boiled beef and beans, many times during the succeeding days of camp life my soul lusted after the flesh-pot and good sweet bread of that little Wilkeson hotel. To our delight we found a good pack trail leading to the mountain, cut by President Villard's orders in 1883. With our sixty-pound packs this occupied us three days, while it could be made quite easily in a day and a half with ponies. Passing through forests of hemlocks like the Adirondacks; then among great three hundred-foot firs; crossing the horse over ravines on bridges of a single log seven feet through; fording the Carbon River, nearly milk color from its glacial origin; up and down hills, gradually ascending till emerging from the almost unbroken tunnel of trees, we entered three beautiful little prairies with soft green grass and flowers. There first we obtained a good

*Sketch of Carbon Glacier, 1881, by one of Mount Rainier's leading early geological explorers, Bailey Willis. (Courtesy Aubrey Haines)*

view of the mountains about us, their rough, reddish rocks towering up
and shutting out half the sky. Great patches of white snow told us we
were already far above the level of the Sound, and caused us to hurry
on with enthusiastic excitement. Then the trail led us along by zigzags
up the mountains, the barometer showing four, five, six thousand feet
of altitude. As we skirted along the crest of this ridge, over gulches
filled with snow, we made our first August snowballs. Taking a forced
rest, we turned to our left, and just a few feet below we saw the most
beautiful little lake that ever rested weary eyes. We were tired no
longer, but hurried down to it. Crater Lake, as it is called, lies right in
the tops of the mountains, and is snow fed only. There is an open
meadow, with plenty of grass and flowers, at the outlet, forming a magnificent camping ground. At the further end, half a mile away, rocks
rise abruptly from the water to jagged points a thousand feet above.
Snowdrifts in every deep ravine and northern slope keep pouring into
the lake their pure supplies, and half a dozen beautiful cascades break
the solitude with their endless monotone. There are fish in the lake,
and although it is of melted snow it is not so cold but that a shallow bay
gave us quite a pleasant swim. Having pitched our tent we passed a
most comfortable night, four blankets keeping us warm till we awoke
refreshed from undisturbed slumber at daybreak.

From Crater Lake the trail descends a little for about four miles along
the side of the Puyallup River gorge. From one point on this part of the
road there is one of the most beautiful views in America. The point of
view is a great rock a few steps from one side of the trail. Two thousand
feet below the Puyallup River comes out from beneath the glacier and
goes dashing down the gorge in a line of white foam, with a roar that
comes up plainly to the ear. To the right the mountains rise up—first
forest covered, then barren rock. To the left a little creek breaks over
the rocks and plunges down five hundred feet. Up the front is the
glacier—first brown and covered with débris, then gray and blue, crev-
iced and bored like a honeycomb, then whiter and higher till it shades
off into the clear white of the mountain side. Above all is the old
mountain itself, rising in its pure, shining whiteness higher than the
winter's sun.

The road soon turns up again, and after a thousand feet of upward
windings, passes the timber line on the base of the mountain. There we
made our permanent camp; walls of sod with the tent for a roof, a few
scrub firs furnishing us with wood and a snow bank giving us water. It
was Friday night when we were ready to turn in on our bed of fir

boughs. Two weeks was the time calculated for the ascent, but that evening, as we threw on the biggest logs for our night fire and sat around waiting for them to light up, we were happily confident that before our next night fire was lighted we would have explored the summit.

Saturday morning, bright and early, we started up, one carrying a small axe and aneroid barometer, another the lunch, and the third one hundred feet of light rope. Each had a good ash alpine-stock, steel pointed, and six feet long. Unfortunately we had come without ice-creepers, but had logger's corks (nails an inch long) in our shoes. There was first a short grassy slope and half a mile of rocks to climb, then came the snow. This snow was hard, having thawed every day and frozen every night for weeks, and so made quite easy walking when at all level, and on the slopes was no more difficult than rock climbing. In the fresh of the morning we took the ascent very bravely, but by degrees it became rather monotonous lifting one foot above the other, even when the snow was an easy slope and we did not slip. Then crevasses began to appear. We did not quite understand them at first; we would walk up near them, try the snow all about with our staves, then creep up gently and, holding our breath, peep over and gaze down their depths with greatest awe. But how familiarity breeds contempt; within three days we would with the utmost nonchalance walk up to their very edge, poke down pieces of snow, contemptuously spit into the abyss, and discuss the idea of jumping across when not more than twelve feet wide. These crevasses are all through the sides of the mountain; they are made by the snow contracting by the cold or sliding down a little. They vary from a few inches to a hundred feet in width, and are the depth of the snow. Often hundreds of feet of their walls of cold blue ice can be seen, with seemingly no bottom. They are a great hindrance to the climber, and frequently it is necessary to go half a mile to get around one, then often to find the way blocked by another. But they were not our greatest difficulty that first day. We had marked out a course over the long snow incline between two rock peaks, up a rocky spur, then by a depression of the main cone to the top, very nearly straight up the north side of the mountain. We had climbed the first rocks quickly and plodded up the long fields of snow, though our feet did not pick themselves up quite so briskly as at first. Noon had passed before the barometer told off ten thousand feet, but we clambered up the highest spur of rock to eleven thousand feet, when we were brought to a sudden halt by finding ourselves on the verge of an immense abyss.

What we had supposed to be simply a protruding ridge of rock was the rim of a great crater basin, and instead of being on the main mountain we found ourselves cut off from it by this valley five hundred feet deep, terminating in almost perpendicular walls of rock thousands of feet in height. As far as we could see on either side it was the same, save in one little ravine, where the snow lay at an angle of about seventy degrees, but seamed with ugly looking crevasses. Everywhere else were walls of black, forbidding rock. The lawyer managed to cross over to the foot of the main dome, in search of a point where these walls could be scaled, but turned back without discovering a spot offering the least encouragement. After shivering awhile on the sunny side of the rocks we returned to camp, satisfied that it was next to impossible to make the ascent from the north. That evening as we sat about the camp-fire, and the huge white mass of mountain loomed up in the moonlight, our admiration of its beauty was accompanied by a respect for its ruggedness we had not the night before possessed.

Sunday was a much-needed day of rest. We slept late, enjoying the pure, light air and the restful stillness. These mountain tops are by no means an uninhabited desert. The hundreds of park-like valleys furnish pasturage for elk and deer, and the mountain goat follows the melting snow to crop the freshest herbage. Almost every open space contains the burrows of the marmot, the mountain woodchuck, and their shrill whistle as they dart into their holes sounds much like a man's signal call. As we came down the mountain Saturday afternoon we passed within easy shot of a flock of ptarmigan, on the rocks way up among the snow. They are a species of grouse, twice as large as the ruffled variety, almost pure white, and a native of the higher latitudes. Saturday evening about dusk a flock came down by our camp, and I missed an easy shot at one trying to take his head off. The whole flock lit on the snow a couple of hundred yards away, and we all tried our skill on them with our only weapon, a Winchester rifle, but with no other result than to frighten them away. Sunday morning I was up early and busily chopping kindling wood when there came trotting over the snow drift toward me what at first seemed a huge collie dog, but which I was soon satisfied was a wolf. He was a great gray fellow, twice as large as a Newfoundland dog, long and lank. As he came up within about fifty feet he grinned savagely, showing his long white teeth. I called to the boys, who were still in bed, to hand out the rifle quick. As they came crouching up the wolf ran off about eighty yards and turned, when I fired quickly at his shoulder, feeling perfectly certain that his skin was ours. But the ball must have struck too far back, for he doubled up and started with his tail between his legs on the keen jump down the snow drift. There were no more cartridges in the rifle so I could not shoot again. We expected at every jump to see him roll over, but he went down the drift at an angle of forty degrees, leaving a crimson trail as he ran. Over the rocks and across the valley he went at full speed till we lost sight of him a mile away.

After a late breakfast we started out for a ramble, each in a different direction, I passing down a valley to the northward. Those mountain valleys, how delightful in the quiet morning, warm in the sunshine, sheltered from the wind, the pure, light air crisp and exhilarating; rills of cool water everywhere, fresh from melting snows; green pastures of softest spring grasses; crystal lakelets born of a snow drift; and through the meadows and along the rills, even against the snow, singly and in banks, the most lovely flowers, scores of varieties and hundreds of shades, buttercups and soft white cowslips, astors like our marguerites, but with pink and lavender petals, red daisies and yellow daisies, violets and lilies, and multitudes of those beautiful flowers found only among high mountains! After going the length of this valley I crossed a low divide to the east and there found a glacier, the source of the Carbon River. It was my first experience with one and I advanced with extreme caution. These glaciers present an odd appearance, much resembling a dried worm with its skin all cracked open, only on a somewhat larger scale. This one is about a mile wide and fifteen long. Unlike water one of these ice rivers cannot widen out after being confined by rocky sides, but maintains nearly the same form throughout. Striking it below a narrow gorge, I had to climb up a hundred feet to reach the surface. The lower end, reaching far below the snow line, was almost entirely covered with rocks and sand from the continued slides and avalanches it had encountered along its course. The upper surface of a glacier is full of crevasses, its profile being much like a saw. Where the top surface is convex these cracks are more open, but where it is concave they are closed. I first tried a convex surface and found it practically impassable, the ice ridges being sharp and the chasms very deep; but going up further there was a concave surface, where there was not much difficulty in crossing by jumping some crevasses and going around others. Crossing here and going up the little mountain opposite, I had a view of the eastern slope of Rainier, and could see what appeared to be a possible way of ascent. Then recrossing the glacier by quite an easy path I returned to camp. The surveyor was already there.

Coming home over a high ridge he saw an immense bear down five
hundred feet in a valley, and as he had the rifle with him he concluded
to give bruin a shot. He started down, but after descending about half
way came to the conclusion that the bear ought not to be so rudely disturbed, and struck out for camp. We never could determine whether
the fact that it was Sunday, the depth of the valley, or the size of the
bear, was the most instrumental in bringing him to this conclusion.
The lawyer came in about two hours later, as we were at supper. He
looked pale and tired, and I never before saw a man so glad to see
friends again after so brief an absence. He shook hands all around, said
the camp seemed so home like, and smiled all over. We finally got it out
of him that he had been on the glacier near its head, where it lay in a
valley, with icy sides. He found it pretty hard going down, but coming
up he had a terrible time. He fell into a crevasse and had to climb up
two hundred feet through a hole in the ice, where hanging masses kept
falling, threatening to immolate him, and he did not expect to get out
alive.

Monday we started to change our camp around to the northeast side
of the mountain, across the Carbon glacier, so as to ascend from the
east. We were crossing over the snow fields on the base of the mountain
when, coming around some rocks with patches of young grass, we surprised a large mountain goat feeding. I had the gun and had been
watching a pair of ptarmigan ahead, and did not see him till he went
galloping across in front of us. I had always longed for hunter's laurels,
mostly in vain, and a goat was just what I had been hoping for. My
nerves were all on end in an instant, and my heart in a flutter. I was
trying to get a good aim; how the gun shook! could I shoot with the
pack pulling my shoulders back? would I lose him as I had the wolf?
there he goes behind a rock, but out he comes again going more slowly;
crack goes the gun, and he changes his course but does not increase his
speed; crack again, and he comes toward us to the edge of a precipice.
He is a perfectly dead shot now, and I shoot for his heart. Then his
head goes down and he struggles on the snow, and we all three are running toward him; but as soon as he is off his feet he begins sliding, and
before we can reach him over he goes. It is only a very steep snow slide,
and we are after him full tilt; and there he lies at the bottom, not
bruised a particle, but with bullets in his shoulder, neck and heart. We
judged that he weighed considerably over three hundred pounds. His
body and neck were very thick, legs short, and head almost as long as
that of a horse, so that he had a very awkward lumbering gait. If

chamois shooting is much like goat hunting, it seems to me that cow shooting in a big pasture might be as difficult, and the romance of the brave chamois hunter suffers severely. We took off the skin and short little horns of our goat, as it was impossible to carry him along. The rings on his horns showed him to be of a venerable age, in fact a patriarch. He was what is vulgarly called a "billy," of a very pronounced order, the kind Virgil speaks of in the "Eclogues." Both of these facts appeared very plainly when we tried to eat him; for though we took his tenderest porterhouse steaks, and tried them boiled, fried and roasted, and all three together, still the billy taste and the seventeen-year toughness were there. But his skin is a beauty, pure white, with long soft hair.

After our little affair with the goat we skirted along the base of the mountain, down across the Carbon glacier, then up again through flowery fields and scrubby fir on to a spur of Rainier, where the last wood could be found. Here again we pitched our tent, gathered a bed of boughs, spread our blankets and made our last camp, as only three days' provisions remained. Our camp was very near the edge of the glacier, and that night, as soon as the sun went down, the ice began to freeze and crack, big pieces continually falling down. Sometimes a mass of the hard, overhanging snow would break off from the brow of the mountain and crash down upon the glacier, sending up clouds of snow dust like smoke. Several times during the night we were awakened by great masses of falling ice, thundering and shaking the ground like discharges of artillery.

The next morning, as the early light was changing the pink of the overhanging mountain into dazzling white, we started up again. We followed the rocky spur on the northeast corner of the mountain for about two miles, ascending about three thousand feet, the Carbon River glacier lying below us on our right, and the double White River glacier to the left. Soon the rocky path ended in a perpendicular wall, and we were obliged to turn toward the east on to the White River glacier. Unfortunately we had climbed the rocks too far, and it was necessary either to go a mile back, or to reach the glacier by a natural bridge of ice several hundred yards long and inclined about fifty degrees. Here a little incident occurred, not very pleasant at the time, but which has been a great source of pleasure since, as with variations it has been made the base of a most thrilling tale to nervous lady acquaintances. We were crossing along this inclined plane, cutting steps with the axe, about one hundred feet above a very wide and deep crevasse, into which a misstep might plunge us at any instant. We were proceeding finely and were more than half way across when it seemed to one of the party that we were going needlessly slow, so he started ahead of the cut steps. It went all right for a few feet, then he slipped a little, and then began sliding toward the big crevasse at a fearful rate of speed. The only hope of safety was in his alpine-stock. Grasping this close to its sharp point, and turning over upon his face, he stuck it into the ice with all the force he could command and clung to it for dear life. It had the desired effect. The point cut a deep ridge in the ice, making the frosty chips fly into the air, and taking a liberal quantity of skin from off his hand, but it checked the speed, and brought him to a halt just above the crevasse. It was the most exciting three seconds of his life.

On the glacier we found the traveling comparatively easy, for the head of a glacier is really the long snow slope of the mountain, with but few crevasses in the higher altitudes. We encountered two places where the ascent was extremely difficult, points where a great thickness of snow had cracked and the lower part slipped down, leaving a wall twenty-five feet high. After climbing these by aid of the axe, plodding steadily up the steep incline of the main cone, on the north side of the eastern spur, we found that we had reached a point quite above the landmarks of our former attempt. The barometer indicated an altitude of eleven thousand five hundred, then twelve thousand feet, and at five hundred more it stopped altogether, although it was graduated to sixteen thousand feet. At one o'clock we rested behind a little shelter to eat our cold lunch, moistening our lips with pieces of ice; but the wind was too raw and cold to permit us to sit still long with comfort. We plodded away again, sometimes going directly up for a quarter of a mile on a smooth incline of about forty-five degrees, then turning to one side to escape a crevasse. But our continued exertions and the rarity of the atmosphere at that high altitude told upon us severely. Fifteen, then ten, minute rests were necessary. Still we were making excellent progress. When a point which, from below, had seemed one of the peaks of the mountain was about on a level with us, the altitude began to affect the surveyor seriously. We were compelled to chafe his feet to keep them from freezing, and with open mouth he could not inhale enough air to fill his lungs. He became pale and faint, and finally said he would have to give it up, but urged us to go on. I was very tired also, and as it was after two o'clock was not very anxious to proceed. However, the lawyer pushed on and I followed. Going up a hundred yards and looking back we saw our companion staggering as if he could hardly stand. That decided us, and we turned back. After descending a thousand feet he recovered considerably, and we made good progress, finding a better path to camp than the one by which we had come.

We felt rather depressed that evening. There was only enough flour and bacon remaining to last two days. I was mixing slapjacks by the brook when the lawyer came down to me and said that he had made up his mind to go up the mountain next day, and if I would not accompany him he would go alone. We knew the route better, and it would be easier than the day before. I agreed to go with him. The next morning the surveyor announced that he would also make the attempt, and if the faintness came on he would return alone. With that understanding we started about seven o'clock, following our last evening's trail. By noon we reached our lunching place of the previous day, and were thus nearly an hour in advance. We soon passed our highest mark of the day before, and going around a point of snow discovered that the summit lay only a short distance beyond. The inspiration of success was upon us and overcame our fatigue, though we had to stop every five minutes to catch a full breath. We found that what appears to be the summit from the north and from Tacoma is not in reality the highest point, but only a northern ridge. We passed up the valley connecting this ridge, then ascended the little round snow-covered dome which forms the real summit, and, arm in arm, so that we might all be first, marched to the topmost point. We had just given three wild Western cheers to express our exultation at being, as we supposed, the first human beings to stand upon the white summit of Mount Rainier, when our eyes fell upon a walking stick protruding from the snow. It was a most common, scrubby looking affair, but was sufficient evidence of the previous presence of some human being who had planted it there as a warning to all who came after him not to claim too much for themselves, and our ardor was considerably dampened.

It was now half-past two, and we had but a brief time to make observations. The summit consists of two basin-shaped craters, side by side, each a quarter of a mile in diameter, the ridge between them being the highest point. These were full of snow, but their rocky rims were bare. We observed several holes in the snow by the edges, where the strong odor of sulphur indicated that heat had been given out not many months before. On the western edge there is a large chamber in the snow, and from a hole six or eight inches in diameter a continuous column of steam and sulphurous smoke arises, showing that the internal fires of Mount Rainier are not yet extinguished. We stood about it to warm ourselves, and endeavored to peer into the hole, with no other result than receiving a burnt hand and inhaling a disagreeable quantity of sulphur and brimstone fumes. Near this chimney hole we found a piece of lead with four names inscribed upon it. We examined the summit carefully, though we did not visit the western peak, which is about four hundred feet lower. The rocks are all volcanic, with considerable of scoria. Curiously enough we found a butterfly fluttering over the snow. We had observed numerous others in going up. The day was bright and clear, with no clouds and but little fog or smoke hanging over the low places, offering a splendid view of the surrounding country. It is a common but erroneous idea that the view from the top of our great mountains is grander than that afforded by lower altitudes. We found that the view does not increase in grandeur with the altitude. In this respect a high mountain is somewhat disappointing; the sight is much less impressive than one naturally expects, the one redeeming feature being the knowledge of the fact that the eye ranges over a vast extent of territory. It is too much like a bird's-eye map, like the prospect from a balloon; the range of vision is too comprehensive and the eye cannot take it all in. The view through gaps in lower mountains is far more impressive.

We spent much time in studying the details of the great panorama spread out before us, which, as a whole, was so confusing in its vastness. To the north Mount Baker, one hundred and fifty miles distant, seemed near at hand, and we could plainly see the mountains of British Columbia, more than twice the distance. We traced the shores of the Straits past Victoria far up the side of Vancouver Island. Below us the Cascade Range, with its peaks six and eight thousand feet high, seemed scarcely more than a potato patch. Westward, over the tops of the Olympic Mountains, the Pacific Ocean formed a level horizon, and nearer, through a semi-transparent sea of haze, were seen the tortuous outlines of Puget Sound. The cities were marked by their smoke, and even the steamboats announced their position in the same manner. The grain fields and prairies seemed like little islands in the vast blue sea of forest. To the south the sharp peaks of Adams and St. Helens loomed up grandly, with their long snow-covered sides. Oregon was shrouded in smoke, Mount Hood and a few other points alone lifting themselves above the gloom. On the east the spurs of the Rocky Mountains closed our horizon, though because of the smoky haze they were but dimly seen. We could count seven distinct glaciers running down from the mountains, the heads of six rivers. We experienced no peculiar physical effects from the high altitude. It was not extremely cold, thawing a little in the sun and freezing in the shade; but a sharp, cold wind chilled us very quickly whenever we ceased exercising, and we were glad enough to start down again after spending an hour on the summit. The only actual fun of such a journey is in the descent. It took us eight hours to ascend and only two to return. Squatting on our feet, and using our alpine-stocks as a kind of third leg and break, we would sometimes slide down a half mile of smooth slope in about two minutes. We reached camp at six—satisfied, jolly and hungry.

New trials were in store for us. For three days we had been among the whitest snows, with the August sun shining. We had two pairs of goggles, but did not use them, because we could not see so well with them, and sometimes a misstep of an inch would have thrown us down a crevasse. However, we kept our faces in the vicinity of the eyes well blackened with charcoal. My two companions had been troubled more or less before, but that night their eyes became very much inflamed and pained them so that they could not sleep. The next morning they could scarcely see. We had only one day's rations, and there was the Carbon glacier to cross, which required the most careful watchfulness, and a mile of hard climbing, besides three of rough traveling to reach the trail. But it was a case of necessity, and we started, progressing slowly and painfully the first day, but more easily the second, as the sore eyes became better in the shade of the woods. We reached Tacoma thirteen days from our start, with hands and faces so burned that the skin was peeling off, but with added health of body and that satisfied condition of mind which comes only from success.

Warner Fobes

# 9

# Allison Brown[*]
# 1886

Allison Brown's brief tale is almost as lighthearted as J. Warner Fobes's, lacking only a complete ascent to make it the second neophyte victory over the mountain. Brown's account is also interesting because it shows how familiar the Yakima Indians were with the eastern side of the mountain and its nearby foothills, where they hunted and gathered. The Yakima lived east and south of the mountain.

Brown and the Indians approached from the Ohanapecosh River valley, eventually making their final ascent on the glacier that was later named Ingraham. It is not known how high they climbed, but it is clear that they did not reach the summit. It was, as Brown said, just a "lark," but it is the first known attempt made on the peak from the east, and it showed the promise of that route.

In his excellent book *The Challenge of Rainier*, Dee Molenaar pointed out that the following account is an unusually early mention of Indians climbing high on the slopes of the mountain. Limited archeological evidence suggests that Indians did visit the mountain often, especially the lower meadows, but we have no way of knowing how many may have tried for—or reached—the summit before whites were around to chronicle such adventures. Remember that Sluiskin, in Hazard Stevens's account in Chapter 6, said that his grandfather had once climbed high on the mountain but had turned back short of the summit because of the dangers. It is unclear if Sluiskin was referring to physical or supernatural dangers, but it is plain that some tribes believed the mountain's summit had spiritual powers that should not be disturbed. As Brown points out in this chapter, the Yakimas accompanying him were reservation educated and had no such fears.

*Reprinted from Allison Brown, "Ascent of Mount Rainier by the Ingraham Glacier," The Mountaineer 13(1920): 49–50.

In 1885 and 1886 I spent the summers in Eastern Washington, making my headquarters on the Yakima Indian Reservation. I became very chummy with the Indians, and in the fall of the latter year when they organized their annual hunting trip, I was invited to go with them. Being a boy, I readily accepted. I was the only white person in the party of some thirty odd people.

As near as I can remember, we crossed the Cascades through what was then known as Packwood Pass, going north up the Ohanapecosh Valley to the Cowlitz Divide country, a region which the Indians considered one of their best hunting grounds. Finding no game here, we were forced to hunt near the snow-line.

As the Indians were not killing the quantity of game they expected to, and for a little diversion from hunting, several of the more adventurous ones suggested that we get up a crowd and climb to the top of the Mountain. My recollection is that seven or eight made the climb, and I, being in for anything, went along.

From the contour maps I have seen since, my impression is that we continued to the end of the Indian Trail on the Cowlitz Divide, and from there made for the lower end of Whitman Crest, skirting the end of the Ohanapecosh Glacier and from there to the ice field now called Whitman Glacier, crossing it and the ridge between the Whitman and Ingraham, and dropping down upon the Ingraham Glacier. At about 8500 feet we crossed to the south side. We had used our horses as far as the near side of the Ingraham—much farther, probably, than would be considered possible by a white man, and from this point we sent them back to our camp at timber-line.

Continuing on foot, we followed up the west slope of what is now known as Cathedral Rocks on the Ingraham Glacier, making use of the well defined goat trails. As I remember, there was a short distance of 40 to 60 feet where we were compelled to work ourselves along a ledge by gripping the side wall with our fingers, the ledge being very narrow, apparently just wide enough for the wild goat to travel over. After crossing this small strip, we found ourselves again on the glacier snow, and from there had an unobstructed, though rather steep climb over the snow to the top. We did not try to reach the highest pinnacle. The snow, as I remember, at that time was rough and granular, and the walking was comparatively easy. Most of the party wore the usual Indian moccasins and some of us had alpenstocks which we cut from the mountain ash and other shrubbery along the wooded spots. We took rations and axes, and carried one or two lariats to use in case of emergency, but never found it necessary to use them.

In descending we tried to retrace as near as possible our own footsteps. Late in the afternoon we put up for the night at the base of the rock I have always believed to be Gibraltar. We found a rather sheltered place, and the following morning descended to join the rest of our party and continue the hunting expedition. We were in the mountains approximately six weeks in all.

You will note from the foregoing that as far as I was concerned this mountain climb was just a lark with me. I was out with a crowd simply to be doing something. It has never occurred to me as being of any historical value, and it is reasonably certain that the Indians never gave it a thought.

In view of Sluiskin's warning given to Hazard Stevens and P. B. Van Trump, it is interesting to know that the Indians who composed this party were all educated at the Yakima Reservation and therefore had no superstitions with regard to the spirit of the mountain.

*Woman climber enjoying view of Cowlitz Glacier from Cowlitz Rocks. A Curtis & Miller photograph from the Washington State Historical Society. (Courtesy Aubrey Haines)*

## ～ 10 ～

# John Muir[*]
# 1888

John Muir's ascent of Mount Rainier came about because he was editing a book about the West Coast. Historians and biographers have suggested that the climb of Mount Rainier brought him out of a dry period in his writing and set him off on new literary and wilderness adventures. Through George Bayley he met Philemon Van Trump and invited him along for what would be Van Trump's third ascent.

Two other members of this party deserve special mention. Edward Sturgis Ingraham, a teacher from Seattle, had made his first attempt on the peak in 1886, displaying a knack for naming prominent geological features. On this second climb he renamed the "high camp" in honor of the trip's most famous guest; thus "Cloud Camp" became "Camp Muir." (Eventually a glacier on the east side of the mountain was named for Ingraham.) More important in some ways was a young Massachusetts-born photographer named Arthur Warner. Warner carried his huge camera and related equipment (more than fifty pounds of gear) all the way from Seattle to the top of the peak, getting the first and still some of the most famous photographs of the top of the mountain. This is surely one of the most singular personal achievements of the early days of climbing on Mount Rainier.

Once again Van Trump was frustrated in his goal of reaching the North Peak. The party stayed only two hours on the summit, leaving in anticipation of a storm. But Van Trump would be back, and more than once.

Ambitious climbers, seeking adventures and opportunities to test their strength and skill, occasionally attempt to penetrate the wilderness on the side of the Sound, and push on to the summit of Mt. Olympus. But

*Reprinted from John Muir, "The Ascent of Mount Rainier," The Pacific Monthly 8(1902): 197–204.

the grandest excursion of all to be made hereabouts is to Mt. Rainier: to climb to the top of its icy crown. The mountain is very high, 14,400 feet, and laden with glaciers that are terribly roughened and interrupted by crevasses and ice-cliffs. Only good climbers should attempt to gain the summit, led by a guide of proved nerve and endurance. A good trail has been cut through the woods to the base of the mountain on the north; but the summit of the mountain never has been reached from this side, though many attempts have been made upon it.

I gained the summit, from the south side, in a day and a half from the timber line, without encountering any desperate obstacles that could not in some way be passed in good weather. I was accompanied by Keith, the artist, Prof. Ingraham, and five ambitious young climbers from Seattle. We were lead by the veteran mountaineer and guide, Van Trump, of Yelm, who, many years ago, guided General Stevens in his memorable ascent, and later Mr. Bayley of Oakland. With a cumbersome abundance of campstools and blankets, we set out from Seattle, traveling by rail as far as Yelm prairie, on the Tacoma and Oregon road. Here we made our first camp, and arranged with Mr. Longmire, a farmer in the neighborhood, for pack and saddle animals. The noble King mountain was in full view from here, glorifying the bright, sunny day with his presence, rising in god-like majesty over the road, with the magnificent prairie as a foreground. The distance to the mountain from Yelm in a straight line is perhaps fifty miles; but by the mule and yellow-jacket trail we had to follow it is a hundred miles. For, notwithstanding a portion of this trail runs in the air where the wasps work hardest, it is far from being an air-line, as commonly understood.

By night of the third day we reached the Soda Springs on the right bank of the Nisqually, which goes roaring by, gray with mud, gravel and boulders from the caves of the glaciers of Rainier, now close to hand. The distance from the Soda Springs to the Camp of the Clouds is about ten miles. The first part of the way lies up the Nisqually canon, the bottom of which is flat in some places and the walls very high and precipitous, like those of the Yosemite Valley. The upper part of the canon is still occupied by one of the Nisqually glaciers, from which this branch of the river draws its source, issuing from a cave in the gray, rock-strewn snout. About a mile below the glacier we had to ford the river, which caused some anxiety, for the current is very rapid and carried forward large boulders, as well as lighter material, while its savage roar is bewildering.

At this point we left the canon, climbing out of it by a steep zigzag up the old left lateral moraine of the glacier, which was deposited when the present glacier flowed past at this height, and is about eight hundred feet high. It is now covered with a superb growth of *Picea amabilis;* so, also, is the corresponding portion of the right lateral. From the top of the moraine, still ascending, we passed for a mile or two through a forest of mixed growth, mainly silver fir, Paton spruce and mountain pine, and then came to the charming park region, at an elevation of about five thousand feet above sea-level. Here the vast continuous woods at length begin to give way under the dominion of climate, though still at this height retaining their beauty and giving no sign of stress of storm, sweeping upward in belts of varying width, composed mainly of one species of fir, sharp and spiny in form, leaving smooth, spacious parks, with here and there separate groups of trees standing out in the midst of the openings like islands in a lake. Every one of these parks, great and small, is a garden filled knee-deep with fresh, lovely flowers of every hue, the most luxuriant and the most extravagantly beautiful of all the Alpine gardens I ever beheld in all my mountain-top wanderings.

We arrived at the Cloud Camp at noon, but no clouds were in sight, save a few gauzy, ornamental wreaths adrift in the sunshine. Out of the forest at last there stood the mountain, wholly unveiled, awful in bulk and majesty, filling all the view like a separate, new-born world, yet withal so fine and so beautiful it might well fire the dullest observer to desperate enthusiasm. Long we gazed in silent admiration, buried in tall daisies and anemones by the side of a snow-bank. Higher we could not go with the animals and find food for them and wood for our own camp-fires, for just beyond this lies the region of ice, with only here and there an open spot on the ridges in the midst of the ice, with dwarf Alpine plants, such as saxifrages and iribas, which reach far up between the glaciers with low mats of the beautiful bryanthus, while back of us were the gardens and abundance of everything that heart could wish. Here we lay all the afternoon considering the lilies and the lines of the mountains with reference to a way to the summit.

At noon next day we left camp and began our long climb. We were in light marching order, save one, who pluckily determined to carry his camera to the summit. At night, after a long, easy climb over wide and smooth fields of ice, we reached a narrow ridge, at an elevation of about ten thousand feet above the sea, on the divide between the glacier of the Nisqually and Cowlitz. Here we lay, as best we could, waiting another day, without fire of course, as we were now many miles beyond the

*Arthur C. Warner in a self-portrait taken during 1888 ascent by the Muir party. Note line leading from his hand—he is holding the bulb shutter release for camera. (Courtesy Aubrey Haines)*

timber line, and without much to cover us. After eating a little hard tack each of us leveled a spot to lie on among lava-blocks and cinders. The night was cold, and the wind, coming down upon us in stormy surges, drove gritty ashes and fragments of pumice about our ears, while chilling to the bone. Very short and shallow was our sleep that night; but day dawned at last, early rising was easy, and there was nothing about breakfast to cause any delay. About 4 o'clock we were off, and climbing began in earnest. We followed up the ridge on which we had spent the night, now along its crest, now on either side, or on the ice leaning against it, until we came to where it becomes massive and precipitous. Then we were compelled to crawl along the seam or narrow shelf, on its face, which we traced to its termination in the base of the great ice-cap. From this point all the climbing was over ice, which was here desperately steep, but, fortunately, was at the same time carved into innumerable spikes and pillars which afforded good footholds, and we crawled cautiously on, warm with ambition and exercise.

At length, after gaining the upper extreme of our guiding ridge, we found a good place to rest and prepare ourselves to scale the dangerous upper curves of the dome. The surface everywhere was bare, hard, snowless ice, extremely slippery, and, though smooth in general, it was interrupted by a network of yawning crevasses, outspread like lions of defence against any attempt to win the summit. Here every one of the party took off his shoes and drove steel caulks about half an inch long into them, having brought tools along for the purpose, and not having made use of them until now, so that the points might not get dulled on the rocks ere the smooth, dangerous ice was reached. Besides being well shod, each carried an alpenstock, and for special difficulties we had a hundred feet of rope and an axe.

Thus prepared, we stepped forth afresh, slowly groping our way through tangled lines of crevasses, crossing on snow bridges here and there, after cautiously testing them, jumping at narrow places, or crawling around the ends of the largest, bracing well at every point with our alpenstocks and setting our spiked shoes squarely down on the dangerous slopes. It was nerve-trying work, most of it, but we made good speed nevertheless, and by noon all stood together on the utmost summit, save one, who, his strength failing for a time, came up later.

We remained on the summit nearly two hours, looking about us at the vast map-like views, comprehending hundreds of miles of the Cascade Range, with their black, interminable forests and white volcanic cones in glorious array reaching far into Oregon; the Sound region, also, and the great plains of Eastern Washington, hazy and vague in the distance. Of all the land only the snowy summits of the great volcanic mountains, such as St. Helens, Adams and Hood, were left in sight, forming islands in the sky. We found two well-formed and well-preserved craters on the summit, lying close together like two plates on a table with their rims touching. The highest point of the mountain is located between the craters, where their edges come in contact. Sulphurous fumes and steam issue from several rents, giving out a sickening smell that can be detected at a considerable distance. The unwasted condition of these craters, and indeed to a great extent, of the entire mountain, would tend to show that Rainier is still a comparatively young mountain. With the exception of the projecting lips of the craters and the top of a subordinate summit a short distance to the northward, the mountain is solidly capped with ice all around; and it is this ice-cap which forms the grand central fountain whence all the twenty glaciers of Rainier flow, radiating in every direction.

The descent was accomplished without disaster, though several of the party had narrow escapes. One slipped and fell, and as he shot past me seemed to be going to certain death. So steep was the ice slope no one could move to help him, but fortunately, keeping his presence of mind, he threw himself upon his face and, digging his alpenstock into the ice, gradually retarded his motion until he came to rest. Another broke through a slim bridge over a crevasse, but his momentum at the time carried him against the lower edge, and only his alpenstock was lost in the abyss. Thus crippled by the loss of his staff, we had to lower him the rest of the way down the dome by means of the rope we carried. Falling rocks from the upper precipitous part of the ridge were also a source of danger, as they came whizzing past in successive

*Poor quality but unique historical photo: the Muir party on the summit, photographed by A. C. Warner with the first camera ever carried to the top. (Courtesy Aubrey Haines)*

volleys; but none told on us, and when at length we gained the gentle slopes of the lower ice-fields we ran and slid at our ease, making fast, glad time, all care and danger past, and arrived at our beloved Cloud Camp before sundown. We were rather weak from want of nourishment, and some suffered from sunburn, notwithstanding the partial protection of glasses and veils; otherwise all were unscathed and well. The view we enjoyed from the summit could hardly be surpassed in sublimity and grandeur; but one feels far from home so high in the sky, so much so that one is inclined to guess that, apart from the acquisition of knowledge and the exhiliration of climbing, more pleasure is to be found at the foot of the mountains than on their frozen tops. Doubly happy, however, is the man to whom lofty mountain tops are within reach, for the lights that shine there illumine all that lies below.

*An older A. C. Warner with the camera he carried to the summit as a young man. (Courtesy Aubrey Haines)*

The weather continued fine and we lingered in these lower gardens of Eden day after day, making short excursions of a dozen miles or so to lakes and waterfalls and glaciers, resting, sketching, botanizing, watching the changing lights and clouds on the glorious mountain until, all too soon, our Rainier time was done and we were compelled to pack our spoils and take the wasp-trail to civilization and Yelm.

# 11

# Fay Fuller[*]
# 1890

We now pass a few climbs, including an 1890 ascent by Ingraham, and come to a notable milestone in the mountain's history, the first time it was climbed by a woman.

Fay Fuller taught school in Yelm, a small town southeast of Olympia, where her father owned the local newspaper. She was about twenty in 1890, and was already social editor of her father's paper. She had met Philemon Van Trump a few years earlier and was filled with admiration for his exploits on the mountain. (It is from these early climbing accounts that we comprehend the full magnitude of Van Trump's influence on the mountain's growing fame.) Fuller first visited the mountain in 1887, climbing some distance above Paradise Park, though she obviously wanted to go higher. She got her chance in 1890, as she explains in the following account.

It appears that when she set out from Yelm it was by no means clear that she would be allowed to attempt the full climb, but her determination was no doubt apparent to the group as the ascent was organized and headed up.

Historians give Fuller considerable credit for exciting interest in the mountain and the climb. She wrote frequently of the mountain, doing much to popularize the sport of climbing.

A second important element of the trip was photographic. Though his lens was broken, W. O. Amsden was able to make a few photographic views of the mountain; his pictures were eventually used to promote the movement to create Mount Rainier National Park.

Twenty-five miles from Tacoma, on the railroad to Portland, the little town of Yelm, named after an old Indian chief, is situated on the broad prairies, from which point may be obtained one of the best views of

*Reprinted from Fay Fuller, "A Trip to the Summit," Every Sunday, August 23, 1890.

Mount Tahoma to be anywhere seen. The three peaks are very distinct
and the apparent absence of foothills seems to make the grand old
mountain appear much higher than elsewhere. Here lives Mr. P. B.
Van Trump, of mountain fame, the man who on first seeing the grand
peak, resolved to reach its summit, and who has three times looked at
the world from an elevation of 14,444 feet. I had readily accepted the
invitation from Mr. and Mrs. Van Trump to accompany them on their
summer outing, and having climbed the mountain in 1887 to an altitude
of 8500 feet, knew the pleasure in store. That year I was very anxious
to reach the summit but was allowed to go only a certain distance and
then expected to return to camp. It was a great dissapointment, [*sic*] and
one that made me resolve that some time I would go as high as possible,
but hardly daring to hope

## WHAT THAT MIGHT MEAN.

In starting this trip, therefore, although knowing of no party that
would attempt the full ascent, not supposing Mr. Van Trump would
care to undertake the trip again, I prepared for it, hoping some opportunity would present itself. Dressed in a thick, blue flannel bloomer
suit, heavy calfskin boys' shoes, loose blouse waist with innumerable
pockets in the lining, small straw hat in order to get the benefit of the
sun, and astride my horse I left Yelm Monday, August 4, at 10 a.m.,
with Mr. and Mrs. Van Trump and their ten year old daughter, Chris-
tine. We had a pack horse for carrying provisions and tent and our extra
clothing was carried in saddle bags. Soon after leaving Yelm, we
crossed the Nisqually river bridge, arriving in Pierce county, through
which the route is made all the way to the Nisqually glacier. The prairies were soon of the past, and we travelled slowly through the timber
land during the rest of the day. A good wagon road has been made over
the first twenty miles, which greatly eases the trip. We lunched on the
way beside a clear cool well, and refreshed again, mounted the horses
for the rest of the day's journey. Houses are passed every few miles,
showing a wonderful growth of the country in the last three years. In
the afternoon we came to the steep Owhop hill, where we dismounted
and drove the horses down, crossed the river of the same name, and
then climbed a long sloping hill beyond. About 5:30 p.m. we reached
the Mishell prairie,

*Fay Fuller, first woman to climb Mount Rainier. (Courtesy Aubrey Haines)*

## THE ABODE OF INDIAN HENRY,

a smart old Klickitat who has lived there for sixteen years and owns a very valuable farm. Unsaddling and unpacking took only a few minutes and soon the fire burned brightly and the camp kettle was thinking about boiling. After supper was cooked and enjoyed, the beds were made on the new hay in the barn and we were ready for the night. As darkness came on we heard familiar sounds and soon recognized a party of mountaineers who had left Yelm a few hours after us.

## THE PARTY FROM SEATTLE

was composed of Rev. E. C. Smith, pastor of Unitarian church of that city, Miss Katie Smith, Miss Tillie J. Piper, Mr. W. O. Amsden, of the Seattle Photo firm, Dr. J. J. Sturgus and Mr. R. R. Parrish. The Yelm people were Miss Maud Longmire, Mr. Leonard Longmire, Washington Longmire and Miss Edith Corbett, of Des Moines. Elcaine Longmire was the guide and packer for both parties. One tent was pitched but all our party left the prairie, the others not being ready, and we did not meet again until upon the mountain and in camp a day. The second day's travel is long, being

## IN OUR SADDLES FOURTEEN HOURS

before we reached the Succotash valley, and Mr. J. B. Kernahan's home. The trail winds through dense forests of grand old cedars and firs, gardens of beautiful ferns over the Mishell mountains and across chattering brooks, where the tin cups strapped to our backs came in use. It is a beautiful ride through the wilderness, alone with nature and her wonders, with scarcely a sound to break the silence. Great tall trees line the winding trail, so tall you can not look up to the tops, so straight they seem like pillars of an ancient building, and this trail the aisle through which one passes to admire. It is then one can realize the resources of this state and dream of its future preeminence. But soon a dream of any kind is broken and the clanging of tin pans and kicking of hoofs ahead remind one that the train has struck the famous yellow-jacket nests and that the pack horse is having his share of the fun. It is a lively break of the monotonous gait which we were obliged to follow and the Indian cry of

## "HYACK-SOJERS"

Rings out warningly on the air. The horses feel the whip and a furious rush is made over the swarming insects whose domestic feelings have been somewhat aroused. Riding in the rear, one not only gets considerable benefit of the enraged hornet's stings but also the pleasure of watching the procession ahead, and it is amusing to note how alike in disposition are horses to human beings, shown by the different ways they take their troubles. The yellow-jackets are not to blame; their homes are molested and they wound their enemies in self-defense, rarely stinging persons. The Succotash valley, as it is now called and spelled, derived its name from the Indian word, Suh-ho-tas, which means the black raspberry, this fruit being plentiful throughout the valley. It is a fertile tract of land and well settled. Mr. Kernahan, a former Tacoma resident, moved there about five years ago and has now an excellent farm, with about forty acres of cleared land, a comfortable house, a young orchard and a well cultivated garden. Considering that everything has to be carried there about forty miles on pack horses their comforts are luxuries. It is a delightful place to visit and the night spent

*Virinda Longmire at the Longmire Hotel and springs she and her husband, James, operated about the time of Fay Fuller's climb. (Courtesy Aubrey Haines)*

there was greatly enjoyed. The next morning riding begins again and for eleven miles the trail is followed until the

## LONGMIRE SODA SPRINGS

are reached. One dangerous river, the Rainier Forks, has to be forded, and a relief is felt when the rapid rolling stream is left behind. For several miles the route is over rocky river beds, crossing small tributaries again and again, and then the Longmire springs come into view beneath the lofty mountain. It was in 1883 when James Longmire, George B. Bayley and P. B. Van Trump were returning from the mountain that these mineral springs were discovered and explored. Soda, magnesium and iron are the principal elements of the water. Mr. Longmire afterward discovered mineral paint on the land and took it up as a mineral claim, cleared the swampy ground, built dwellings and bath houses and established a summer resort there. Many invalids have been benefited by the waters and baths and the clear air, and Mr. and Mrs. Longmire make it a very attractive place for a summer outing.

About four miles ride through woods and over river beds take you to the murky, glacial Nisqually river, near the foot of the Nisqually glacier, where the river finds its source. Formerly it was necessary to ford this stream near the glacier, a hazardous task for both horse and rider, the swift water bringing down huge boulders, continually roaring and rolling from the glacier. About two years ago Mr. Longmire built a log bridge over the river, which is now crossed without difficulty. After crossing, the saddles and pack are carefully adjusted before the steep ascent begins. This eminence is called the switchback, from the way the trail has been recently improved, and is almost perpendicular and is estimated to be

BETWEEN 1000 AND 1200 FEET HIGH.

It is no easy work to reach the top, for people rarely ride up this hill, and you can climb up and up without seeing daylight above. Anxious to get to the top before the horses, three of us made this ascent in twenty-five minutes, and were weary when we mounted again. Then for about an hour we traveled higher and higher through timber land till, at an elevation of about 4000 feet, we entered the most beautiful parks that could be created. A tiny patch of snow covered part of one of these rolling praries [sic], which are composed of the greenest grass, prairie firs and myriads of flowers. Occasionally a little lake surrounded by beds of asters comes into view and the purple Scotch heather brightly colors the scene. These green slopes continue for 2000 feet or more and are seen on all sides of the mountain. They are what Mr. Muir so prettily called "The Lower Gardens of Eden," and he thus expressed his appreciation.

Still farther back rise the Cascades, and by climbing a few feet higher than Camp of the Clouds, St. Helens, Adams, Hood and Jefferson appear in the scene, the first two looking nearly as large as Mount

Tahoma does from our homes. One more glance gives you a view of the winding Nisqually, rushing in and out the forest, down towards its mouth. Hills rise and fall in all directions, and as you look in astonishment on the Great Artist's picture your eye slowly wanders back till you gaze on the grandest work of all. The next day, Thursday, was spent in gathering and pressing wild flowers, arranging camp comforts, and exploring the near beauties. Towards evening the Seattle and Yelm parties arrived and passed on across the valley, pitching tents at Paradise and Yelm camps, about 500 feet higher than ours. Visiting and talking with these parties the next day, I found several anticipated trying the ascent, and they made me happy when they kindly invited me to join them. That day, Friday, after climbing about 7500 feet to view the Nisqually glacier with others of the visitors, I packed what I needed for climbing in my blankets and went to their camp to spend the night. The next morning we prepared for the trip, and at 11 a.m., Saturday, August 9th, five of us bade good bye to those who remained in camp and started, promising to await the coming of others who were delayed. Before starting I donned heavy flannels, woolen hose, warm mittens and goggles, blacked my face with charcoal to modify the sun's glare, drove long caulks and brads into my shoes, rolled two single blankets containing provisions for three days and strapped them from the shoulder under the arm to the waist, the easiest way by far to

## CARRY A PACK,

shouldered one of Uncle Sam's canteens, grasped my alpenstock and was resolved to climb until exhausted. Rev. E. C. Smith, of Seattle, who made the ascent last year with Ingraham was the guide and a heavily laden one too. Besides his provisions and blankets he carried a mercurial barometer three feet long, a prismatic compass, hatchet and the greater part of the time about fifty feet of rope. Mr. W. O. Amsden carried the heaviest pack that anyone ever took to the summit. It consisted of his blankets, provisions and a large camera with two 8 x 10 plates. A field glass was added to Mr. R. R. Parrish's bundle and thus we started. The sun was hot, the packs then seemed heavy and warm, but we soon became accustomed to them, as we toiled upward, first over long steep snowfields, then over ledges of rock, onward and upward throughout the afternoon. There was no danger this day only one small crevasse appearing in our way and that easily jumped; but it was the first day and the

## PERPENDICULAR ROCKS AND FIELDS

seemed miles away before we reached them. We passed Plummer's camp at 9,000 feet, and Camp Ewing at nearly 10,000 feet, and after an unusually long steep hillside landed at Camp Muir, between ten and eleven thousand feet at 5 p.m. and there waited for the rest of the party. Mr. Smith wanted to reach Camp Seattle that night where the Ingraham party had slept the previous year, but it was 6 p.m. when the others joined us and too late to travel further. The others were Elcaine Longmire, Miss Maud Longmire, Miss Edith Corbett, Leonard Longmire and Washington Longmire, a boy about twelve. Instead of carrying a blanket, Elcaine Longmire packed a tent, hoping to be the first one to carry a tent to the summit. It was a welcome protection at Camp Muir, 3,000 feet above wood and fire, and stretching it on the alpenstocks we prepared our beds. However we first supped from corn beef sandwiches, cheese and a little chocolate which had been heated by the blankets lying next to my pockets. As all are interested in the provision question, the names of the articles carried may be given here. Among us we had dried beef, fried ham, cold boiled eggs, sardines, bread and butter, extract of beef, cheese, chocolate, dried peaches, raisins and prunes; a bottle of brandy and a small flask of whiskey were also carried. Just before our arrival at Camp Muir, an unfortunate accident occurred which marred our pleasure. In putting on his pack, the caulks of Mr. Amsden's shoes caught on his blanket and the ground glass of his camera was ruined. Soon after reaching Camp Muir, Mr. Smith, in following instructions in regard to taking an observation, broke the barometer. No pictures, no observations. Mr. Smith put the instrument away until his return and philosophically concluded that the accieent [sic] had changed his trip

## FROM BUSINESS TO PLEASURE

and he would make the best of the loss and enjoy the climb. The most beautiful cloud effects below us were visible. A sea of snowy and pearl-colored clouds floated over the lower hills looking like great white waves playing with each other on the ocean. The sunset after glow shons [sic] on the mountain peaks beyond and a light resembling moonlight rested on Tahoma. Mr. Amsden set his camera and found he had glass pieces enough for focusing and took a beautiful view of the valley below. Arrangements had been made to signal our friends, and seeing their camp fires at 9 o'clock we waved

## A LIGHTED TORCH

and candle, which they answered with three reports of a gun. Mr. Parrish, who has a happy faculty of making himself comfortable, prepared a bed on the rocks and sands and spread his oil cloth over the top to exclude the wind. The rest of us slept in the tent. At 4:30 a.m. we rose and shouldered our blankets ready for the hard day's work. Not waiting to eat breakfast, we nibbled some of the melted chocolate, now frozen solid, and began the ascent. Right over high ledges of loose moving rock, where every step started immense boulders down the glacial slopes, only over the ledge when another and higher one would rise to be surmounted, so on hour after hour, growing more dangerous and toilsome as we approached the cliff, we climbed and climbed until we stood at the foot

## OF THE GREAT GIBRALTAR.

This is one of the most dangerous and difficult points of the journey. Standing on some of the high narrow backbones of the ridges we could look down on either side to a long glacier where one wrong step or several loose rocks giving way would land one in the unknown world. Some time after starting, Miss Corbett was taken sick which delayed their party about half an hour; but we could not wait for them as the Gibraltar climb must be made before the sun gets warm enough to loosen the rock, and when they reached that cliff it was too late to climb without the aid of a rope and they were sadly obliged to retrace their steps to camp. Leonard Longmire joined us and there were four men and myself who hoped to reach the summit. It was hard climbing without water, for the canteen was dry, and in the morning the streams were nearly all frozen and for several hours we had nothing to drink and had eaten nothing that day save a few raisins and prunes. We did not think of eating. Time was more than precious, and unless we made Gibraltar early our work was of no avail.

Gibraltar, as is pretty well known, is the rocky cliff about 1,000 feet high which blocks the passage to the summit of the mountain. For half a mile the route lies around that cliff on a shelf along the edge with that great wall above you and the Nisqually glacier stretching away miles below. If this shelf, scarcely three feet wide, were only level, it would make the traveling on it much easier, but it slants down towards the glacier and is composed of nothing but loose sand and rock. There is no way of fastening one's pike firmly and there is only occasionally a solid rock to cling to. Here the rope was useful; although it would not be wise to tie the party together all along here,

## OVER THE MOST DANGEROUS PLACES,

they tied me with a rope and two men ahead and two behind helped me safely over. In crossing one unusually ticklish place Mr. Parrish's bundle, which he had taken off to throw over first, went whirling through space down, down the glacier out of sight. Only one wrong step and that would be the end of all. When the ridge was almost passed we found we had a steep glacial side of solid ice to climb for about fifty feet, and then tied with ropes our guide cut steps with a hatchet and we waited, one step only firmly planted for step after step to be cut out. Already the sun was melting the snow and the rocks came down to our right and left, Mr. Smith being hit twice but able to keep his footing. After the ice one more ridge of moving rock and we had reached the top of Gibraltar cliff and felt free to rest. It was now nearly 12 noon. For seven long hours we had hurried on over these loose rocks without food or drink and only now were able to think of ourselves. We then knew the most dangerous part was over, but were prepared to be disappointed yet, for the crevasses looked broken and numerous, and breathining [*sic*]

## WAS GETTING MORE DIFFICULT.

Here at 12,000 feet we lunched heartily and found a stream of ice water, which was refreshing. Stepping on the edge to get a view of the country below we found the wind blowing a terrific gale, and formed a faint idea of what it would be beyond. At 12:30, tied with the rope at intervals of about ten feet we again started upward on the snow fields, first passing through an ice aisle, walled about to our waists and just wide enough to walk through, with a glacier on each side sloping way below. Of course it was solid, but still one could not help thinking of the peculiar situation of walking on the backbone where two glaciers met and that two feet either way would precipitate one thousands of feet below. Then came the great ridges of snow that can only be likened to high frozen billows where you step down three feet, up to the top of the next, down again and so on. They are too far apart to jump and it is very exhaustive climbing for several hundred feet. The first crevasse we came to was not very large and over it we found a good though narrow bridge where we stood and got the first look inside the mountain. Bluish green ice walls on either side of a big crack look like caves up the mountain sides. Some are large enough

## TO DROP A HOUSE INTO,

and one seemed bottomless. Looking down a crevasse half way up the mountain it appeared not level beneath, but as if a mountain with its hills and valleys, glaciers and rivers were lying below. The great trouble here in this thin atmosphere is in breathing. I could sometimes only travel fifteen feet for loss of breath, being obliged to stop and rest, but only a moment or two is needed to recover, when your lungs are again ready, you think, to climb a long distance, but not so; quickly exhausted, soon refreshed, is the rule, and it is not possible to do otherwise. We soon came to one crevasse where there seemed to be no bridge to cross, and Mr. Smith used his pike to try all the snow before stepping on it, for these blind crevasses are to be watched for. Piece after piece of snow gave way and crashed down to the bottomless depths with loud sounds. One part seemed firm, but only by looking underneath could its strength be calculated. Mr. Smith scrambled over, held the rope below, and planting himself firmly in the snow with his pike and holding the rope we followed hand over hand up this

## ALMOST PERPENDICULAR CLIFF

with the crevasses on either side. Safety accomplished, we moved slowly on with the rim of the crater in sight, but a long way off. We felt the wind growing stronger all the time and the air rarer, making it more difficult to climb. At last, at 4:10 p.m., we stood on the rim of the big crater, where the wind was blowing so strongly we could hardly keep our footing, and oh, it was bitter cold. Several times someone or other slipped, but marched on. The middle peak was some ways off, and for fear anything should happen we hastened on to the great high knob and at 4:30 p.m. August 10, 1890, we stood on the

*Fay Fuller, posed in full climbing regalia, sometime after her successful ascent. (Courtesy National Park Service)*

## TIP TOP OF MOUNT TAHOMA.

It was a heavenly moment; nothing was said—words cannot describe scenery and beauty, how could they speak for the soul! Such sensations can be known to only those who reach the heights. The scene below was a wonderful panorama. Some years when it is very clear the Sound can be seen, appearing like a small straddle bug, and the Olympic range is visible. The clouds prevented that sight this year, but besides Adams, Hood, St. Helens and Jefferson, we could see Mount Baker away to the north and miles of mountains forming one great circle round the horizon. The glaciers of the Nisqually, Cowlitz, Carbon and White rivers were seen, and the valleys and prairies beyond. The White river glacier is the longest, being estimated by Mr. Muir to be twelve miles to the base. An idea of the size of the top of this mountain can be formed when it is said that the distance from the north to the southwest peaks across the top is about two miles. Standing on the summit we see below us two large craters looking like immense bowls with a central common rim. The large crater is about three quarters of a mile across. They are filled with snow and solid ice with the rim around the circumference of bare rocks rising about sixty feet in some places. The

## STEAM KEEPS THESE ROCKS BARE ALL

the time. Coming down from the summit where we could hardly stand on account of the wind, we were sheltered in the crater and examined the steam jets, looking as if a row of boiling teakettles had been placed along the ridge. We sat on the rocks and were soon damp with the moisture and parboiled by the heat, and it was necessary to move. Mr. Amsden, not feeling well, and concluded he would wait until morning before taking a view of the crater, we started to make our beds before the sun went down. We saw it glide behind the summit and before 6 p.m. were all ready for the night. On the east edge of the big crater we entered an ice cave between the snow and rim of the crater, and there, with steam beside us, we spread our blankets, which seemed light enough now, took off our shoes, bathed our feet in whisky, and began the night. After having reached the summit I began to feel sick from cold, exhaustion and the sulphur odor, and for some time suffered from a chill and nausea. After vomiting I felt all right and ready to enjoy the night. Some of the gentlemen were tired and very cold. Eating had no attraction for me, but some ate a little. It is quite amusing to think of cooking at that altitude, but Mr. Smith melted some ice in a cup over the steam, heated the water, dissolved some extract of beef and served good hot

## BEEF SOUP FOR SUPPER.

Two blankets over us seemed little protection for the night. Through the small opening in the cave above we could watch the stars and meteors and all night long hear the awful avalanches roaring down the mountain sides. From the faintest sound of running brook to the fiercest lash of the ocean and the roar of these rock and snow slides, it is all God's music, the sounds being grander than the sights. We will pass over the chilly night, during which I was the only one fortunate enough to be able to sleep. I did not sleep all night on account of the cold, but rested in slumberland for some hours. Mr. Smith was ambitious enough to see the sun rise about 5 the next morning, but he saw it alone. When we awoke our

## SHOES WERE FROZEN STIFF,

and had to be melted in the steam before we could put them on. The blankets where the steam had been were icy. A light snow storm visited us early in the morning and covered all our cave and blankets with snow, the gentlemen's moustaches were frozen like ice, and the wind howled fiercely. There was nothing to do but prepare for the descent. Not much breakfast was eaten. A sandwich handed me was left and relished by the party who came up the next day. Prunes seemed palatable, and were the principal article of food enjoyed that morning. Before leaving

## LARGE PIECES OF GREEN MOSS,

that is kept alive in this cave by the steam, were taken for mementoes of that memorial night. Very little of anything grows over 10,000 feet and to find moss at this height is wonderful. At 6:30 a.m. we started dreading leaving the shelter for the rim of the crater. I tied my blanket right around me and with woolen mittens on nearly froze the fingers of one hand. We had to stop to rub and get some feeling in it, for with that hand my alpenstock must be carried. The wind was blowing so fiercely that several times I fell on the ice unable to keep my balance. The descent had to be made very rapidly to reach Gibraltar at an early hour, and a weary journey it was down through the clouds. We had no water for five or six hours and ate nothing until noon. The steps cut in the glacier the day before had melted and this work had again to be done. It seemed even more dangerous descending along the cliff and especially over the rocky ledges than ascending, the parties behind loosening rocks which might roll on the others. After Gibraltar was passed we toiled slowly down the ledge apparently having no ambition to hurry. At Camp Muir we met the Hitchcock-Knight-Watsou party on their way up, and after a conversation with them we watched them climb, glad our faces were turned homeward. Their party slept higher than any other party have on their up, [*sic*] at Camp Hitchcock, about 12,000 feet right in the ice. I neglected to mention that after Mr. Amsden carried his camera to the summit, the next morning trying to take a view of the party he found the paper slide frozen and the picture impossible. We reached camp that afternoon, enjoying some delightful slides down the steep hillsides and were royally welcomed by our friends. That evening we felt well but the next morning told the tale. The heat, air, cold and wind affect people differently. Three of the party showed the effects of the trip very little, but the guide and myself

## WERE PITIABLE SIGHTS.

Our lips, noses and almost all our faces were swollen out of proportion, eyes sore and wrists peeling and for several days the pain was intense. It was not easy to walk much for a day or two, and camp life seemed pleasant. The appetites were remarkable that we brought back with us and from all reports have lasted ever since. Leonard Longmire deserves a great deal of credit for what he did. Dressed in summer clothing and without gloves he was plucky enough to reach the top, a statement that means something even if one is prepared for it. One day later we explored the wonderful Nisqually glacier, and Mr. Smith and Mr. Amsden crossed the dangerous Cowlitz. Mr. Amsden obtained some beautiful views for which he has large orders. Two kodaks were in our party and added greatly to the interest. I regret I did not carry mine to the summit, but it was probably wise to leave it behind.

This ascent was made on the southeast slope of the mountain, the only way that people have ever traveled to the summit. Year by year it is becoming more difficult along the ledge and those who have made the trip more than once think that soon it will be impossible to go by the old route and that a new way must be discovered. Mr. Van Trump and others are examining the southwest slope now and think it may be the coming route. No one yet has stood on the north peak, owing to the circumstance that the snow melting so rapidly during the day the journey would have to be made early in the morning. It would be almost necessary to spend two nights in the crater in order to do this. Two of our party were willing to stay, but the others were obliged to return. I sincerely hope that

## MR. VAN TRUMP

will be the first one there, and I know he intends making the attempt at an early occasion. It is not so much the difficulty of this ascent as the lack of time that has prevented climbers from reaching the north peak.

As early as 1870 the Olympia papers mentioned the Indian name of the mountain as Tahoma, and this I think it should bear. The Klickitats more than the Puget Sound tribes know no other name for this particular mountain. Yet Indian Henry pronounced it for me in deep gutteral tones. Tacoma has no significance as far as the mountain is concerned, and if it cannot take its original name, Tahoma, let us call it Rainier.

In the crater we left our names in a sardine can, a brandy flask, and a tin cup. The hairpins which tried to serve as a button-hook, but miserably failed, were found by the Hitchcock party, and they laughingly remarked that it proved to them that a woman had been to the summit.

Our party left camp August 16, and arrived at Yelm August 19, the journey home being similar [to] that above described. At the Nisqually the current of the river was found entirely changed, the bridge of no use, and the rapid river had to be forded. All who have the opportunity, and who live in sight of this lofty pinnacle we almost reverence, who have never climbed the mountains, and want to begin life anew might profitably spend a few weeks next summer on its hillside, if they want to fall in love with the world again. The beauty and grandeur and inspiration you will find there will add new life. I want to be able to visit Tahoma each year and explore its mysteries, when the fascination for one more day on the summit may return; but now I am satisfied. I accomplished what I have always dreamed of and feared impossible.

# ℰ 12 ℰ

# George Dickson*
# 1892

George Dickson's short account is a tale of persistence rewarded. Perhaps no other early climber suffered so many defeats before finally reaching the summit.

The Dickson narrative is not included here for any special literary or historical significance. It is the very routine of the journey that attracted me to it. Notice how different the travel route is from those of twenty or more years before. We have seen in the past few accounts a gradual increase in the mileage of approach roads, number of settlements, and number of people, including climbers, met along the way. Gradually the route was becoming developed. This didn't make the climb any easier in itself, but it made contemplation of it a little more interesting to many people. The time when only small isolated parties would approach the mountain one by one was almost at an end.

And with the change came the disadvantages as well as the benefits of more visitors; we hear Dickson complaining about the damage of forest fires, intentionally set, that had ruined parts of Paradise valley. It is a process, and a cycle, common to all newly "discovered" wilderness attractions, until some system of consistent management is established.

In answer to your request to give some of my experience in mountain climbing, I will endeavor to give a brief account of the ascent of Mt. Tahoma by myself and party in the summer of 1892.

I will say first, that I had made several unsuccessful attempts to reach the summit in former years, but had strong hopes of finally getting to the top, which I eventually did in the latter part of July in the year mentioned.

Although I had made a couple of prospecting trips up toward the

*Reprinted from George Dickson, "George L. Dickson's Narrative," Tacomian, January 7, 1893.

north side of the mountain years ago, my first real attempt to reach the summit was in 1889, when I overtook the Dodge party in Paradise valley, on the south side of the mountain.

A large party of us undertook to climb the mountain, but dropped off one by one, until only three of us remained, and the three succeeded in reaching the top of Gibraltar Rock. Here a huge crevice in the ice and snow stopped all further advance. As we were without ropes or any means of crossing a dangerous place, and I was almost crippled with a sprained ankle, so we were obliged to give it up. In reaching this spot in other years I have always found it full of snow and easy to cross.

The following year, 1890, I formed a party and made another trip and succeeded in once more reaching the top of the big rock. There were three others with me, and one of them in passing my pack down a steep place accidently let it fall, and it soon disappeared in one of the glaciers below. The pack contained my coat, blanket and most of our provisions, and its loss threw a damper over the whole party. On reaching the top of Gibraltar we found ourselves in the teeth of a terrible gale, and as I was without a coat it was decided to give it up and get back as soon as possible.

The next year I again made one of a party of six to climb the mountain. Three of the party gave out when about half way up. Two others and myself almost reached the top.

We had become very much exhausted by strong winds blowing in our faces, and the snow was frozen so hard that we could scarcely keep our footing, so that when we were about half an hours climb from the top one of our party gave out completely.

We could not leave the man there in an almost fainting condition, and there remained only one thing to do, and that was to descend, which we did very reluctantly.

My last and successful attempt was made in the latter part of July, 1892. The party consisted of H. W. Baker, Dr. Cassels, my brother, W. H. Dickson, and myself, all of Tacoma, and W. E. Daniels of Sumner.

We left Tacoma by stage via Spanaway on July 24th, and reached Baker's store on the Little Mashel that night.

Having hired two pack ponies from Baker we loaded them up next morning and resumed our journey, but had not proceeded far into the woods before one of our ponies began to "buck" as it is called, and soon succeeded in relieving himself of his pack. The road was strewn for quite a ways with pieces of bacon, rolls of butter, loaves of bread, etc.

*Undated photograph of early party at Camp Muir. (Courtesy Aubrey Haines)*

After much delay, and some swearing, we secured the runaway, re-packed him and proceeded on our way and reached the Nisqually river about noon, where we had dinner at Sully's.

After leaving the Nisqually we had only a trail to follow through the woods, but it was well beaten, and as we had fine weather, we made good time and reached Kernahan's ranch early in the evening, where we pitched our tent and camped for the night.

From Kernahan's to Longmire springs is about 8 or 10 miles. We reached the springs about noon on the third day out from Tacoma. The distance is supposed to be about 70 miles from Tacoma to the springs. All of the party took a bath in the mineral springs and drank large quantities of the waters. One of the springs is very pleasant to the taste, and was much relished by all of the party.

We packed up about 3 p.m. and climbed the steep hills leading to

Paradise valley, which we reached three hours later. I found that forest fires had done much damage since I was here the year before. Some miscreant had set fire to the woods round the valley, and hundreds of acres of beautiful park had been burned over.

We made a temporary camp in the lower part of the valley, and rested and dried our feet, which had become saturated by crossing patches of soft snow on the way up.

The next day as the weather continued fine we moved our camp up the valley about two or three miles, until we were at the highest point of timber line.

A sharp ridge of bare ground rising out of deep snow drifts, with a small groves [sic] of tunted [sic] trees or bushes on it, marked the location of the camp. Making our tent secure against the strong winds that we knew would arise during the night, we turned in early, so as to be well rested for the ascent on the following morning.

We had with us everything necessary in the way of outfit for the ascent, comprising these articles: Each man was provided with an alpine staff and had heavy soled shoes with steel calks in them, and each had a warm blanket of wool and one of rubber. In addition we carried with us a life line of ½ inch cotton rope and a small hatchet to cut steps in the ice where it became necessary. We also carried two canteens, one for water and one filled with what the Indians denominate "fire water." The latter article however we did not have much use for, as the lightness of the air and the exertion of climbing so inflamed our throats and lungs, that we could scarcely swallow anything so fiery as whiskey.

Early in the morning of July 28th we began the ascent. The weather promised to be fine, and all the party felt in good condition. We took our course in as near a direct line as possible for Gibraltar rock. Some of our party thought we could easily reach the big rock by noon, but after a few hours climbing, and the rock still appearing as far away as ever, they changed their minds. The whole forenoon was spent in toiling over vast sloping fields of snow, softened just enough by the warm July sun to let us sink in about to the ankles.

About noon we reached high ridges of bare rocks, and then our real climbing began. We kept faithfully at it all the afternoon, and by the time the sun had disappeared we were close in under the shadow of Gibraltar, where we made preparations to pass the night. Spreading our rubber blankets on the softest rock we could find, we covered ourselves with our woolen blankets and huddled up together, trying to get up a little warmth, and kept on trying all night, but with very poor success. A bitter cold wind blew around us, and we got little or no sleep, and were all very glad when it became light enough to travel. By unanimous consent this place was named "Camp Misery."

We resumed our journey at daybreak July 29th. After trying to swallow a few mouthfuls of breakfast, being too cold to eat, we decided to put it off until we got warmed up climbing. We left all our blankets and extra baggage at this place, and took only our staffs, rope, canteens, ax, and a small lunch. The severest and most dangerous part of the trip was passed during the next two hours, which was the exact time it took us to reach the top of the big rock, we had to use our hatchet in several places to cut steps for our feet in the ice of the glacier, we followed the rocks where ever we could, but in many places were obliged to go out on the glacier. One of our party became very weak at this place and bled freely at the mouth and nose. This seemed to give him some relief, and he was able to go on again slowly. When we reached the top of Gibraltar the wind from the north-east had full sweep at us, and we all shivered in the piercing blast.

We were all very tired, but it was too cold a place to stop long. So after eating a few dried figs and drinking a mouthful of water, we went on. All bare rocks were now left behind, and we were traveling over dazzling white fields of snow.

The sun soon rose high enough to warm us, and as the wind had nearly died away, we soon began to suffer more from the heat than we did before from the cold. Our route took us over huge snow drifts, so steep that we had go [*sic*] around some and others we would zig-zag up the sides.

From the top of Gibraltar rock a small bare spot of rock can be seen, well up toward the summit. This bare spot forms one edge of the crater and it was toward this spot we directed our course as near as we could. This rocky spot, seen from Paradise valley, appears to be the shape of a whale's back. It is however very much larger than it appears from below, and is really a ridge of bare rock mixed with lava, covering several acres.

We reached the top of this bare spot in two hours and fifteen minutes hard climbing from the top of Gibraltar, and had the satisfaction of looking down into the crater.

I will not attempt to give a very accurate description of the crater, as we had no instrument to measure it, and were all too much exhausted to do so, if we had.

The crater appeared to me to be a large oval basin about 3/4 by 1/2 a mile in diameter. It is sunken in the centre and partially filled with hard snow, or probably ice covered with snow. We did not go down into it, but could easily have done so if we had desired.

Two others and myself walked entirely around the crater and in doing so saw the other crater, which is north of the first one and more indistinct being nearly filled with snow and ice. One side of it has apparently fallen out at some former period. The ridge which separates the two craters, rises at one place to a large snow covered mound, and the top of this mound is the highest point on the entire mountain. The so called north peak which some climbers have taken such pains to ascend, is some hundreds of feet below this point, as we could look directly over it and see the waters of Puget Sound in the distance.

We had an exceptionally fine day and the view from this point is one that once seen is never forgotten. We had no glass, but could easily see the waters of Puget Sound glistening in the sunlight, and could make out Commencement bay, but could not see either Tacoma or Seattle. Far to the northward, we could see snow capped mountain [sic], which we supposed to be Mt. Baker and others.

In making our circuit around the crater, we found a small monument of stones and in one of the crevices a small tin box in which was the names of a Seattle party who had visited this spot in 1889. One of the party was a clergyman. I entered the names of our party, with the date and returned the box to its place.

We left the summit shortly after noon and made good time coming down. We only had occasion to use the rope once, and that was in descending from Gibraltar rock.

The strong midday sun had losened [sic] the rocks and they were coming down in showers every few minutes. We had several narrow escapes from being crushed by them, one large boulder weighing about half a ton struck the snow a few yards ahead of us, having fallen from an overhanging ledge fully 200 feet high. Hapily [sic] we passed this dangerous spot without any serious mishap and reached our last nights camp where we rested and packed up our blankets, reaching our camp at timber line about 5 in the evening, having made the descent in less than six hours. We found the horses standing around the camp evidently glad to see us, as there were tracks of wolves all around camp.

We spent the next day resting and rubbing vaseline on our sunburned hands and faces; some of us had badly swollen faces for a day or two, but none of the party regretted having made the ascent.

We arrived home in Tacoma after an absence of five days and at a to tal expense for the trip of $85.00 or $17.00 each.

Some day in the near future, when a good road has been made into Paradise valley, it will become one of the greatest summer resorts on the coast. All the natural resources for such a resort are there now, and it would not require any great amount of capital to develop them. The mineral springs, fine mountain scenery, and clear mountain streams, are certainly worth the journey alone.

It has been suggested to make the mountain and a few miles around the base into a State Park. I think the suggestion a good one and well worthy the attention of our new legislature, when it meets.

Geo. L. Dickson

# ‿ 13 ‿

# Philemon Beecher
# Van Trump[*]
# 1892

Philemon Van Trump had made his fourth successful ascent in 1891, but again was denied the North Peak. At the end of July 1892, a party of climbers became the first to reach this elusive summit, which is now known as Liberty Cap, and so Van Trump was foiled in his hope to be first. But he still felt the challenge, and arranged for yet another try with his old friend and climbing partner George Bayley.

They were struck with the development along the way; few other climbers shared even Bayley's memories of how the route used to be, and none shared Van Trump's. They were one of seven parties to reach the summit that year, a far cry from earlier times when several years often passed between ascents.

Besides Van Trump's triumph over Liberty Cap, this account tells of the extraordinary misadventure of Bayley, who slipped on ice and slid hundreds of yards into a crevasse, a miraculous survival story that seems almost to get worse after Van Trump hauled his companion from the crevasse.

First, a few words in relation to the name applied in this paper to a mountain which has always been named on the official maps of the Government "Mount Rainier," and which for almost three-quarters of a century prior to the early seventies had been exclusively known by that name. Every student familiar with the history of early explorations on the Pacific Coast of North America knows, that when the distinguished navigator, George Vancouver, was in search of the then

*Reprinted from Philemon Van Trump, "Mount Tahoma," Sierra Club Bulletin 1 (1894): 109–132.

fabled northwest passage between the Atlantic and Pacific Oceans, he entered and explored the beautiful inland sea which he named Puget Sound; that as he was sailing over its waters one clear day in May, 1792, he saw looming up on the eastern horizon a magnificent snow-capped mountain, which he named Mount Rainier, in honor of his friend, Rear-Admiral Rainier, of the English navy. When Vancouver thus named this grand mountain, he did so without considering, apparently, whether some other navigator might not have discovered and named it, and evidently without endeavoring to ascertain by what name it was known among the primitive dwellers by the beautiful inland sea. This people, or race of mysterious origin, who had for unknown generations dwelt by this inland sea and on the plains east of the great mountain chain which runs parallel with it, called the mountain by a name which had a peculiar and appropriate meaning. The tribes dwelling by the Sound, which they termed "Whulge," called the mountain "Tacōbet," the nourisher or source of waters, and those tribes (the Yakimas and Klickitats) which dwelt on the plains east of the mountain, called it Tahōma, which means "rumbling sound." How much more significant and appropriate these Indian names for the mountain than is the name of a *man*, one who was an alien, who never saw the mountain, and who was not in sympathy or in touch with the nation which was thus to perpetuate his name! And these Indian names are thus appropriate not only on account of the peculiar significance of them, but because this primitive race were the original discoverers of the mountain, and the original and rightful owners of the country which the mountain so grandly dominated. Even if we leave the Indian out of the question altogether, Vancouver was not the original discoverer of the mountain. The Spaniards explored these waters previous to Vancouver's explorations, and they saw the mountain. About fifty years after Vancouver named the mountain, the brilliant American author, Theodore Winthrop, visited the Sound, beheld the mountain, was piloted first by western Washington Indians over the waters of Puget Sound, and then by eastern Washington Indians across the Cascade Mountains. From the two Indian names heard during this journey he coined the euphonious name "Tacoma," and he thus subsequently named the mountain in his "Canoe and Saddle." Of late years many of the inhabitants of the State of Washington called the mountain Tacoma, while a few others apply to it the Yakima-Klickitat name "Tahōma." The writer believes that the time is not many years distant when the inexpressive and inappropriate name of Rainier will be generally, if not universally, replaced by one of the expressive and appropriate Indian names.

Mount Tahōma is beyond question the grandest of all the peaks of the great Cascade Range, and, Mount St. Elias aside, is without a rival in North America in ruggedness, grandeur, beauty of outline, and in the number and magnificence of its glaciers. It is questionable whether there is in all Europe a single mountain which has a glacial system on so grand a scale. A dozen prominent glaciers are imbedded in its rugged sides, one of which is 12 miles long and nearly 3 miles in width—several others are from 6 to 10 miles long; and if all its glaciers, both great and small, were to be counted, the number would be found to reach 15 or 16. Some further idea may be formed of the magnitude of this mountain from the following statements, which are estimates based on numerous ascents of the mountain and a considerable personal experience in exploration of it.

The main glaciers terminate at points which have a common level. A line passing around the mountain at the terminals of these glaciers, so as to complete the circuit of it, would measure 40 miles, and the circumference of the mountain where its base may be said to begin to swell from the surrounding country is at least 80 miles. The diameter of the mountain at the line of perpetual snow (6000 feet) must be at least 10 miles. The altitude of Tahoma is almost 15,000 feet; yet even at that height the distance across its summit is fully 2 miles. The air at the line of perpetual snow, and above it, is magically clear; yet a man standing at the snow-line on a clear day and gazing at the summit of the mountain would be unable to see a mountain climber moving on the snow at the summit. To an observer standing at a point on the mountain side 10,000 feet above the sea-level a party of tall men just reaching the summit would appear like black specks moving across the snow. Although properly a mountain of the Cascade Range, Tahoma stands some miles to the west of the main chain, rising in solitary and unapproachable grandeur, and immeasurably overtopping the neighboring peaks or elevations of the parent range.

Between the years 1870 and 1884, I made several ascents of the mountain by the south side, and one ascent by the west side in 1891, accomplishing the mastery of two peaks; but several attempts to reach the summit of the North Peak were unsuccessful. In the summer of 1892, determining to make a final and supreme effort to master this coveted peak, and remembering that my friend, George B. Bayley, of San Francisco, had exacted a promise of me to let him know when I intended to make my final effort to scale the North Peak, that he might join me in the attempt, I wrote to him, and in due time he arrived at Yelm, eager for the mountain fray and armed *cap-a-pie*. On the morning of August 16, 1892, we left the little village of Yelm on our journey mountainward, each mountaineer astride of a substantial pony, one of them leading a large horse well-laden with provisions and abundant camp paraphernalia. The mountain lies due east of Yelm, and is distant from it "as the crow flies," a little over 40 miles, supposing the crow to alight at the terminal point of one of the west-side glaciers. The distance in an air-line from Yelm to the actual summit of Tahoma is, by triangulation, just 50 miles; and yet on a summer day, when the atmosphere is pure and clear, the mountain looms up with such vast proportions, with such clear-cut outlines, and seems so neighborly, that a "tenderfoot" or novice from the East would deem it less than ten miles distant. Our general course lay up the valley of the Nesqually River, crossing the latter but twice, once by means of a good substantial county bridge on the edge of Yelm prairie, the second time far up toward the mountain, where the murky, turbulent water of the river has a swift current, where the rolling, bumping bowlders tend much to the discomfiture of the horses in fording, and where, sometimes, a careless rider is unhorsed and forced to take an ice-cold bath not down on the program at starting.

After the broad and bare Nesqually plains are left, or the equally treeless prairie of Yelm, the road to the mountain may be said to extend through one vast and continuous forest; and so dense is it in places and so closely, high overhead, are the branches of the giant firs and monster spruces interlaced, that rarely does a sunbeam penetrate them to fleck with its light the pine-leaf-carpeted floor of "the forest primeval." When the open glades and the beautiful flowery meadows of the mountain proper are reached, after a long journey through these funereal pines, the change is marked and agreeable, and so very pleasing, that the traveler is fully repaid for the fatigue of his journey and for his "moving accidents by flood and field." The entire tourist travel of to-day to the mountain is to the south or Paradise Valley side, the more rugged, picturesque and varied west side being, as yet, a *terra incognita*, except to a few adventurous mountaineers or goat hunters. All the artists, all the photographers, and almost all the kodak fiends even, take the beaten track to the better known and famed Paradise Valley; hence, there are, as yet, no photographic views or sketches extant of the west side of the mountain other than those showing it as seen from the

*Undated photograph of the camp-hotel at Paradise, probably from around the turn of the century. (Courtesy Aubrey Haines)*

Sound, 50 miles away; and hence the fact that the illustrations [originally] accompanying this article do not picture any of the interesting points in and the striking features connected with the exploit of the mountain climbers who figure in this narrative.

Where the Rainier Fork of the Nesqually River makes its confluence with the main Nesqually, a distance of 45 miles from Yelm, we left the Paradise Valley road and turned our course up the Rainier Fork; and in leaving the aforesaid road we left behind us the traces of civilization and what comforts of traveling it afforded—for there was scarcely a semblance of a trail to mark our way, a few scattering "blazes" on the thickly standing trees indicating the course, these few-and-far-between blazes having been made some years ago by the Indians in one of their annual hunting expeditions to Tahoma for mountain goats or to lay in their winter supply of mountain whortleberries. We traveled up the right bank of the river till we reached a point about 3 miles above its mouth; here we left it to climb the outlying spurs and foot-hills that lay between us and the mountain proper. Now the trail became quite discernible in its zigzagging up the mountain ridges. For an hour and a half the climbing was quite arduous. Now up a steep mountain only to go down on the other side, in order to "tackle" another of still greater elevation, and so on, till we reached the first park or mountain meadow of Tahoma, which we entered by passing through a narrow, rocky gorge or natural gateway in a high ledge of rock, which had long hidden the mountain from us as we toiled upward. When the traveler has passed through this gateway, he stops almost involuntarily, not to rest and regain his "wind" after the long, steep climb, as might seem natural, but to "take in" and enjoy the sublime view suddenly revealed to him. Directly in front of him, and filling up the whole range of vision in that direction, is the long-sought mountain, apparently near enough to touch, yet in reality 2 miles and a half distant, its triple summit seeming to pierce the very vault of heaven, three of its magnificent glaciers in full view, the deep, muffled thunder of huge rocks rolling and grinding beneath their mighty movements occasionally breaking the otherwise Sabbath stillness of the mountain air. Immediately before the spectator, and on his right hand and on his left hand, stretch a succession of mountain meadows, or Alpine gardens, richly clothed in grass and brilliant with many-hued flowers, dotted with beautiful groves of firs, and with here and there a crystal lake. Looking back over the region through which lies the course of his journey mountainward, and far beyond the point where it began, he sees innumerable undulating hills, the winding curse of the Nesqually, and a vast sea of green forest stretching westward to the Pacific Ocean; while off to the right, or against the southern horizon, rise the snow-capped peaks of near Adams, more remote St. Helens, and beyond

"Where rolls the Oregon, and hears no sound,
   Save his own dashings—"

the magnificent white cone of distant Hood. A man who thus stands and who is thus blessed with such a vision, yet who feels no exaltation of soul, no supreme delight in the conscious exercise or stirring of that something within us we call the aesthetic,

"Is fit for treasons, stratagems and spoils;
   Let no such man be trusted."

Wending our way through the mountain meadows until we reached the one at the highest elevation, and consequently nearest to the line of perpetual snow on the mountain, we pitched our comfortable wall tent and established permanent camp. One pony and the pack-horse were turned loose to graze at will; the remaining pony was securely picketed, in order that we might be sure of one animal on our return from the summit—a wise precaution in relation to the two biped climbers, but an unfortunate one for the picketed quadruped, as will be shown in each case by the sequel. On the following morning, August 20th, we completed our preparations for the climb. Each of us took a double blanket, an extra woolen undershirt and overshirt and an extra pair of woolen socks, these extras in clothing being intended for use on the summit at night. Each, of course, had the regulation alpenstock. One carried a hatchet, and the other 75 feet of three-eighths rope. A pint bottle of alcohol and a spirit-lamp were part of the outfit. I carried a large reflector made of bright plate tin, fastened to a board of the same size. The edibles for the trip (in quantity sufficient for 2 days ) were equally divided between the two packs. Concluding to use our pack-horse as far as practicable in the ascent, we caught him and strapped our packs, coats, hatchet, rope and reflector on him. Oneonta (for with this poetic and aboriginal name had the pack-horse been christened in his early colthood) did not make any frisky demonstrations of delight over the prospect of an additional climb. He looked sadly and regret-fully at his grazing companions, and heaved a dismal groan as the "cinch" was finally tightened; yet, with that patient docility (or is it animal philosophy?) characteristic of the horse, he submitted to the in-evitable in the shape of domineering man.

Mountaineers and puffing steed now climbed for something more than a good mile over alternate fields of snow and patches of rock to a point where the spur we were ascending connected by a narrow tongue of loose shelving rock with one of the rocky ridges which extend up the mountain toward the south peak. When we reached this narrow tongue of loose rock, to get on which there was quite a jump-off from the spur we had ascended, we discussed whether we should take the horse any further. My companion was in favor of doing so, and it could easily have been done with a sure-footed cayuse used to climbing over rocks; but as the horse was heavy, and not a graduate in mountain climbing, I thought it best to dispense with him there. I thought my companion, as he glanced at his heavy pack, heaved a gentle sigh of protest against this early abandonment of horse-power. We soon stripped Oneonta of his pack and halter, leaving him at perfect liberty to return or follow. For a time Oneonta seemed to be halting between two opinions. He first looked back in the direction he had come, then looked meditatively at the mountain looming up before us, and then after casting a glance at us with an expression of eye which said, "as plain as whisper in the ear," "Well, gentlemen, if it's your intention to scale these awful heights, please consider me not in it," turned in his tracks and trotted briskly off in the direction of camp. Simple and natural as was this desertion of us by our horse for his more congenial four-footed companions at camp, it seemed, as he disappeared over the neighboring snow-ridge, as though we had lost forever a valuable friend, and it cast a sort of damper on our spirits; and as we started off up the mountain, after strapping (by each other's help) our packs to our backs, we seemed to have suddenly acquired a wonderful increment of avoirdupois. A few moments of exercise, however, in the exhilarating mountain air revived our spirits, and we philosophically concluded that horses will be horses, and sometimes forget the hand which cares for them, just as "boys will be boys," and sometimes forget the amenities and proprieties of life. I, for my part, as we swung along under our somewhat heavy packs, was reminded of the early days when I prospected in the mountains of Montana and Idaho with a forty-pound pack on my back; and as I thought of it, and especially of the expected triumph over the North Peak, my muscles seemed to regain something of their wonted vigor and endurance. For about a half-mile from the point where the horse left us we climbed the ridge of rock, extending up toward the South Peak, then descended it on the left and got on to one of the three glaciers alluded to earlier in this paper.

Our object was to cross this glacier to reach the snow-field which extends some distance up the mountain between the first-mentioned glacier and the great Tahoma glacier. The upper portion of this snow-field terminates at the foot of a ledge of rock at an altitudes of about 11,000 feet. On the lower point of this ledge of rock we intended to camp for the night. Where we crossed the glacier it was cut up with many crevasses, some of them wide and deep, and in threading our way among them, and in looking for "bridges" of ice on which to cross the larger and more dangerous ones, considerable time was occupied. When we finally reached the ledge of rock, 11,000 feet altitude, where we intended to spend the night, it was evening, and we were tired enough to stop. Selecting the spot that seemed the nearest level and the *softest* on this rocky point, we unrolled our blankets and prepared our mountain bed while it was yet light. The next thing was to find some water, for our day's climb without any to drink had made us exceedingly thirsty. One peculiarity of climbing on the west side is the absence of running water, except at the lower altitudes of the snowslopes. On the southern slope running water is found in the summer afternoons as high as 10,000 or 12,000 feet. Our spirit-lamp now came in play, and, by melting ice in our drinking-cup, we managed after some time to quench our great thirst. But the fresh night wind blew the alcohol blaze much of the time away from the cup, and our great thirst caused such a drain on the alcohol that we had but a small amount for melting ice with in the morning. Our camping-site was on the edge of the Tahoma glacier, the main glacier of the west side of the mountain. It originates on the very summit of the mountain, the snow sloping from the middle and north peaks forming it. Eight miles would be a very conservative estimate of its length—ten miles would probably be nearer the truth—its width from a half-mile to a mile. From Yelm this fine glacier is discernible from the summit of the mountain, from which it flows down through the wide gap or channel it has worn through the wall of rock forming the west brow of the mountain from the north peak to the extreme south peak, and thence discernible clear down to the timber line. From near the middle of its length clear up to the summit the medial line or center of the glacier is free of crevasses and comparatively smooth; but from both sides to this smooth medial line it is thickly strewn with crevasses, many of them wide and of great depth. Our intention was to cross this smooth medial pathway and climb up by it to the summit. Early in the morning following the cold and disagreeable night we spent in our stony bed at 11,000 feet, we got on the glacier and commenced climbing in a diagonal line upward toward the smooth central snow-line already described. For more than four hours we toiled upward, threading our way among innumerable crevasses, now climbing along the sharp, icy edge of a wide one, where a single misstep would have hurled us down into its blue and yawning depths on the one hand, or on the other down its steep, icy side, to be swallowed by the next yawning crevasse below; again crossing other deep and wider-mouthed ones by means of natural ice-bridges spanning them; at other times leaping narrow ones, and occasionally crossing one and attaining its higher upper wall by means of a ladder which my companion, with sailor skill, constructed of our rope and alpenstocks. When, as stated, we had toiled upward in this way for over four hours, we had the inexpressible chagrin of finding ourselves in a wilderness of crevasses, so wide that there was no practical way of crossing them. There was nothing to do but retrace our steps and begin a new line of ascent in the desired direction. This we did, and after a long and tedious effort, during which we threaded a labyrinth of crevasses, we reached the long-sought and smooth medial line of the glacier; but when we had done so the afternoon was far spent, and there was no possible chance of reaching the summit before nightfall. Climbing such a mountain by night is not without possible danger, and is certainly far from being preferable to climbing by the cheerful and guiding light of day; but thus we should have to climb it or beat an ignominious retreat—and retreat was a word that had no place in our mountain vocabulary.

It was early evening when we reached the foot of the steepest stretch of the ascent (a portion of it that my companion will long remember), namely, where the glacier flows from over the rocky brow of the mountain, 1000 feet below its actual summit. I supposed, from previous experience, that we would have much tedious step-cutting at this point; but much to our satisfaction we found the snow in such favorable condition that our shoe-calks took good hold of the hard snow, and, with the additional help of our alpenstocks, we climbed without having to resort to much step-cutting. When we turned the brow of the mountain the stars were shining with the clear, glittering light peculiar to that high, pure atmosphere; but though they gave sufficient light to prevent utter darkness, they, of course, did not give enough to make our now icy paths very luminous. After traveling for some distance over a comparatively gradual slope, with the North Peak on our left and the middle or Crater Peak on our right, we came to the foot of the dome of the latter, turned our course southward, and began climbing the steep slope of Crater Peak. The night air was now piercingly cold, August though it was, and our shoes, which became soaked with water as the snow had melted on them during the heat of the afternoon, now froze as hard as boards. During a night spent on the summit of Tahoma in a previous season I had my feet badly frosted, and now they pained me very much with cold. Twice that night I bathed and rubbed them in the snow, cutting the crust of ice away with the hatchet for that purpose, and the last time I put on my reserve pair of thick woolen stockings. But for the reserved pair of dry, heavy stockings, I think my toes would have been "done for" this time; as it was, I suffered with them for many weeks after our expedition. Every winter now I am a martyr to painfully cold feet; and I presume that I shall suffer thus every winter with cold feet till they have traveled to the end of life's journey. Should some person chance to read these humble lines who has never caught the contagion of mountain-climbing, who has never known the proud delight that thrills and swells the breast of the happy mountaineer who has planted his foot triumphantly on the crest of some sublime peak which, through generations, had baffled the efforts of man to conquer it—should such a one, I repeat, read these pages, he will wonder where is the pleasure, or profit, or honor of mountain-climbing under such circumstances. Does this skeptic suppose that a true mountaineer regrets any heroic mountain exploit because of some mishap, or of some after pain or suffering entailed by reason of its accomplishment? Does he suppose that any of the many zealous navigators who sailed in that vain quest, the discovery of the mild open sea about the North Pole, bewailed the suffering he endured or the brave efforts he made? Does he imagine that man will ever cease his attempts to unravel the mystery of the North Pole, or to reach the summit of unconquered peaks, simply because of possible mishaps and sufferings attendant thereon?

We now began the steep ascent of the north slope of Crater Peak's dome. Occasionally we would come to a broad patch of peculiarly hard, glassy ice, caused, I think, by swirls of steam from the crater depositing moisture which the keen night air converted into sheets of glassy ice. Our shoe-calks seemed to make no impression on it, and many were the sudden falls we got; it was difficult at times to prevent our bodies from rolling down toward the dangerous brow of the mountain. Once my companion, in a sudden slip, had the coil of rope loosened from his grasp, and it rapidly slid down to the foot of the dome, where we regained it on our descent. At last, at about 11 o'clock at night, we reached the rim of the small crater, and our climbing for the night was done. Had we been strangers on the summit, we would have found it difficult—it may be, impossible—to find a suitable resting-place for the rest of the night. For me, however, this was the fifth visit to the crater, and Mr. Bayley had spent a night with me in the crater on my second visit to it in 1883. So we each knew, even by starlight, where to find our bed in the crater tavern without the aid of landlord or call-boy. We were soon lying prone on the warm inner rim of the crater, in the mouth of one of the ice caverns formed by the jets of scalding steam which issue from the hidden but still smouldering furnace of the old volcano. After resting a few moments, the first thing we did was to prepare some drinking-water, which was done by filling our large drinking-cup with ice and then holding it over a steam jet till the ice melted.

This night in the crater was remarkable in my experience. The air was so calm that scarcely a breath was stirring, whereas always before a fierce, breath-quelling blast swept over the summit. In 1883, when Bayley and I, and our companion, James Longmire, in the morning climbed out of the crater, where we had steamed all night till our clothes were reeking with moisture, the fierce, cold wind in five minutes froze our clothing stiff, and we became so numbed with cold that the wind repeatedly prostrated us among the sharp rocks of the crater's rim, and for some time it seemed that we must succumb. This time the air in the morning was still calm, and the sun rose gloriously to convert the summit of Tahoma and its companion peaks into domes of burnished gold. We now revisited familiar points, and searched in particular for the lead plate we had left in the crater in 1883. We could not find it, though I had seen it in August, 1891, just where we left it. It was somewhat corroded, but the names were still legible. We learned on reaching the lower country that a mountain-climber, who had visited the crater a week or two before us, had taken the plate away as a trophy, and to exhibit it as an evidence that he had reached the top, it being known to many persons interested in mountain-climbing that we had reached the crater in 1883, and deposited a lead plate there.

Mount Tahoma, in addition to its superior height and magnitude, differs from the other volcanic cones of the Cascades in the fact of its having two craters. They occupy the summit of the middle peak, which is the true summit of the mountain, the larger crater inclining or dipping toward the east, the smaller one dipping slightly westward. Their two rims coincide or touch at the top of the peak, and at the point of actual contact of these two rims a vast pile of snow, of a dome-like shape, has accumulated, through how many generations it would be difficult to tell, but interesting to calculate or to speculate about. The persons who have visited the craters and given estimates of their dimensions differ considerably in their estimates. Some give the diameter of the larger crater as 300 yards, others estimate it at half a mile. No one has ever made any actual measurement of them. Such a deliberate and painstaking process would hardly be in keeping with the feeling of discomfort, uneasiness and eagerness to get down again which usually affects those who succeed in reaching the summit. My own impression of the size of the larger crater, based on several inspections of it, is that it is a mile, or nearly a mile, in circumference, and that the smaller crater has a circumference of about 300 yards. In August, 1891, I fastened a good-sized mirror to a rock on the west side of the small crater's rim. We found the mirror still there, but with a large block of ice adhering to it. On breaking the ice away, the glass was found to be intact. Parties in Olympia thought they saw flashes from this glass soon after it was placed there. After re-examining the craters all we cared to, we re-shouldered our packs and started for the North Peak, between 7 and 8 o'clock in the morning. We found the snow in good condition both for descending the middle peak and for climbing North Peak. We accomplished in a little less than two hours this feat, which we had long been desirous of accomplishing, but which one adverse circumstance after another had hitherto prevented; and now, when victory at last crowned our final effort, the long-coveted peak was not, as it had been for so many years, a virgin and unexplored peak—for just about two weeks before our mastery of it Dr. W. Riley, of Olympia, and two companions reached its summit. It was my good fortune (so a mountain-climber considers it), in 1870, in company with my friend, Gen. Hazard Stevens, to be the first to reach the summits of the south and middle peaks, which we named respectively Peak Success and Crater Peak.

In August, 1891, I attempted the ascent of the peak in company with Dr. Riley. The snow was very unfavorable for climbing that season. We were a day and a half reaching the base of North Peak from permanent camp at 7000 feet, and we were 300 or 400 feet below the summit of the peak, toiling through new snow, knee-deep, when night overtook us, and we were compelled to abandon North Peak to ascend the middle peak, so that we could spend the night in one of the crater caverns. Bayley and I, as before stated, reached the summit of North Peak from Crater Peak in a little less than two hours' time. North Peak, as seen from the crater rim of the middle peak of the mountain, and as shown by the illustration [originally] accompanying this article, seems to be a cone-shaped mass of snow, fringed on the left or west with a ledge of serrated volcanic rock. It is in reality a vast mass of rock, very rugged and precipitous on its west and north exposures, and covered with snow of great depth on its summit and southern slope. We climbed to the very apex of its snowy summit. We met with one great disappointment. The whole of the landscape below us was blotted from view by a dense pall of mist and smoke, except where rents in the pall gave us but glimpses of it. Through several of these rents we caught

*The mountain's foremost promotor and champion, Philemon Beecher Van Trump, late in life. (Courtesy Aubrey Haines)*

glimpses of Puget Sound, shining like patches of burnished gold. Rarely does the climber who succeeds in reaching the summit of Tahoma have the good fortune to find the whole of the prospect commanded by that lofty altitude free from smoke and clouds. Only once during my experiences on the mountain-top did I have this good fortune, and then only for a brief hour. The air was very clear, no clouds at the cloud-level below, and no obscuring mist or haze. I saw nearly all of the then Territory of Washington, much of the State of Oregon, far into British Columbia, and far out to sea on the Pacific. In this view were included half a dozen of the snow-capped peaks of the Cascade Range and innumerable mountains of less magnitude. It was a sublime vision, and included a scope of country whose circumference must measure close to a thousand miles.

From "Liberty Cap," or the snowy apex of North Peak, we descended about 80 feet to the bare rock below it on the west. Here to a projection of the rock we wired the tin-plate reflector, facing it toward Yelm. It was, doubtless, useless trouble and labor carrying and fixing the tin-plate there—for I have never heard of any one seeing reflections from it. It will serve as a relic or proof of our visit to the other explorers who reach the summit. Mr. Bayley deposited on this rock another lead plate with our names and the date and year engraved on it. About 11 A.M., on the 22d, we began the descent of the mountain by the route we had climbed it. When we were at the steepest part of the descent, and where the surface of the snow was hard and icy, at a point probably 2000 feet below the summit, my companion, who was in the lead, stepped on an icy and treacherous place where his shoe-calks seemed to be useless. His feet flew from under him, and he fell with such suddenness and unexpectedness that he lost the grasp of his alpenstock and left it sticking in the crest of snow where he had planted it when making the faulty step. As soon as he struck the snow his body began rolling, and he rolled with great velocity for some distance down the steep, icy slope. Then by some means, probably by his own efforts to that end, he managed to assume a sitting posture, with his feet pointing down the mountain. He now bravely endeavored to check his speed by striking his calked shoe-heels into the icy snow-crust and using his gloved hands as drags or brakes; but it was all in vain. His efforts may have had the effect of preventing an acceleration of speed, but it did not stay his fearful progress down the mountain-side. It will be remembered that it was stated earlier in these pages that there was a smooth medial pathway up the glacier from a certain point, toward which smooth line we ascended in an oblique direction from the labyrinth of crevasses at the side of the glacier. Now, it was directly down over this smooth pathway that my companion was involuntarily descending with such fearful rapidity, and toward a point where its smoothness was terminated by crevasses which crossed it. About 600 or 700 yards below the place where he lost his footing the first of these crevasses stretched across the smooth snow-line. I remembered noting, as we passed around the far end of it in ascending, how broad and deep it was. I saw that it was inevitable that he would be lost in this crevasse unless he could succeed in stopping his progress before he reached its yawning mouth. From where I stood there seemed to be quite a broad strip of snow in front of the crevasse that was comparatively level. My one hope was—and no doubt such was the thought and hope that filled his mind—that the snow on this level stretch in front of the crevasse would be so softened by the sun's heat as to make successful his efforts to stop his progress; but, as I gazed, I saw his body pass over the first of this level space, with less-ened speed it is true, but with velocity enough to carry him to the crevasse. Nearer and nearer to that yawning crevasse did his body ap-proach, till at last I saw it go over the brink and pass out of sight. Never shall I forget my feeling of horror as I stood, spell-bound, watching my friend's body approaching that fearful crevasse. I felt morally certain that when he disappeared from view his body lay a mangled corpse at the bottom of it. At first horror at his fate crowded all thought of self out of my mind; but with the re-action that followed came the thought, or self-asked question, "Can you pass with safety the fatal spot where your friend fell, or will you, too, fall and speed helplessly to and into that insatiable crevasse?" Taking my friend's alpenstock, from an inex-plicable feeling that I ought to do so—for it certainly was going to in-commode me rather than be of any benefit—I began to descend slowly and cautiously. After descending about 100 yards I stopped to rest, and to watch with a strange sort of fascination that crevasse. And now oc-curred one of the deceptions of the mountain. About 200 yards below the crevasse in which my companion had disappeared, on another com-paratively level stretch of snow, I saw the figure of a small man. At first he was standing still, but, as I watched him, he began to walk, and seemed coming in my direction. I could plainly see the swinging of his arms and the motion of his legs. "Could it be possible," I thought, "that my friend is not dead after all; that he had miraculously escaped, and found some hidden passage from the crevasse to that level stretch of snow below it?" But, as I studied this figure from successive resting-places, I found that it did not make any real progress in my direction, and later I discovered that it was a point of rock sticking out of the snow, and not unlike a man in shape. The summer heat playing around it had given it apparent motion, and my imagination had further aided the deception by giving it arms and legs, and therefore a more perfect resemblance to a man. I could relate other instances (if this paper were not already so long) of this sort of mirage or mountain deception in my experience. At last I reached the crevasse, but some distance to the left of the point where my friend had disappeared over its edge. This was owing to the oblique line of my descent to avoid the danger of a fall which would have been more likely to happen in a direct descent of the steep, icy slope. Approaching the edge of the crevasse, I called my friend loudly by name, but with no hope of getting any reply. To my great surprise, and no less joy, I got a feeble answer from him, and almost underneath where I stood. To my eager questions he replied that his fall had been a fearful one, but that he had escaped with some broken ribs and some bruises of the body. His body had struck the opposite side of the crevasse over 20 feet in width, and then dropped to a shelf of ice on the wall of the crevasse at least 60 feet down in it. When my friend recovered consciousness he found himself lying on this shelf or ledge of ice, and he noticed that it slanted gradually toward the mouth of the crevasse. He had dragged himself up this ledge, and this accounted for his being so nearly under the point where I stood on the edge of the crevasse when I shouted his name. Passing around the end of the crevasse, still considerably to the left, I got over to the side on which the ledge was and directly over the place where he was standing. Letting one end of the rope down to him, I managed to helphim out and over some huge blocks of ice that lay between the end of the crevasse and the line of descent to our 11,000-foot camp. My companion when he fell was carrying his coat slung over one shoulder, and I think when his body struck the ledge of ice upon which he lodged, this coat broke the force of the blow, and probably was the means of saving his life. When he emerged from the crevasse, my companion was as pale as a sheet and suffering great pain, but with great pluck and endurance, made the long and toilsome tramp to camp. We used the rope in descending the remaining dangerous slopes.

Owing to Bayley's condition necessitating cautious traveling, to the large number of crevasses to be crossed, to the still larger number to be wound around or circumvented, and to the additional fact that I was carrying both packs now, our progress toward the 11,000-foot camp was slow and tedious, and it was nearly sundown when we reached it. The next morning (23d) the steep snow-field down which we had to journey was hard and slippery and my companion did not dare to travel over it till the sun had softened the surface of the snow—for a fall now would be very disastrous to him. The sun did not soften the snow till nearly noon. We now started again, after throwing out of the packs everything not absolutely needed. So slowly did we have to travel that not till nearly sundown did we step off the glacier which we first crossed in beginning the ascent. Just before we left the glacier clouds began to roll up from the south, and when we reached *terra firma* again we were in a thick, driving mist, or, rather, we were enveloped in the clouds. Soon every rock, bush and tree a dozen feet away vanished from sight as completely as though they never had existed, and the wind began blowing hard from the south. It now became apparent to us that we could not find our way to permanent camp in that obscuring mist before night set in, so we decided to camp again on the mountain side. Finding as suitable a place for our camp as I could, I laid in a supply of wood, and after our frugal meal improvised a tent with our alpenstocks, rope and one of our double blankets. The wind kept increasing during the night, and shook our tent fearfully, and often I got up and out to put an additional bowlder on the end of the blanket, to keep it from blowing away. It did not rain or snow, as we feared it would, but in the morning the obscuring mist or clouds remained. We waited till late in the forenoon for it to clear off, and then, despairing of it, we started for our permanent camp. In descending the spur of the mountain, up which we took the pack-horse on the 20th, we several times lost our course in the blinding fog, and when we finally reached our long-sought tent it was late in the afternoon. The first thing done was to make my companion a comfortable bed; the next was to look after the horses, and finally to get supper—for we were hungry as wolves. And now I found our picketed pony in a sad plight. She had evidently, soon after we left on the 20th, caught her lariat in a small bush which had escaped my notice as being within reach of her tether, and had gone round and round it till her nose almost touched the bush, and there she had been held a prisoner, without food or water, and had been the helpless prey of myriads of flies and mosquitoes during the heat of the day for two days or more. Nearly the whole of her body was covered with sores or crusted with blood, where numerous horseflies had been feasting on her. I had to give her water in small quantities, to prevent her killing herself with over-drinking in her water-famished condition. Then a prospecting tour of the neighboring parks developed the comforting fact that we were in all probability minus one pony and the pack-horse—for they were nowhere to be seen. That night my eyes began to pain me, and the next morning when the sun was shining (for the clouds had cleared away without giving the threatened storm), it was with difficulty that I could use them, and I became aware of the fact that I was having a touch at least of "snow-blind." As soon as I

could, on the morning of the 25th, I started out on a final search for the
lost animals. Nowhere in the mountain meadows could I find the missing pony, but I came upon Oneonta more than a mile from camp. As I
approached him, with a small pan of tempting oats in my hand, he
watched me with a strange and suspicious eye, and whenever I tried to
get near enough to lay my hand on him he bounded away with a snort.
Round and round I followed him, calling, coaxing and wheedling, but
all in vain. Once, when I made a dive to catch him around the neck, he
jumped away, kicked up his heels, and disappeared over a neighboring
ridge. I was puzzled, nonplussed. Here was a horse disowning me, utterly repudiating me, when always hitherto, from his colthood up, I
could catch him anywhere and at any time; whom I had frequently had
at the mountain before; to whom I had always before gone up and
caught in the mountain parks, even out of a band of horses; who many a
time came into camp and poked his head into my tent to be petted and
to have the flies rubbed off him. And now, in the sorest need of myself
and friend, he "went back on me." I could only account for it on one of
two hypotheses. Either he did not recognize me with my red, swollen,
peeled and sunburned face and purblind eyes, to say nothing of my
clumsy gait, on account of tender feet from freezing on the mountain-
top, or he believed that if he allowed himself to be caught, my companion and I would insist, this time, upon his packing our bundles clear
to the top of Tahoma. I went back to camp in no amiable frame of mind
—for I very well knew that this whim of Oneonta and the disap-
pearance of the other pony would necessitate the abandonment of our
tent and provisions for the present, and a journey on foot, for me, to the
settlement. When I got back to camp I informed my companion of the
state of affairs, and we at once prepared to start for my friend
J. B. Kernahan's, in the Succotash Valley, 15 miles distant. The pony
(Nellie) was saddled, my companion was helped to mount her, and we
moved off slowly—for the pony was anything but strong after her long
fast, and my companion, in his condition, could not stand much jolt-
ing. We arrived at Palisade Farm late at night. The last 3 miles of the
journey were traveled in such utter darkness that my companion could
not see the road nor even the head of the pony he was riding, yet she
carried him safely over the mountain road and never stumbled once.
We received a hospitable welcome at Palisade Farm. My companion's
broken ribs were set and skillfully bandaged, and the disabled mountaineer was kindly and carefully nursed back to health. During the several days that I spent at Palisade Farm to recruit, our missing horses,

tent and provisions were brought in by a party which we sent out for them. After 8 days' sojourn at Palisade Farm, Mr. Bayley returned to Yelm, our starting-point, where I had preceded him. Thus ended our finally successful, but almost tragical, ascent of the North Peak of Tahoma.[1]

YELM, WASH., March 26, 1894.

NOTE

1. "While the final proof of this article was being read at the foot of Mt. Tamalpais on the afternoon of April 30th, Geo. B. Bayley was caught by the ascending elevator, at his place of business in San Francisco, and instantly killed." HB.

# 14

# Olin Wheeler*
# 1894

Though the previous chapters have demonstrated a variety of writing styles—
from innocent boyishness to military austerity, none of those could fully prepare you for Olin Wheeler. Brace yourself for the full gale force of florid late-
Victorian travel writing. This is truly a period piece, written as much to promote travel as to tell the story.

Wheeler was a well-educated man who had done many kinds of work in
business and government, but he is now remembered, when remembered at
all, for his promotional writing on behalf of the Northern Pacific Railroad.
Working out of St. Paul, he wrote the *Wonderland* travel guides for that line, including the one in which the following account appears. Several of the earlier
writers were openly enthusiastic about the possibilities for tourist development
of the mountain, but as far as I know none of them were being paid for their enthusiasm, at least not so directly as Wheeler was.

Yet, I wanted Wheeler in this book. His account, and his style of telling the
tale, were common currency among travel writers of the day. Though I
couldn't imagine wading through a whole book of this kind of stuff, I think it's
interesting to become acquainted with it. After a few opening paragraphs that
sound as if writing them was almost a religious experience for him, Wheeler
does settle down into something like normal narrative. He is effusive, yes, he is
overwrought, yes, but he is also quite descriptive, sometimes more so than his
predecessors in this book. Wheeler, like Van Trump and Fuller, was influ-
encing the way America perceived the mountain. His influence may have been
the broadest of all.

The following is not Wheeler's full account, however. In order to keep the
excerpts readable, I've removed a brief history of earlier ascents, as well as ex-
traneous matter not related to Mount Rainier and some shorter sections on life
in camp. What is left is the heart of his story of the climb.

*Reprinted from Olin Wheeler, "Mount Rainier. Its Ascent by a Northern Pacific Party,"
Wonderland (1895):52–103.

Thou lord of mountains, majesty of majesties, peak of peaks, the pride of every true American; thou who in thine long, glistening robe, woven by the winds of the ocean from the mists of the night, standest in thy might and grandeur, touched by the calm waters of our western sound, with brow laved by the gentle dews of heaven, and vision reaching out across Pacific's heaving bosom toward the Orient, to thee would I pay my tribute.

Grant, I beseech thee, oh! hoary monarch, that the remembrance of my wanderings in Paradise; the Camp among the Clouds; the sound of thy waterfalls; the flowery banks amid the snow; the thunderings of the avalanche; the frowning cliffs of Gibraltar; the tramping over thy snowy fields; the swift slide down the snow-cliffs; the stand upon thy topmost point in cloudland, where one felt as if in communion with the Almighty God himself, ruler of heaven and earth, of mountain and vale, of torrent and rock, of man and nature; grant, I entreat thee, that of these may come an inspiration that will enable the brain that directs the hand that holds the pen, to, in a measure, depict for others who would know more of thy great presence, some of thy glories and attributes.

In the midst of a swelling maze of noble mountains thou rearest thy tri-crested form. Not as do many, from a mountain plain itself thousands of feet in midair, but from the level of old ocean itself. Straight aloft thy dome-like, spectral shape stretches toward heaven the full measure of the more than 14,000 feet which compasses thy stature. About thee, regal too in their ample proportions, rise thy fellows, also attired in their garments of white. High as they reach toward the azure vault, endowed as they are with dignity and grandeur, none of them, oh! greatest of all, nor Adams, nor Baker, nor St. Helens; nor yet Hood, most graceful and symmetric of them; none of them approaches thee, the highest and mightiest of mountain chiefs. Supreme, omnipotent of thy kind, thou standest. Mountain and valley, river and glacier, sea and forest, the fowl of the air, the beast of the field, the creeping thing of earth, and greater than all, man himself, made in the image of the Almighty, make their obeisance to thee, and acknowledge thine exalted character.

And as for a time we do thee homage, let it be that in studying thee, we study Him who made thee, the great I Am, at whose will the mountains are brought forth, the valleys are clothed, the rivers are poured out, and man himself created.

In the summer of 1894 the North Pacific Railroad, believing that the time had come when this peerless mountain should be more prominently brought to the attention of tourists, geological and glacial investigators, and students of universities and colleges, given to summer scientific excursions, authorized the writer to organize a party for the ascent of the mountain. This was done and the party left Tacoma the evening of July 31st, returning thereto, after successfully accomplishing its purpose, August 13th. The party consisted of Henry M. Sarvent, a young civil engineer, of Tacoma, as guide; Dr. Lyman B. Sperry of Bellevue, Ohio, an educator and lecturer; Ross Comstock of Elbe, Wash., general assistant; George M. Weister of Portland, Ore., as photographer; and the writer.

## OFF FOR THE MOUNTAIN

### TACOMA TO LONGMIRE'S SPRINGS.

On Tuesday evening, July 31st, we took the street-car on Lower Pacific Avenue, Tacoma, that connects with the steam motor line for Lake Park.

Leaving Lake Park the following morning, the road wound for a few miles through the park region heretofore mentioned that lies at the base of the range. The grass was cured and of a yellow brown, and the green, shapely evergreens, standing now in family groups, again in rows, or perchance singly, furnished some beautiful little pictures of parkland. Nature can surpass noblemen in laying out fine parks.

And now the road climbs the eternal hills that gradually lead up to the big mountain itself. In pushing in among the mountains, we plunge into the depths of the massive forest. Left behind the softer touches of the open country, the bright evergreens, the hard, level prairie. Before us, for mile after mile, broken only by a few clearings and ranches, are the cool arcades of the wilderness, whose mighty cedars, firs, and occasional hemlocks and pines of the coniferous family, stretch their giant trunks 100, 150, aye, even 200 feet heavenward. Mingled with these old rustlers of the centuries, almost indeed under their protecting branches, in the less heavily timbered spots, are the ashes and maples, the alders and poplars and box-elders, etc., of the deciduous sort. Small, slender, and lithesome, they gracefully bend to the murmuring breezes that gently creep through the aisles of the mightier forest. Up hill and down, along slight grades and o'er level pieces of road, across small water-courses, by oozing springs, but ever through the grand growth of trees, we ride or walk as inclination prompts, and learn new lessons of God's goodness and Nature's manifold greatness.

Long after the sun has passed its meridian, we reach Eatonville, a little hamlet of a half-dozen houses.

Between Eatonville and Elbe, our stopping-place for the second night, the forest grew denser and more interesting. It was not only a novelty, but a delightful pleasure to slowly thread the narrow road cut through the very heart of this timberland. Between Eatonville and Longmire's Springs it stretches in unbroken continuity, a "forest primeval" indeed. 'Tis true there are little clearings where some hardy settler has bravely attacked the mighty giants, and with fire and axe beaten them back, but they form a high cordon about and hem him in and again sweep onward.

At Elbe we obtain another satisfactory meal, then arrange our beds and lie down for a good night's rest. We here reach the Nesqually River, fresh from the glaciers, and feel that we are drawing near our goal.

Reader, have you ever seen a glacial river, a river of water flowing from a river of ice? If not, you have something to see that will interest you, and if you are of an observant nature, you will experience emotions and sensations of an unusual sort.

Well, did you ever see a river of milk? No? This can hardly be called that, it is true, but it is of a drab color that makes you think of dirty milk. This is characteristic of glacial rivers, the sediment being of such a character as to impart this somewhat milky hue to the waters.

Let me state another peculiarity of this and other glacial streams. During the day the sun of course causes the glacier to melt. Millions of tiny streams thus go coursing over the surface of the ice, and the heat naturally causes the quantity of water running from the glacier to be much greater in daytime than at night. Now, this causes a complete reversal of this state of affairs farther down stream.

Elbe is just far enough down stream to illustrate this. During the night the stream here rises, and in the morning we found it considerably higher than the previous evening. That is to say, the distance between the mouth of the glacier and Elbe is such that the higher water of the daytime, *at the mouth of the glacier*, flows past the latter place each succeeding night, and the low water of the night *at the glacier* is found at Elbe during the day.

*Views of Paradise River and Glacier, and Sluiskin Falls. From Olin Wheeler's* Mount Rainier: Its Ascent by a Northern Pacific Party.

We now follow the course of the Nesqually River, the road keeping to the right bank. This day in the woods is replete with surprise.

Vegetation is luxuriant, especially so in spots. The trees have large quantities of moss on them. This is of two kinds. A pale, pea-green, stringy kind, dry and like corn-silk in its nature, is the more uncommon species. It is found in quite long masses, and ofttimes hangs from the limbs in great quantities. Another sort is the common moss, and of a darker green than the former. It clings to the dead and decaying trees, and invests many of them with most grotesque forms. It is no uncommon sight to see the dead trunks and limbs of a tree entirely enveloped in this covering, and the appearance is striking in the extreme.

Here we stumble upon a strange freak of nature. A monster tree rising high overhead and as straight as an arrow, has clutched in its massive roots, and *above the ground*, an old log. It stands astride the log with the roots sinking deep into the ground upon each side.

What is the explanation? Another phenomenon met with, perhaps, at the same locality, may suggest the philosophy of it. Glance at that old decayed stump, ten or twenty feet high. Dead, it yet bears aloft a young forest of its own. One tree as tall as the stump itself sways gracefully in the slight breeze that kisses it. The entire surface of the top of the ancient monarch is covered with a heavy growth of foliage—smaller trees. Possibly a chance seed took root on the old log as on yon stump, and waxing strong, its roots followed around the sides of the log in their search for mother earth.

Devil's clubs, a species of plant that grows high, with thick stems and large leaves the size of a palm-leaf fan, are a feature of the vegetation. They bear long spines that penetrate the flesh and inflict much pain upon the unwary.

The evening found our road journey ended by arrival at Longmire's.

Here one can drink a pure, unadulterated soda water. Not the snapping, fizzing, artificial stuff of the soda fountain, but such as God Almighty provides for his children in Nature's own laboratory. It comes, not through a metal worm, artificially cooled by ice, but, fresh and pure from its reservoir in the bowels of the earth, it filters upward, and sparkling and bright bursts forth into the sunlight, a cooling and delicious beverage. It is not all cool either. Some of it is lukewarm, yet pleasant to the taste. These warmer waters are used for the baths, and the writer's experience in them is an agreeable recollection.

*Early view of Longmire Hotel and springs development. (Courtesy National Park Service)*

### LONGMIRE'S TO PARADISE PARK.

From Longmire's into Paradise Park the road is succeeded by a mountain trail. This is usually traversed afoot, because a good part of it is a switch-back or zigzag up a steep mountain slope. It can be, and often is, traveled on horseback. The distance from the springs to the usual camping spots in the park is between six and seven miles, and the difference in elevation about 3,000 feet.

Leaving the springs the trail strikes directly into the timber. For the first three miles or more, to the crossing of the Nesqually, it is an easy and pleasant one. The foliage, as heretofore, is interesting, the huge trees garlanded with festoons of moss being still a conspicuous feature.

The route is along the north bank of the Nesqually, in a deep gorge in the mountains, at least partially cut by the rapid stream. Across from it rises a wild, craggy range, the Tatoisch. The western end of it, Eagle Peak, a splendid sharp rock, juts heavenward to a dizzy height. When the Nesqually is reached, a wonderful scene is presented. To one who has never before seen such an one—and one may see hundreds of mountain torrents and *not* see such as this—there is a great unfolding of the prodigious power of such a stream.

The width of the river proper is only fifty feet or such a matter, but the width of the stream bed, where at one time or another the torrent has torn along, is all of an eighth of a mile across. At the extreme western side of it—the hither side—a very small part of the river now flows, but the stream proper, 99 per cent of it, is at the other side of the channel, hugging closely the base of the mountain.

The middle of this channel or river bed reached, one gazes about him in silent astonishment. He has often heard and read of the almost unmeasurable power of water. I never before, felt so forcibly the utter inadequacy of language to describe, to convey to the reader correct and actual impressions—ideas that really carried with them some sense of the actual conditions, or facts described—as I did here.

We were in the midst of a perfect sea of boulders, or shingle. Of all sizes, too—large and heavy, requiring a derrick to lift one, down to a small, round stone, easily hurled from where we stood to either shore. As far as the eye could reach this boulder-plain extended, white and beautifully clean from the scouring action of the water.

But it was not the vast area of this formation, nor even its glaring appearance, that caused one to marvel. *It was the manner in which the boulders were placed and laid.* They were not in beds, comparatively level, except here and there. They were in piles, embankments, knolls, natural cairns. They were tumultuously heaped and piled in all directions. The entire mass was one immense system of hillocks and hollows, banks and gullies, small hills and valleys.

At first I was dazed, and then, as I gradually grasped the idea, observing the same phenomena all about me, the feeling changed to one of wonder and admiration. The meaning of it was as plainly expressed as the printed page expresses the thought of the writer. Here God Almighty was the author; this rocky bed was the page upon which was expressed his meaning, and the Nesqually Glacier and Nesqually River were the agencies through which the work was wrought. If you doubt this, come with me to the verge of the river. How many miles an hour do you suppose it is tearing along? Twelve or fifteen, or even more. Man would breast its mad current at the risk of his life, and a horse does it certainly at the risk of limb, if not of life.

And listen! No, you don't *have* to listen. That sound you hear you have heard ever since leaving Longmire's, whenever you drew anywhere near the river. If you had no idea then what caused it, you know now. Dull, heavy, hollow, like muttered thunder, a sound is heard up and down the river, louder than the roar of the torrent as it dashes along in great waves, that curl and break back in angry spray. Do you need to ask what it is? Do not these millions of rocks all about you suggest the answer, even before the question is fairly shaped in your mind? It is the fearful current forcing along over its bouldered bottom other and heavy boulders, and they go pounding and knocking along against each other.

The carving power of water upon land; its ability to fashion valleys, plow through mountains, cut down cañons, and to modify and diversify the topography of a region, borrows a new meaning, takes on a new significance as you see what it has done over this boulder-strewn river bed.

Over the crude affair of a bridge that has been thrown across the raging current, we trudge, and then comes the climb up the mountain. At the summit of the switchback we reach the first snow, and thenceforth the trail leads over snow-plains. The afternoon sun has softened it to such a degree that travel is difficult, and our alpenstocks save us from many slips and falls.

Soon we obtain a glimpse of our tent pitched on an eminence some distance ahead and much higher than we are. We hasten forward, and about 4 P.M. reach our permanent camp.

#### PARADISE PARK.

The place thus designated includes, in a general way, all the country between the Nesqually and Cowlitz glaciers on the south side of the mountain, being overlooked by the magnificent range of the Tatoisch on the south. Its longest side—east and west—at the base of the Tatoisch, is perhaps eight miles, and its length north and south on a medial line between the two glaciers, not more than five miles. The region is more generally called, at the present time, Paradise Valley, but this is a most unfortunate name and entirely inappropriate.

It may, however, very suitably be applied to the small valley of the stream that flows from Sluiskin Falls at the base of Paradise Glacier, and winds to its junction with the Nesqually, and which is itself an important and beautiful feature of the greater park. Indeed the stream is known as Paradise River, and by the more thoughtful and discriminating this lovely valley is also called by this name.

The Park is a wild, romantic place. Rivers and brooks dash headlong down the cañons; mountains of striking character hem it in; plains of snow, seemingly illimitable, plunge into cañons over cliffs of ice and snow; waterfalls whose cadences continually sound in the ears, leap from the cliffs in tangled cascades of spray; ridges and hills crowned with evergreens rise at various points. Lakes are recessed in the mountains; glaciers fill the gorges; park spots, ideal camping places, alternate with cedar, fir, and hemlock groves. In nooks and hollows, creeping over the slopes, on the rocks, at the edges of the receding snow, are myriads of wild flowers. The region is rough and broken, but not to such a degree as to prohibit climbing and roaming about. Men and women, boys and girls, will find innumerable excursions to occupy their time, and most of them can be made either afoot or on horseback.

Our camp was established at what is known in the history of the mountain as Camp of the Clouds.

The elevation of this knoll is given as 5,360 feet above sea-level, and considering its comparatively low altitude, the first thought that presents itself is, why is a name that savors of cloudland given to a spot so low down? I confess that at first this was a poser, and I ascribed it to an exuberant fancy. Not so, however. It must be remembered that the locality is on the seaward side of a range of mountains that obstructs the free passage eastward of the moist winds from the Pacific, and thus causes great condensation, or clouds. For days at a time this whole park will be so thickly filled with clouds that objects fifty yards distant will be invisible. While the name thus fits this particular spot much of the time, it would apply equally as well to many other places in Paradise Park.

Camp of the Clouds is a small, narrow ridge or tongue of land that extends from a larger and higher ridge, toward the south. It is on the edge of the western slope of Paradise Valley. Of the many grand views from the spot, the most beautiful is that of Sluiskin Falls in its curvilinear leap into the valley that then, with its swirling river, winds first, westward toward us, then bends to the south, and then again to the west, out of sight down among the frowning, timbered slopes of that magnificent Tatoisch Range, seen from here in all its glory.

The higher ridge back of us lies deeply buried under the snow. The slopes upon both sides of us are slopes of snow, spreading out from the snowy ridge behind. Our knoll is a little island rising out of the snow. The water that we use in cooking, for "the toilet," that we drink,

trickles from the snow above, and is caught during the day in holes dug
in the ground. The snow is omnipresent. Look where you will, it is before you. Turn to the north. You see it in the vast, rolling, white plains
that sweep back for miles to the base of Gibraltar and are merged in the
Nesqually Glacier, that rolls up, up, up, until it is lost in the great
white sheet holding the old peak in its icy embrace. Look to the west.
There again, in isolated patches, small in comparison with the large
fields behind us, but large enough when your trail at noonday leads
across their slushy surfaces; there you see them, beautifully contrasted
against the groves of evergreens that rise above them. Now turn your
eye to that Tatoisch Range again. Did you ever see anything finer than
the way those deeply gored flanks are splashed by God's ermine, that
fills the cañons, gorges, hollows, and dares to push up even to the very
pinnacles themselves, where it lies cold, and white, and still?

Glance down into Paradise Valley, and then back at those glorious
cliffs that form that tremendous amphitheater at its head. How white
the latter are as they sweep around the curve, and as you look down
into the valley you wonder where the river is. I will tell you. It flows
down there in the bottom under the ice and snow. At intervals you can
see it, and afar down the valley you can discern that it at last breaks free
from the ice tunnel. From the foot of Sluiskin Falls, for a mile or more,
it is hidden entirely by this universal white blanket.

An odd sight is seen on the eastern slopes of Paradise Valley, and on
the flanks of the Tatoisch Range. The inequalities of surface, with the
dark ridges, knolls, and higher elevations, set against the hollows and
cañons filled with snow, work out strange and even grotesque figures.

At one place a comic valentine sort of Irish Biddy is viciously biting
an animal in front of her, that, doubled up in pain is trying to escape.
An old hen flying; a woman with closely-clinging skirts dancing a clog
dance; a double-humped camel patiently standing; a monstrous negro's
foot standing out in the snow in bold relief, are some of the crude figures seen close at hand.

The Tatoisch flanks are very acute and high, and there the snow and
rocks form large, wide fields of irregular shapes, rather than profiles of
animals and humans. Long, slender, attenuated snow-banks stretch
from the base well up to the very tips of some of the craggy peaks.

MOUNT RAINIER FROM CAMP OF THE CLOUDS.

From this point, turn in whatever direction you will, the eye is regaled by a sight new and uncommon. The particular one that trans-
cends all others, the one to which you turn time and again in silence
and wonder, never surfeited, never satisfied even, is that of the mountain itself.

As I write, I am 2,000 miles distant from it, and yet it rises before me
in all the calm grandeur, the noble dignity, the spacious amplitude, the
mighty elevation, that it did when I stood and contemplated its enormous bulk, as it lifted itself, rocks, ice, and snow, nearly 9,000 feet
above me.

It is difficult to describe a sight such as this, so as to really convey
any idea of the real object to the reader. It is difficult to write of it with
any sense of satisfaction to one's self. Only a small part of the whole
mountain is visible, large as is that which we do see. It is between three
and four miles from Camp of the Clouds to Crater Peak, the highest
point, horizontally, and this part of the mountain and all north, west,
and east of it, is entirely cut off from view.

Peak Success, the farthest point to the west, stands out in all its alpine and whitened glory, and Gibraltar Rock, the flaming beacon that
springs from the Cowlitz Glacier below, is a fitting termination of the
mountain to the eastward.

From the apex of Peak Success, the general slope at the top is eastward, the lowest point being reached at the western limit of Gibraltar.
From this peak, there extends down nearly to Longmire's Springs a
long, rocky ridge, heretofore described, and the one which Kautz
climbed. At the springs we faced the comb of this ridge; here we see
it in profile. Its drop from the peak is rapid, and as now seen a very
rough one.

The slope of the mountain toward us is sharp, abrupt, and it is thousands of feet long. In the vicinity of Gibraltar the character changes.
The flanks drop away more and more acutely, until they become a
sheer precipice of ice and snow, save for a small tongue or strip that
hugs Gibraltar itself, and affords the line of ascent to the summit of
Crater Peak.

This region of ice precipices is the head of the Nesqually Glacier,
and whether studied at close range or viewed from afar it rivets attention. Here the glacier is practically a wild, tumbling, frozen cascade,

or, more truthfully, a congealed cataract. It is warped and broken and twisted. Cracked, fissured, and rent in all directions, it goes tumbling down, a confused mass of heterogeneous shapes and blocks. Fragments of ice are strewn in chaotic confusion over a slope of hardened snow and ice. Large crevasses yawn across the glacier; ragged cliffs of bluish-green ice hang from it; deep cañons are cut into it. Enormous blocks of ice, some angular and jagged and pitched into inconceivable positions, are lodged far down the face of the frozen stream, broken from the impending heights above, and hurled by the inexorable law of gravitation thousands of feet down the mountain. It is a wild, dangerous spot, one that no man in his senses would dare undertake to cross. At intervals during both day and night the thunders of the avalanche are heard, and the cloud of snow that masks its grosser character can be seen rushing down the declivity, sure death to one caught in its mad career.

## THE PUSH FOR THE SUMMIT.

### CAMP OF THE CLOUDS TO THE COWLITZ CLEAVER.

In maturing our plans we had decided to make the great climb on the Tuesday following our arrival.

Sunday and Monday we were held fast in camp by the prevalence of masses of vapor that effectually hid every semblance of valley or mountain. On Monday morning it was thought wise for Sarvent to carry one of the larger packs up to Gibraltar that day, so that the burdens on the morrow might be lessened. Sarvent left us about 10 o'clock A.M. and was soon lost in the mist. At dark he returned, and reported having gotten above the clouds at about 8,000 feet. From thence the atmosphere was bright and warm.

When daylight appeared the following morning, it was seen that heavy, damp clouds still enveloped us. But as we knew that "above the clouds the sun was shining," it rather added to our anticipation to feel that, while we would not, like Joe Hooker at Lookout Mountain, be fighting above the clouds, we would be climbing through and then above them, and have thus a double experience to look back upon. And

*Preceding pages: Views around Mount Rainier, including Gibraltar Rock, the summit, Longmire Hotel and springs. From Olin Wheeler's* Mount Rainier: Its Ascent by a Northern Pacific Party.

that is exactly what happened. For about 3,000 feet we trudged upward, surrounded by curtains of mist that refused to dissipate.

We left Camp of the Clouds at 10 o'clock A.M., the party now increased to seven. As became his position as guide, Sarvent took the advance, and the others strung out behind, following largely in his tracks. Each man had a pack on his back. These were made up of provisions and blankets, with some extra clothing, and were encased in canvas knapsacks made for the purpose, and having arm-straps. We were of course warmly clad. The soles and heels of our shoes had sharp spikes about half an inch long driven into them, covering the surface of the bottom of the shoe, and affording secure footing on the ice. The glare of the sun on snow and ice was trifling throughout the climb, and none of us smeared our faces with charcoal and vaseline, as is customary, or used goggles, and we returned comparatively little sunburned and with no cracked and bleeding lips. Our noses suffered the most, and these were burned so that the usual process of exfoliation was undergone.

The alpenstock was an important part of our outfit. These were of strong, tough wood, with iron or steel spikes at the bottom end. Two hundred feet of the very best window-sash cord completed our special outfit for the ascent, save an aneroid barometer I carried, not for its actual value, but for its relative value in the elevations we might note.

We started with the best wishes of our friends left behind, and climbed the snow-hill above camp, from which we soon descended to a snow-field that led to a steep, rocky hill and ridge. This we attacked in a sidelong fashion, climbing now a little way on snow, then on the ground, and again among rocks. For some time this was our course, and our route alternated between snow-plains and rocky ground. The snow was wet and soft, and on this account the rocks, which were usually not massive, made much the better footing. Fortunately we all proved to be in good climbing condition and no one lagged behind. We thus made good progress, but halted frequently for short intervals of rest and to blow. About a mile from our starting point and several hundred feet above it, we mount the last ridge and now strike out over a wide, whitened plain of snow. Here, too, at about 6,000 feet above the sea, the timber line is reached and left behind. After a long pull, at 12.45 P.M. we reach a lava ridge thrust up in a bald, jagged way through the snow. Through the clouds we have heard the tinkling of a stream we could not see. When we reach it we find it proceeds from the melting snow, and is very small. As it drops from rock to rock the sound at this elevation, and on these ringing volcanic rocks, is clear and musical.

We are hungry, and the first hours of climbing in the morning are always the hardest, so we cast our packs upon the rocks and by the side of the tiny brook and to its musical drip, drip, drip, eat our cold lunch. Our elevation is about 8,000 feet, and we are still in cloudland. The atmosphere is damp, and misting heavily. Soon the mist changes to fine, granular snow-flakes, and these again into pellets of hail. All this within the space of a few minutes. The sun begins to make an impression, however, on the aqueous vapor. The stratum of clouds grows thinner and they drift about in a spirit of unrest. Through the occasional rifts we see the strata below us banked in magnificent masses of cumuli.

And the Tatoisch! Will the memory of that black and white, startling, turreted range and its varying appearance ever fade? Never tame, never dull, never seen twice alike, from wherever man's eyes beheld it, it dared him, as it rose before him, mighty, gigantic, abrupt, cragged, and snow-slashed, to find adjectives to fitly characterize it. Now, conjoined with the fleecy battalions hurled in precipitate flight from Rainier's brow far down the slopes, it took on a new and glorified light.

In prodigious masses of thick white and gray, the aqueous particles crowded against the foot of the range. Far to the west, away down the valley and the lower Tatoisch, the great banks of floating water push their way. Not content with this, they rolled up the slopes, crowding into every cañon, impinging upon every bluff, encircling every crag. Here and there a black, rocky precipice protruded its angry nose through the white blanket, and a great tongue of snow would gleam faintly through the mist covering, *so* faintly that it was impossible to discern where snow faded into cloud.

As the vapors were wafted higher they stretched to the east among the cliffs, cañons, and continuing range that succeeded the Tatoisch. Completely as the clouds covered the scene, their dominion was not universal. A high range is the Tatoisch. And as high as the clouds reached, the crags reached higher. Thrusting their bare, jagged points up through the mantle of vapor, ruthlessly piercing its filmy folds, the magnificent obelisks of the range rose triumphant, and one could almost expect to hear wafted from them, across the intervening space to the great peak that rose behind us, the shout of the victor.

One can go from the Camp of the Clouds to the Cowlitz Cleaver without putting foot to the ground. There really extends down from the Cleaver a field of snow of enormous extent that comprises plains, cliffs, and precipices. Dotting this extended field are islands, usually of bare lava, in a few cases at the lower extremity, scantily clothed with trees and verdure. These islands appear to be points of ridges punched through the snow, and are for the most part decidedly sharp, and composed of small lava rocks. The lavas found here are most interesting in appearance. They are of different colors, some of a pink or reddish-pink, some of them drab, and then a lot of it black or brown. Pieces of it seemed to have flaked off from larger masses; others were exquisitely banded, and still other pieces were polished almost as finely as if from a lapidary's lathe.

In our ascent thus far we had made use of most of these rock oases or islands that came in our way, but we at last reached a point where there were none. In all directions nothing, save snow, snow.

The snow that falls on the higher parts of a mountain undergoes a double change before it becomes a glacier proper. Professor Geike says: "The snow in the higher regions is loose and granular. As it moves downward it becomes firmer, passing into the condition of *nevé*, or *firn*. Gradually as the separate granules are pressed together and the air is squeezed out, the mass assumes the character of blue, compact, crystalline ice."

Our route now led over and across an ascending plain of *nevé* ice that seemed limitless. It reached from the Nesqually Glacier on the west to the Cowlitz on the east. It was nearly the middle of the afternoon when we started out upon it, and it was evening when we reached the foot of the Cleaver, and we toiled steadily on all the time, with short halts to get our wind. The surface of this *nevé* plain was that of a choppy sea. It was cut up into small concavities or hollows, from two to five feet in diameter, that made trailing over it hard work. This we found especially the case on the return descent. A peculiarity of this particular *nevé* ield was the fact that our vision was so circumscribed that we appeared to make no progress. There was ever just ahead of us a rounded white brow that neither advanced nor retreated, but remained just the same. It was at times a little discouraging not to be able to see anything but that cold round line extending to right and left as far as one could see.

Pushing out from Gibraltar Rock, and nearly at right angles to it in a south-southeast direction, runs a sharp knife-like ridge, wide at the base, generally narrow, sometimes a knife-edge at the top. It rises hundreds and hundreds of feet above the ice plain below; is on one side, for much of the distance, an absolute precipice, and on the other side but a degree or two removed from it. This immense wedge drives straight out between the heads of the Cowlitz and Nesqually glaciers, cleaves its way between, hence the name, Cowlitz Cleaver. Up this rocky wedge we needs must go, and away we start, anxious to see the end of our day's work.

For a little way we travel on the ice-snow, now quite hard and slippery, but its irregularities cause us to seek the rocks. It is necessary to use both hands and feet. At first the trail leads over steep, crumbling ground and around large rocks, and we slide back every other step nearly as much as we work ahead. When we reach the more rocky ground everybody is well tired out. While the rocks now afford more substantial foothold, the steps are long, and the rocks sometimes roll or slide. We work upward, though slowly, climbing among sharp angular slabs, about rough rocky points, now edging to one side, now to the other, of the ridge. As we rise the view is a superb one, and we almost forget our fatigues. But in climbing the Cleaver one must watch his steps closely or he may rue it, so that the view must remain for a time a secondary consideration. Finally, twisting among great rocks on the side that looks straight down upon the Nesqually Glacier, and carefully working around a rock of the centuries that rises high above us, and where a fall means sure destruction, we come to a little widening of the ridge, where it is protected from the wind, and our day's work is done. We are several hundred feet below where we intended to bivouac, but it is 7 o'clock, night is coming on rapidly, and so we throw our packs on the rocks, while Sarvent hastens up to the Gibraltar Camp for our provisions, left there the day before.

We all needed rest, and we sat on the rocks for a time and took it, and compared notes. Our cold supper was not long in being eaten, for strange to state, none of us seemed very hungry. Then we arranged our sleeping places. By the side of a protecting slab of lava we found a level spot about six feet wide and eight feet long, upon which four of our party made their blanket beds.

We were in a little cove formed by rocks on one side, an ice-wall on the other. At a point where the ice came in contact with a large rock there was a good-sized hole or cave. The remainder of the party conceived the idea of enlarging this icy aperture, leveling the floor, and spreading their blankets there. This they did after a good deal of scraping and digging, and after they were ensconced therein, sardines were never more snugly packed.

Twilight lingered with us a long, long time. During its continuance I enjoyed the prospect that opened on every side. Twilight reveries are dear to me, and it was with a feeling of innate satisfaction that I stood leaning upon the rocky rampart that formed the backbone of the ridge, and looked out over the world below—aye, and that that still rose above us.

The great, wide snow-fields over which we had plodded, they and their tremendous ramifications extended everywhere.

Paradise Park seemed a magnificent mountain court.

Afar to the west were Goat Mountain and Eagle Crag, rising splendidly out of the congeries of mountains about them. Still westward, fainter but showing well the peculiarities that gave them name, rose the Sawtooth Range, dark and arrogant. And below, the Tatoisch lifted itself out of the depths with that infinite grandeur that seemed enshrined within it. Away down its slopes, lying on the very edge of a cliff, was a small lake, lonely and lovely. In the midst of the forest, with huge peaks frowning above it, and an abrupt cliff below, down which a long line of spray marked the course of the stream that was its outlet, it was a mountain gem of rare beauty.

To the east is new country. Until now almost entirely shut off, the Cowlitz Glacier and its branches, cañons, and cliffs, the main range of the Cascades rising farther to the eastward, excite my lively interest.

The head of the glacier is before me as I turn around, steep, harsh, forbidding, and below, it leaps down into the cañon, a broken, crushed, contorted ice-fall, while in plain view near by a crevasse yawns. The clouds of the day are now in the east, hanging over the vast depression or valley between us and the main range.

A great sea of glorious, white, balloonic clouds, absolutely motionless, apparently, to their minutest particles, in an ocean of space.

Ah! but Gibraltar. It rises in its sentinelship higher and grander than ever. No sun though now to lighten up its vertical expanse, and it appears gloomy, austere, cold, but as full of majestic proportion as ever. A noble rock, noble in shape, noble in appearance, noble in its dignity, noble in dimensions, and most nobly placed, long may it stand, a bulwark fitting and appropriate to the king of peaks!

As I stand, enraptured, charmed with the vastness of the scene and the vastness of the solitude as well, a deep boom and crash and roar breaks upon the quiet night. Springing to a higher rock, I gaze in the direction of the sound. No need to tell what it is. Each one knows the meaning of the direful sound, and yet the shout of "The avalanche! the avalanche!" breaks from each throat.

I see hurled from the heights above the Nesqually Glacier, from near where our route on the morrow leads us, a large, rolling, tumbling cloud of finely pulverized, comminuted ice and snow—snow-dust. Behind this effectual veil we know, but can really see little, that great boulders of ice, snow, and rocks are pitching headlong down the glacier. As it rolls downward the cloud expands and we see better. Some of the debris meets an obstacle and stops then and there; some of it tumbles into the first crevasse that lies athwart its path; some of it in its fearful momentum leaping this, but meets the same fate in the abysses farther down. For hundreds, perhaps a thousand or two thousand feet, some of it continues its unchecked course before the last sounds die away and the snow-dust has vanished. The sound and thought of it is more awful than the sight. The latter has its harsher, more terrible aspects hidden by the beautiful snow-cloud; and it is well.

We have no gorgeous sunset, such as we had hoped might be our good fortune; only a rather commonplace one, yet attractive. As it grows colder, we turn in under our blankets. It is pretty tight squeezing. I lie and watch the stars, and am disappointed at the lack of brilliancy they show. We are in a night of deepest solitude. No note of bird nor hoot of night-owl breaks the silence; not the chirp of an insect is heard. Even the canine-like bark of the coyote, wherein one fills the void that seven ought to, is conspicuous by its absence. The rocks speak not; there are no trees whose leaves rustle in the night breeze. Naught of life or sound save the stertorous breathing of a sleeper, or at long, long intervals through the night the muffled speech of the avalanche.

Nor was the sunrise on the morning following all that we might have desired. We were out of our cold, hard beds at 4.30 o'clock. The air was very cold. My shoes were cold and stiff. As fast as each man got on his foot-gear—our clothes were already there, we having slept in them—he began to dance about on the rocks and ice to warm his feet and start the circulation. The spot soon resembled a nest of jumping-jacks, or a retired nook where a small band of Indians were engaged in a war-dance. This seance continued for a full half-hour, and then when somewhat comfortable we munched our frozen breakfast and drank iced coffee.

The clouds were still crowded in apparently immovable masses high above the sleeping earth, in an extended plain. The track of the sun across them, as it slowly rose over the Cascades to the east, was a golden pathway. To the south, Mounts Adams, Hood, and St. Helens were plainly visible, that is their tips were, and Jefferson's outlines, to the right and far south of Hood, could be faintly made out.

### COWLITZ CLEAVER TO THE SUMMIT—GIBRALTAR ROCK.

At 6.30 o'clock the upward climb was resumed—by five of us. Two of them felt that they had lost no craters, and that the Gibraltar trail and the ice slopes ahead had no charms for them. They, therefore, bade us Godspeed on our farther journey, and at our halting-place on the rocks, some distance ahead, we saw them carefully picking their downward course among the huge rocks of the Cleaver.

Our route led over the highest portion of the Cowlitz Glacier. The ice now was hard and slippery, and it required hard thrusts to make the points of our alpenstocks penetrate the ice sufficiently to afford one a hold should he unfortunately slip. Should one fall, the unlucky man would have a rapid and dangerous descent, for the slope was very steep, nothing to break his momentum, and only a short distance below, a crevasse.

We were compelled to work over this spot with the utmost caution, and to my mind it was by all odds the most dangerous part of the entire ascent. After a time we reached the rocks again, and it was necessary to cut some few steps in places where it was half ice, half rocky material pulverized. This climb of 750 feet was undeniably hard on all of us. A cold supper the evening before, a cold night of discomfort, and a frozen breakfast were by no means conducive to rapid nor easy climbing. We were well satisfied when in little more than an hour we found ourselves at the bivouac at the foot of Gibraltar, which we had hoped to reach the evening before.

To fill in the time, while waiting certain necessary repairs to our outfit, some of us rolled rocks down to the Nesqually Glacier. The upper heights, the formative parts of this great ice river, lay spread out before us. The ridge upon which we were was a perfect precipice on its western side, and from its base, hundreds of feet below, the glacier stretched away across the cañon, to the white wall that dropped down from Peak Success to meet it. Loose rocks of all sizes abounded at the edge of the ridge, and these we pushed over the cliff and watched them as they leaped downward. The first drop was of course a dull, sheer, lifeless one to the first place that it struck. This was 20, 50, 100, 200 feet, as it might be, depending upon the size of the boulder and the force with which it was hurled over. But the moment it struck it was transformed. It seemed as if imbued with demoniacal life. With a malicious spring it bounded far out into the air and downward, revolving at the same time upon its own axis. At a distance of another 50 or 100 feet it again came in contact with the rocky ground or the ice, and the same jump outward was seen. Over and over again this was repeated, until the rock plunged down into one particular crevasse that none of them could clear. There was a great fascination in this, and every man of us indulged in it. The fate of any one unlucky enough to slip or fall was plainly seen.

### GIBRALTAR ROCK.

I have made mention frequently of Gibraltar Rock. In writing of Mount Rainier, especially the southern side of it, one must necessarily do so. The literature of the mountain is full of it. The mountaineers are full of it. In the views of the peak from the south, southeast, and southwest, it is a conspicuous feature of them. In the climb to the summit its narrow ledge that must perforce be traversed, is felt by many to be the most dangerous part of the way. The danger consists in the fact that, during the warm hours of the day, stones are continually falling over its sides and are not unlikely to strike the passer on the trail, which might indeed be serious. No rocks are ever mentioned as falling at other places, and it seems somewhat anomalous that here alone they should be found. Now as I sit at its base and cast my eye up and down its swarthy, vertical sides, and study its structure, I understand what this all means.

One of the products of volcanic eruptions or explosions is known as volcanic breccia. This consists of angular fragments of volcanic rocks cemented together in a paste of volcanic dust or mud. It is often intercalated, or interstratified, with layers of lava, and this is the case with Gibraltar. It is not therefore a mass of hard, volcanic rock, but an indurated, pasty composition easily affected by the rain, snow, frost, and ice, in conjunction with the heat of the sun. The moisture of the atmosphere permeates it, and penetrates its crevices and fissures. The alternate freezing and thawing to which it is subjected disintegrates it, loosens the rocks, which drop during the heated portion of the day, and works in its surface great holes, almost caverns in some instances.

This great landmark, nearly 2,000 feet high, is conspicuous from the fact that it rises in the sea of white about it, almost barren of snow. Just east of it rise the Cathedral Rocks, a fine palisade with a sharply-notched comb.

*Some "ascendants to top of Mount Rainier": (from left top) P. B. Van Trump, Fay Fuller, Hazard Stevens, Helen Holmes. From Olin Wheeler's* Mount Rainier: Its Ascent by a Northern Pacific Party.

### GIBRALTAR TO CRATER PEAK.

Before reaching Gibraltar I had serious misgivings whether I should undertake to pass it. I had made a promise that I would not imperil my life needlessly merely for the glory of the ascent, and rather expected, from reports of this dangerous passage, that I would proceed no farther. I therefore, upon arrival, examined it with much interest and anxiety, and soon concluded that I had many times risked my neck in as dangerous places without thinking much of it. Of mountain-climbing among rocks, cañons, cliffs, etc., I had done a good deal, and when I discovered that the ice factor was mostly eliminated from the problem, I felt very little concern. Ice-climbing was new to me; the rocks and I were old companions.

When all was ready and we were again pushing ahead, it was with a peculiar feeling that I found myself really working around the base of the mighty rock, the *bete noir* to so many. The distance that must be covered is about one-quarter of a mile, but the time required to do this is considerable. The face of the cliff at this point is cut away into a number of small ledges, so that one not familiar with the spot is more than apt to take the wrong one, and in the end find himself in an embarrassing and probably dangerous position.

The ledge along which leads the trail lies at the base and at an outward angle from the cliff, and in places this angle is decidedly acute, the ground hard or stony, so that a firm foothold is next to impossible.

It is also very, very narrow; and below, the inclination is such that should one slip and fall, nothing short of a miracle would prevent being carried down to the glacier and into the crevasses, even if not dashed to pieces on the sharp rocks first encountered.

For most of the distance the face of the precipice above the trail slopes toward and under the cliff, so that a man passing along, even at midday, can be protected from falling stones by hugging the rock closely.

To make sure that no accidents should befall us, an inch rope left at this point by Sarvent in 1893, was used at the worst place, being wound about nubbins of rock at each side of the spot, and held to with one hand. One can find slight projections of rock to grasp for the greater part of the way. At the farther end the ice is reached, a long tongue extending down from the top of the rock. It appears almost insanity to think of ascending this, gazing upward from its base, and from

Camp of the Clouds seems absolutely impossible. As we found it, it was not difficult after a little experience and our nerves were steadied.

The manner in which the sun strikes this mass melts it in such a way as to form an infinite number of terraces or steps, very small, but, if the ice be not too soft, just the width for convenient climbing. They are, too, for the most part, at easy distances from each other.

Sarvent would climb up for the full length of our rope—200 feet— then sitting down, plant himself firmly, with one end of the rope fastened to his waist. Then grasping the trailing rope, at intervals of twenty-five feet apart, we would "follow the leader." We soon found that simply holding the rope line in the left hand without bringing any strain to bear, was all that was necessary. It gave us the confidence required to get along by ourselves, practically.

It is lunch time, noon, when we find ourselves at the top of Gibraltar. We have climbed well since the ice was reached, and are now warmed to our work, and the cold night and cold breakfast are forgotten.

Anxious to proceed, we dispatch lunch rapidly, and now, as our route is entirely over ice, comes a new wrinkle. Our strong sash-cord is doubled, and at about twenty-five feet distant from each other, it is firmly tied about each man's waist and we are off.

Instead of zigzagging up the ice, Sarvent goes straight up a slope that makes me hold my breath for an instant. As we go right along, easily and without slipping, our alpenstocks in our right hands, our left hands grasping the rope that trails from the man in front and keeping it taut, I feel no alarm.

We are doing splendidly—every man holds out well. No nose-bleed, no nausea, no faintness nor giddiness, and seemingly no tired legs, weak lungs, no fluttering hearts.

We are aiming for a point midway between Peak Success and Crater Peak. A crevasse or two are headed. Deep, narrow, clean-cut in cleavage, the ice stratification beautiful, they are fascinating to gaze into— but to fall into—ugh! Two or three smaller ones are jumped across or passed over on ice—snow bridges—treading lightly.

Our course has been to the west. Now, as we are well up the side, we turn toward the north, and at last the divide is reached. Hastening on, a stout pull and a long one, and we are on Crater Peak and crossing the western crater, so-called.

Before us, higher yet, rises a white, glistening dome of snow, not unlike a human skull in contour. It is a beautiful sight, *and the highest point of Mount Rainier*. We hurry onward, and at 2.15 P.M. of August 8, 1894, we are standing on the topmost point—Columbia's Crest, as Major Ingraham's party have happily termed it—of the great mountain chieftain, the King of Peaks.

### THE SUMMIT OF MOUNT RAINIER.

At last the time is come, the eventful day has arrived, when a long cherished plan has reached its fruition. From far over in the Yakima Valley I had seen this peak peeping above the main Cascade Range, and wanted to stand thereon. From Tacoma and Seattle I looked across the intervening space, and gazed upon this Colossus of mountains, wrapped about by ethereal mists, and wanted to tread that pinnacle of earthly glory. From my hotel window at Tacoma, I once more saw it suffused in all the glory and soft radiance of a sunrise, when in its light bath of the morning it seemed as if it might be the herald, the harbinger of the coming millenium—and more than ever I wished to breathe the air that circled about its immaculate crest. The dream had come true, the wish was gratified, and now I stood 14,444 feet above the ocean's surge, 6,000 feet above the clouds, 2¾ miles above Manhattan Island, Florida Keys, and San Francisco's Golden Gate, and looked out upon a scene that any man might thank God for enjoying.

In front of us yawned a chasm, a white *nevé* ice cañon, hundreds of feet deep. On the other side of it rose the sharp rock and snow-peak of Tahoma, or Liberty Cap, more than a mile distant. The eastern prolongation or spur of Tahoma Peak was sheared off, parabolically, at a very steep angle, as clearly as though done with a mammoth knife, and the entire slope was a shining crystalline bed of *nevé* ice. This cañon is stated by Mr. Emmons to be the interior of a very old and very large crater, of which the peaks are remnants.

To the southwest we looked down on Peak Success, a mile away. The Tahoma Peak is about 13,800 feet high, and Peak Success 14,000 feet above the sea. The sides of the mountain in all directions were composed of glaciers—ice everywhere! It tumbled down in great waves, cascades, cliffs, and extended, shining slopes, scarified by the ever-present crevasse that yawned and gaped in deep and fascinating terror.

To the south, back of us, and now hidden from sight, was the familiar Nesqually Glacier. To the southeast was the Cowlitz, another and smaller branch of which we now saw, and the main body of which was visible in the distance; also the cañon through which the river itself flows. To the northeast an immense body of *nevé* ice, considerably more than a mile wide, swept down in a dazzling sheet, giving birth to three large glaciers, the White River, Inter, and Winthrop. Flowing from the terminals could be seen the three branches and main White River, white indeed as they issued from the glaciers. On a dome of ice and snow we stood midst an unbounded sea of the same; a majestic, a god-like peak, overspread with the immaculate enameling of nature, which in turn became the mother of numberless rivers that hied themselves to the sea. It was indeed wonderful, and well worth the toilsome climb to reach it.

On either side of our white, rounded crest lie the craters, the western one the smaller and rather indefinite; the eastern, oblong, well marked, with its black, serrated rim inclining inward, and rising 10, 15, 20, 40 feet above the interior that is a floor of snow, sloping toward the center.

Craters—that means volcano, and it flashes over me that I am standing at the extreme point, the top of *a volcano*. Once there burst from this very place clouds of steam and ashes; rocks were hurled aloft—those over which we have but just been climbing; rivers of burning lava, fantastic, fiery serpents, that wriggled and hissed, and scorched and devastated, as they trailed down the sides, issued from these vents.

Now all is changed. The fires are quenched; the serpents scotched. The Fire King is conquered by the Ice God, and death and destruction are no more; the deluge of fire is smothered under the deluge of snow.

*Is* that true?

Glance down yonder ridge that slopes eastward from where we stand. See how red and bare it is. No snow there. Small puffs and fleecy jets of steam emanate from it. Let us leave this cold icy poll of the mountain, for the wind blows hard from out the west, and we are chilled and shivering. Let us go down and investigate.

What find we?

A rounded reddish ridge, barren of snow, leaning toward the interior of the crater, and evidently a part of its rim. The ground is moist and warm, so warm that we lie down upon it that our bodies may gratefully absorb some of its heat. By some process the rocks have been changed into a clayey mass, through which the steam issues from a jet the size of a pin-point to a respectably-sized column. If you place your hand over one of them it will scald you. Down among the rocks are more steam-clouds, and thus we see that even yet the internal heat of this old pile still maintains the unequal struggle.

The grandest sight vouchsafed us from the summit was that of the clouds that lay beneath and all around us. The land below was completely hidden from view. It seemed as if all the clouds of the North Pacific Coast had arranged themselves about this peak. Never saw I anything like it before.

A magnificent plain of clouds, the most imposing, and of tremendous depths, encircled us except immediately about the mountain itself. The surface was choppy and hummocky, much as I fancy an arctic land-scape to be. We seemed completely shut out from the world that we knew, and in a strange, weird, lifeless one. It is almost beyond the power of description, either written or verbal, to convey the faintest idea of the sight that greeted us, turn whichever way we might, and of the feeling that came over us. A perfect ocean, a wilderness of clouds, stretching in illimitable plain to the farthest realms of vision, motion-less, as though they always had been there, always would be. The only features that seemed real and familiar to us were the peak upon which we stood, and the others that projected above the vapory plain.

To the north, the noble head of the Baker of Vancouver, the more euphonious Kulshan of the red man, showed itself; to the southeast, the truncated cone of Mount Adams, the Indian Pah-to, rises not far distant; south, the graceful, symmetric, Hood pierces the clouds to the height of 11,225 feet; while southwest, St. Helen's, as the white man calls it—Lah-me-lat-clah as the aborigine knows it—broke upon the horizon.

### THE DESCENT.

At 3.45 o'clock we began the descent and made rapid progress. Re-tracing our upward trail, when we reached the top of Gibraltar and looked back at the slope over which we had come, it was hard to believe that we had climbed down it. The sun had set when we passed the great rock safely.

There is little danger in climbing around this place in the early morn or late afternoon, if one has good nerve, a cool head, and uses ordinary caution. No one, though, deficient in the above qualities has any business there, and one unused to it should not *dare* to try it without a good guide.

We hastened down to our old bivouac, hastily ate a little lunch, donned our packs, and started down the Cleaver. It was quite dark when the snow-field was reached, and the distance to Camp of the Clouds was made by moonlight.

We were all fatigued, and this part of the descent was hard on us, and especially trying to me. The uneven surface and no daylight made it impossible to see, and our steps were taken on faith. My knees gave out for a time, and I had half a dozen falls, none of them serious. Then my knees braced up, and I reached camp in better condition than when half-way there. We kept on the snow; sat and slid down two or three snow-hills, bumpety-bump, and arrived at Camp of the Clouds at 10.30 o'clock, and were received by our friends with three cheers and a tiger.

Since the above narrative was written great changes have taken place about the mountain. In the autum [*sic*] heavy avalanches fell on the western side, and during the winter on the north side. So tremendous have been the latter that the aspect of that part of the peak has undergone a profound change, and at one time it was thought the mountain was in a state of eruption. A winter expedition led by Major Ingraham, after many hardships and dangers, ascended the mountain on the north side sufficiently high to verify the fact that these avalanches occurred.

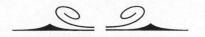

# Index

Paul Schullery, a resident of Hershey, Pennsylvania, is editor of the publication *Country Journal*. He was researching a history of the native elk in Mount Rainier National Park when he came across these first-person accounts of the pioneers on Rainier, scattered throughout dusty journals and out-of-print publications from the era. Finding them quite inspiring and entertaining, he decided to collect them into a single volume for the enjoyment of others who love The Mountain.

Schullery holds both bachelor's and master's degrees in American history (Wittenberg University, Ohio University). He worked at Yellowstone National Park as ranger-naturalist for five summers, and as historian for three winters, during the 1970s. An avid fisherman, he spent five years as executive director of the American Museum of Fly Fishing, Manchester, Vermont.

He writes regularly for publications in the outdoor and history fields, including *National Parks, Field & Stream, Montana, Environmental Review* and *The Journal of Forest History*.

Schullery is the author or editor of a number of books, including *The Bears of Yellowstone, Mountain Time, Old Yellowstone Days, The Grand Canyon: Early Impressions, Theodore Roosevelt: Wilderness Writings*, and *American Bears: Selections from the Writings of Theodore Roosevelt;* and is co-author of *Freshwater Wilderness: Yellowstone Fishes and Their World.*

*For an illustrated catalog of the more than 100 outdoor titles published by The Mountaineers, write:*

The Mountaineers Books
306 Second Avenue West
Seattle WA 98119